Wiley Series in Software Design Patterns

The WILEY SERIES IN SOFTWARE DESIGN PATTERNS is designed to meet the needs of today's software architects, developers, programmers and managers interested in design patterns. Frank Buschmann (Series Editor), as well as authors, shepherds and reviewers work collaboratively within the patterns community to strive for high-quality, highly researched, thoroughly validated, classic works, which document accepted and acknowledged design experience. Priority is given to those titles that catalog software patterns and pattern languages with a practical, applied approach in domains such as:

- Distributed systems
- Real time systems
- Databases
- Business information systems
- Telecommunications
- Organisations
- Concurrency
- Networking

Books in the series will also cover conceptual areas of how to apply patterns, pattern language developments and architectural/component-based approaches to pattern-led software development.

TITLES PUBLISHED

- PATTERN-ORIENTED SOFTWARE ARCHITECTURE, Volume 1
Frank Buschmann, Regine Meunier, Hans Rohnert, Peter Sommerlad and Michael Stal
978-0471-95869-7 476pp 1996 Hardback

- PATTERN-ORIENTED SOFTWARE ARCHITECTURE, Volume 2
Douglas Schmidt, Michael Stal, Hans Rohnert and Frank Buschmann
978-0471-60695-6 636pp 2000 Hardback

- A PATTERN APPROACH TO INTERACTION DESIGN
Jan Borchers
978-0471-49828-5 250pp 2001 Hardback

- SERVER COMPONENT PATTERNS
Markus Völter, Alexander Schmid, Eberhard Wolff
978-0470-84319-2 462pp 2002 Hardback

- ARCHITECTING ENTERPRISE SOLUTIONS
Paul Dyson, Andy Longshaw
978-0470-85612-3 384pp 2004 Hardback

- PATTERN-ORIENTED SOFTWARE ARCHITECTURE, Volume 3
Michael Kircher, Prashant Jain
978-0470-84525-7 312pp 2004 Hardback

- SECURITY PATTERNS
Markus Schumacher, Eduardo Fernandez-Buglioni, Duane Hybertson, Frank Buschmann, Peter Sommerlad
978-0-470-85884-4 600pp 2005 Hardback

- PATTERN-ORIENTED SOFTWARE ARCHITECTURE, Volume 4
Frank Buschmann, Kevlin Henney, Douglas C. Schmidt
978-0-470-05902-9 363pp 2007 Hardback

- PATTERN-ORIENTED SOFTWARE ARCHITECTURE, Volume 5
Frank Buschmann, Kevlin Henney, Douglas C. Schmidt
978-0471-48648-0 490pp 2007 Hardback

- PATTERNS FOR COMPUTER-MEDIATED INTERACTION
Till Schümmer, Stephan Lukosch
978-0-470-02561-1 600pp 2007 Hardback

- PATTERNS FOR FAULT TOLERANT SOFTWARE
Robert Hanmer
978-0-470-31979-6 308pp 2007 Hardback

- WHERE CODE AND CONTENT MEET
Andreas Rüping
978-0-470-74845-9 216pp 2009 Hardback

- PATTERNS FOR PARALLEL SOFTWARE DESIGN
Jorge Luis Ortega-Arjona
978-0-470-69734-4 440pp 2010 Hardback

- BUSINESS PATTERNS FOR SOFTWARE DEVELOPERS
Allan Kelly
978-1-119-99924-9 408pp 2012 Hardback

Business Patterns for Software Developers

Business Patterns for Software Developers

Allan Kelly

WILEY
A John Wiley and Sons, Ltd, publication

This edition first published 2012

Registered office
John Wiley & Sons Ltd, The Atrium, Southern Gate, Chichester, West Sussex, PO19 8SQ, United Kingdom

For details of our global editorial offices, for customer services and for information about how to apply for permission to reuse the copyright material in this book please see our website at www.wiley.com.

A catalogue record for this book is available from the British Library.

ISBN 978-1-119-99924-9

Set in 10/12 point Utopia by WordMongers Ltd, Treen, Penzance, Cornwall
Printed in Great Britain by TJ International

Спасибо Таисии, Грише и Антону за все

Thank you for everything to Taissia, Grisha and Antonska

Publisher's acknowledgements

Some of the people who helped to bring this book to market include the following:

Editorial and Production
VP Consumer and Technology Publishing Director: Michelle Leete
Associate Director–Book Content Management: Martin Tribe
Associate Publisher: Chris Webb
Executive Commissioning Editor: Birgit Gruber
Assistant Editor: Ellie Scott
Copy Editor: Steve Rickaby, WordMongers Ltd
Editorial Manager: Jodi Jensen
Senior Project Editor: Sara Shlaer
Editorial Assistant: Leslie Saxman

Marketing
Associate Marketing Director: Louise Breinholt
Senior Marketing Executive: Kate Parrett

Composition Services
Steve Rickaby, WordMongers Ltd

Contents

Foreword

I love books. I believe that all patterns fans love books. I remember in the early evangelical days of patterns introduction, arriving at a corporate site to talk about design patterns, hauling in my usual stack of patterns books: the Gang of Four (of course), the first of the PoSA series, several by Christopher Alexander and a PLoPD book or two. It was a lot of work, especially in the summer in Phoenix when the temperatures could be above 110 F. But it was worth it. Participants would immediately gather round, pick up, leaf through and start to read those books. It's often been said about Alexander's *A Pattern Language* that you start thumbing through, and then it happens – the book draws you in and soon you're reading and reading and reading.

Good pattern books are all like that. Actually all good books are like that. It's one reason why I miss bookstores. You can't, even when selections are available online, browse books in the same way. I think you'll find Allan Kelly's book is the same. You'll pick it up. You'll see a particular pattern that catches your eye because it calls up a problem you've had or are having, and pretty soon you, too, will be reading and learning. One participant at a long-ago patterns talk, when asked about the attraction of books, said, "Some of my happiest memories are about books".

I think that books have this power for us because they are proxies for the longest-lived form of learning – listening to others tell a story. Allan mentions Steve's Denning's work on corporate storytelling – how a good story is the most effective way to persuade others to hear your compelling idea. Readers will like the format for Allan's patterns, because each one opens with a short story.

Mary Lynn Manns and I decided to adopt that format for the patterns in *Fearless Change* after feedback from our reviewers. We had not taken the time to find good images for the patterns, believing that we could do that at a later date. We did, however, include a lot of known uses – stories from contributors all over the world who had used the patterns. Our reviewers noted that these stories, especially the more powerful ones, seemed to embody the message of the pattern – they were almost a stand-alone explanation. The suggestion was that we move an archetypal story to the opening of the pattern as a replacement for the image. Readers could then create their own images, in the same way that radio listeners used to. I remember many happy hours after school listening with my brothers to The Lone Ranger on the radio, and was almost disappointed the first time I saw an episode on television – it seemed to be missing all the detail from my eight-year-old imagination.

Good stories reflect the author's expertise. It's why we want to hear good storytellers. We're all looking for answers. We want some suggestions for new directions, experiments we might try in our organisations and in our lives. You will definitely find that in Allan's book. The expertise shines through – in the stories, in the understanding of the challenges we face and in the powerful solutions. This is one reason why patterns books take a long time to produce. It's not a simple matter of documenting the idea we had in the shower this morning. Patterns capture expertise, that of the author and of those who contribute known uses, examples or stories of their experiences using the pattern. It takes considerable effort to gather all that valuable material.

I can recall the first time someone asked me a very important question about books: can you think of at least one book that changed your life? I struggled with this question when I heard it, but then the obvious answer appeared. The book with the most impact on my life was one I had written: *Fearless Change*. Over the ten years it took to produce that book, I changed from a techie, a software designer, to someone intensely interested in the people side of development, especially the psychology of human interaction. The amount of research from the cognitive scientists that appears almost daily is overwhelming. It all has to do with us as humans, and has enormous impact on our software development and business process. It wasn't an overnight change, since the book took ten years to create, but it turned my life and career upside down. My personal mission statement is to translate as much of the research in this area to those in software development who are willing to listen.

Now that I teach others these patterns, I'm constantly reminded of how I saw the world. I encounter participants who want to introduce new ideas by 'forcing people to use patterns' or any new technology. There is a strong sense in many people that, if you just had enough power, you could get others to change. Even when I spent time discussing the difference between 'compliance' – where others toe the line and give the appearance of adopting the new idea – and 'commitment' – when others sign up for the innovation because they also believe it is the right thing to do, I often feel that many innovators would prefer a club to using influence strategies.

I experienced this again when my boss stopped by my cubicle one day and asked me to look into some possible patterns for customer interaction. Our small teams were moving to Scrum, something that I had found on the web and thought it might help. No books on agile development were available in the mid-90s, but `controlchaos.com` and some e-mails with Ken Schwaber and Mike Beedle helped us jump-start agile in our organisation. There was just one small problem: we expected developers to interact with customers. Developers are, for the most part, good-hearted technical people. Their people skills may be limited. It was unfair of us to expect them to understand immediately how to work with customers effectively.

That was not a simple assignment. I was not an expert in customer interaction, but I spent considerable time interviewing our business and marketing folks and others throughout the company who interacted with our customers successfully. The result, *Patterns for Customer Interaction*, again taught me that while we techies believe that a good technical solution is what the customer really wants, determining the true nature of that solution and how best to implement it requires more understanding of human interaction than computer performance. It was another wake-up call.

I hope you're wiser than I am. I hope that you already understand the importance of the business and human side of development. You don't need a wake-up call to see how critical Allan's patterns and others like them are to successful software development. You won't make the mistakes I have made. You know you need this book!

I first saw Allan's patterns at VikingPLoP in 2004. They resonated with me because I was working on some patterns for building beautiful companies with Daniel May, Steve Sanchez and Caroline King. I thought at that time that Allan had the beginnings of a book, and I am so happy to be able to introduce it to all of you. The *Beautiful Company* patterns were never finished – a casualty of lack of time, so common these days (the initial cut is on my website, `lindarising.org`) but I'm delighted that Allan has been diligent and has produced his own patterns to help you build your own beautiful company. Enjoy.

Linda Rising, Independent consultant

Mt. Juliet, Tennessee, USA

Acknowledgements

In some ways this book is accidental. Initially I wanted to see if the pattern form could add anything to the thinking and writing about business strategy. The experiment took the form of two papers, one at EuroPLoP and one at VikingPLoP (Kelly, 2004a; Kelly, 2004b). The experiment eventually worked: I learned a lot about what would work and what wouldn't. I also found insights into the original source material.

The more I looked at patterns of business strategy, the more I saw. Patterns to the left of me, patterns to the right of me. There are still many more business strategy patterns I have identified but have not had the time to write up.

It took me a while to come around to accepting there was a book in these patterns. Which is strange, because two people saw the potential almost immediately and have encouraged me along the way: Lise Hvatum and Cecilia Haskins. These two Norwegian–American crossovers have encouraged my writing, supported me when I've had doubts and been generous with their comments, criticism and advice.

Strangely enough neither Lise or Cecila actually shepherded any of the patterns in this book. As every pattern author knows, the shepherd plays an invaluable role in the creation of every pattern. I have been truly fortunate to have had some wonderful shepherds during this project: Manfred Lange, Daniel May, Alan O'Callaghan, Klaus Marquardt, Michael Weiss and Uwe Zdun.

Klaus, Daniel and Michael deserve special mention for shepherding several pattern papers. Daniel's advice, both in the early patterns and the later ones, was critical in shaping the work, challenging me and pushing me to go further.

Manfred also deserves special mention for being the first. Although the 2004 *Porter Patterns* are not included here, they were the start of the project, and Manfred's advice was particularly useful in shaping the business patterns that came later.

But shepherds are not the only PLoP reviewers: many more people commented on these patterns in workshops during VikingPLoP and EuroPLoP. Thanks too to: Ademar Aguiar, Albena Antonova, Valerie Brown, Jim Coplien, Lotte De Rore, Andreas Fießer, Alexander Fülleborn, Ian Graham, Birgit Gruber, Cecila Haskins, Kevlin Henney, Florian Humplik, Lise Hvatum, Halina Kaminski, Maria Kavanagh, Gwendolyn Kolfschoten, Herman Koppleman, Dinesha Koravangala, Wim Laurier, Andy Longshaw, Stephan Lukosch, Nora Ludewig, Jorge L. Ortega Arjona, Klaus Marquardt, Linda Rising, Pavel Hruby, Rebecca Riker, Jan Reher, Jürgen Salecker, Martin Schmettow, Lubor Sessera, Kristian Elof Sørensen, Hans Wegener, Claudius Link, Anne Hoffman, Neil Harrison, Aliaksandr Birukou, Christoph Hannebauer, Elissaveta Gourova, Yanka Todorova and Tim Wellhausen.

Thanks too to the reviewers who worked with me and Wiley at various stages to help improve the book: Charles Weir, Phil Nash, Mark Dalgarno, Linda Rising, Daniel May, Klaus Marquardt, Cecilia Haskins, Carl Åsman and Filipe Correia.

At VikingPLoP 2004, still early in the experiment, I experienced a degree of doubt and uncertainty concerning the pattern form for business patterns. I found the answers I needed in the writing of Dick Gabriel and Stephen Denning, and later in conversations with Klaus Marquardt and Jorge L. Ortega Arjona.

Dick Gabriel is a long-standing member of the patterns community and one of its more noteworthy philosophers. He is also a poet, and compares writing software and patterns to poetry. His *Patterns of Software* (Gabriel, 1996) had significant influence on my thinking about patterns, poetry and stories.

For me patterns, like poetry, are stories told in a specific way. I arrived at this conclusion after reading Stephen Denning's *The Springboard* (Denning, 2001) and *Storytelling in Organizations* (Brown et al, 2005). Denning, like Gabriel, has left his mark on this text without knowing it – and possibly without actually knowing about patterns!

Klaus Marquardt suggested that it may be the pattern writer, not the pattern reader, who gets the most out of a pattern. In effect, by writing the pattern we are forcing ourselves to understand it in depth. Writing the pattern is itself a 'sense-making' process for the writer. While I believe readers will certainly learn from this book, the author has learned far more during its writing.

Jorge L. Ortega Arjona pointed out that in most forms of art and literature, such as novels, films and music, it is normal to have many stories about the same subject. So why should pattern writing be any better? Duplication may run counter to minimalist instinct, but it certainly helps to tell a story.

In late 2009 I started to assemble the patterns so I could see *the whole*. Once whole it was clear that there was a book, and from that point on another group of people become involved: from 2009 Birgit Gruber at Wiley played midwife to the book. Thanks Birgit! Birgit was just one of many at John Wiley & Sons who helped this book come into being: thanks are also due to Chris Webb, Leslie Saxman, and Ellie Scott, and especially to Steve Rickaby of WordMongers for editing, typesetting and everything else.

Thanks too to Peter Sommerlad for the Itopia story, and to Nat Pryce, who in an off-hand, beer-enhanced, rant against pattern books at XTC unwittingly contributed to this book by listing things he didn't like about them. When agonising about how to present the patterns and book, I often heard Nat and Daniel's voices in my head.

As should be clear by now, lots of people had a hand in helping to create this book. Inevitably I will have missed some people, so thank you too, and my apologies.

Finally, thank you Taissia, my loving wife, for supporting me in the years of pattern writing and book construction, and thank you Grigory and Anton for being there to distract me, interrupt me and for generally being good sons.

1 Introduction

'Software entities are more complex for their size than perhaps any other human construct because no two parts are alike'

No Silver Bullet, Brooks, 1986

Building software is hard: successfully bringing a new software product from conception to market is harder. Building a successful software company that develops and markets multiple software products is harder still.

The days of 'build it and they will come' are over. Simply creating a great piece of software and waiting for the customers to knock on your door no longer works – if it ever did.

Nobody should ever think that building software is easy: some small application may indeed be easy to build, but meaningful software applications and platforms are extremely complicated things to create. However, building software is at least a reasonably well-defined task which isn't true of many of the other things that need to be done. Indeed it isn't even clear what needs doing.

Creating a successful software product, and building a successful software company, involve a myriad of other activities that are far less easy to define and put boundaries around. The first of these is just deciding what it is that should be built. But perhaps the most difficult task of all is bringing all these activities – well-defined, poorly defined and never defined alike – into alignment so that they move towards a common goal. This is akin to an exercise in formation flying in which the individual pilots have their own opinion on where they should be going. The bigger the company, the more complex the environment, the more difficult the task.

Focusing on the customer helps: after all, we all agree the customer comes first (don't we?) But while it might be clear what an individual customer says they want, what they are willing and able to pay for might be something different. When individual customers are aggregated into a market – be it millions, thousands or just dozens – it can be extremely difficult truly to know what the customer wants.

Customers are not homogenous: they want different things, but if you intend to build a product to sell to many of them, you need to determine common needs. Great leaders help, but great leaders are not a panacea. Leadership can give direction and common goals, but if a company can only survive with a truly remarkable leader, then the leader has failed. Leaders lead, but they also need to put in place mechanisms to prevent single points of failure.

Given all these difficulties, and more, is it a any surprise that many choose to focus on something right in front of them? Something here and now? We might call it 'goal displacement'. Building a company is an engineering task to parallel the construction of the software itself.

The patterns in this book describe many of the recurring problems software companies face and details the solutions found by existing companies. The patterns follow the well-known pattern format: a problem statement, a set of forces that make the problem difficult, a solution, with details of how to build it, the consequences of the solution, and examples and related work.

The Whole

'No plan survives contact with the enemy.'

General Helmuth von Moltke

Each pattern in this book contains one part of a solution. It may be used in isolation – a component if you like, dropped in to fix an issue. But each pattern also links to other patterns, and together they build towards a complete thing, a whole.

The whole is more than the sum of its parts. The whole is the thing you see when everyone is flying in formation. The whole happens when all the different parts of the organisation – engineering, sales, marketing – are coordinated, aligned, heading in the same direction. In business, making this happen is *strategy.*

Strategy sets organisational goals, objectives and direction. It is embodied in structures and organisation. It is planned, but it is also dynamic. It is changing in response to events and learning. Strategy looks forward and looks backwards to make sense of events. Strategy may be equated with a plan, something that is determined by a few – top management, consultants, planners – and executed by the many. But the devil is in the detail: things are just too complicated for a comprehensive plan.

While there are elements of forward-looking planning, strategy is equally the result of what happens; it emerges from events and decisions: what happens in the market, what engineers learn as they build the product, what competitors do. Strategy is backwards-looking; it makes sense of what has happened in order to direct the future.

Patterns are ideal for describing strategy, because they share these characteristics. Patterns are descriptions of what happens – like strategy, they emerge from looking backwards, adding to understanding and making sense. They are also forward-looking: they describe what to do.

Used alone, an individual pattern might be strategic, or it might just be something done to fix a problem – that is, tactical. When brought together, when used in a sequence to form a whole, they work strategically. Patterns direct and inform, but they are not a straight-jacket; you can, and should, vary a pattern as you see fit. This is how new patterns come into being.

Patterns describe the problems and the solution, and importantly, they name these things. Perhaps the most important thing a pattern adds to a discussion is a name. Patterns bring a shared vocabulary, which raises the level of the discussion.

Rather than talking about 'that thing you do when you involve the customer in creating the product but don't create the product only for that customer' you can say CUSTOMER CO-CREATED PRODUCT. This raises the level of the discussion and the abstraction level, it moves the conversation along more quickly and gives everyone, from CEO to lowly software engineer, a common language.

Patterns

> *'According to leading management thinkers, the manufacturing, service, and information sectors will be based on knowledge in the coming age, and business organisations will evolve into knowledge creators in many ways.*
>
> *According to [Peter Drucker] we are entering 'the knowledge society,' in which 'the basic resource' is no longer capital, or natural resources, or labour, but 'is and will be knowledge…'*
>
> *(Nonaka & Takeuchi, 1995)*

Patterns are all around us; it is simply a question of whether we see them and whether anyone has documented them. Patterns are recurring events, situations, constructions and ideas. They occur over and over again. Things that happen once are not patterns, but when they recur several times we label them patterns.

A pattern exists for a reason. A pretty design on a tie, on a sheet of wallpaper or on a dress is just that, a pretty design. These patterns exist to decorate people and places; attractiveness is no small matter. When these designs are used again and again, they take on meaning: they are used again and again for a reason.

The pattern on a tie may simply be there to make a businessman look good, but it may also serve to identify him as a member of an association, a clan or an alumni of a college. Similarly, a pattern on a dress may make the woman wearing it look good, but it may also help to identify her or convey authority and legitimacy (think of a nurse). Wallpaper may look nice, but we would choose different wallpaper for a gentleman's club to that for decorating a baby's nursery.

Things recur for reasons; things repeat for a reason.

In the 1970s the architect Christopher Alexander devised the 'pattern form' to codify his thinking about architecture. Using patterns, he documented the way in which buildings are located, laid out and constructed in recurring ways for reasons – reasons he came to call *forces*. Traditionally the logic behind these designs was handed down by word-of-mouth and through participation. Today those who study these things would call this 'tacit' knowledge and would say it was communicated through stories and *legitimate peripheral participation*.

Alexander also believed that this knowledge was being lost. Modern architecture and modern society separates architects and builders from those who use the buildings. So he set about codifying the patterns that made buildings the way they are.

By the early 1990s the software engineering community faced a knowledge transfer problem. Knowledge of how to build computer systems effectively existed, but was confined to a few experts. Even when the knowledge was widely known it was difficult to talk about. The rapid growth of the discipline needed a new way of communicating this knowledge.

In the late 1980s a few engineers in the software development community began to look at Alexander's pattern ideas. Bruce Anderson, Kent Beck, Grady Booch, Jim Coplien, Ward Cunningham, Erich Gamma, Ralph Johnson and others set about applying Alexander's ideas to software. One result of this was the formation of the Hillside Group (`www.hillside.net`) to promote these patterns. Like Alexander, they used this approach to codify tacit knowledge so that it could be communicated and shared in a wider community.

The patterns identified by Alexander and the software community were not created by them. Patterns can, and do, exist independently of documentation.

The world is full of undocumented patterns. Only a few of all possible patterns are documented. To those which are documented, the title *pattern* is awarded. These patterns codify the events and constructions that happen again and again.

Building on Alexander's ideas, each formally documented pattern contains:

- The problem the pattern is addressing
- The context in which the pattern is found
- The forces that make it hard to solve
- The solution
- How the solution is constructed
- The consequences of implementing the solution

Patterns that adopt this approach may be called *Alexandrian patterns*. There are different formats and styles in which such patterns might be written (see Appendix A) but, in general, as long as they consider these elements, we may call them Alexandrian patterns, or just *patterns* for short.

Ever since software professionals started writing patterns there have been some patterns which concern themselves more with the business side of the profession than the technical side. For example, the patterns in *Organizational Patterns of Agile Software Development* (Coplien & Harrison, 2004) are more about organisational form than software development. *Fearless Change* (Manns & Rising, 2005) originated in the software community, but is really about introducing organisational change.

This book sets out to show how the pattern approach can tackle the major issues of business – strategy – and specifically, business strategy as deployed by companies that create software.

All that jazz

The formation flying metaphor works – especially for engineers – but business people have long preferred the analogy of the symphony orchestra. The famous business writer Peter Drucker compared the executive's role to that of a conductor coordinating an orchestra (Drucker, 1985). Yet even the most famous symphony orchestra conductors only spend a small proportion of their time actually conducting in performance. After observing an actual conductor at work for a day, one writer suggested that 'rehearsing is the work of the organisation' (Mintzberg, 2009).

Rather than symphony orchestra, jazz offers an alternative metaphor – that of coordinated improvisation (Weick, 1997; Weick, 1999). Jazz musicians actively engage in improvisation and variation; *free jazz* in particular deliberately sets out to extend the score, to alter it and to break the rules with the aim of improving the experience.

There is no dedicated, isolated, conductor/leader here: maybe the drummer sets the beat, or maybe the sax takes the lead, but the leader is part of the band, the team. And while the team have a goal – a particular melody or sound to perform – each performance is different and contains improvisation. Experimentation is encouraged.

Formation flying is highly risky: improvisation is discouraged, for obvious reasons. But in business we have no choice; there are too many unknowns, many unknowables – we need variation and improvisation.

The difficult part is improvising while remaining coordinated. Individuals and teams need to be innovative, they need to experiment, they need to try new things, but simultaneously they need to be consistent and to work with others in the organisation.

For musicians the score gives an approximate map: however, things will definitely not unfold exactly according to the score. Patterns can help here: like a music score, they provide a shared understanding and language, a framework within which the players can perform while understanding the kind of moves others might make.

The Journey to Business Patterns

Many patterns have been written about the design and architecture of software systems. Other patterns have been written that describe the structural development of software organisations.

The more established patterns of software design exist within the context of organised software development. As long ago as 1968 Mel Conway pointed out that the organisation structure will influence system structure (Conway, 1968). Consequently, some architecture designs and patterns are more applicable in some organisational contexts than others. For example, an organisation with a large centralised team and several smaller distributed teams may find *Patterns for Plug-ins* (Marquardt, 2006) perfectly applicable. Conversely, developers working separately and under time pressure may find their design degenerating into a BIG BALL OF MUD (Foote & Yoder, 1999a).

Similarly, organisational structure will constrain the strategies available to an organisation, while the strategies a company pursues often dictate organisational structure. For example, staffing levels will be effected by the use of DOMAIN EXPERTISE IN ROLES (Coplien & Harrison, 2004). Similarly, a strategy of utilising offshore development may make use of JOIN FOR COMPLETION (Bricout et al, 2004). Organisations, their structures, culture and constraints provide context and forces within which patterns form.

Through such mechanisms, the patterns used at one level in the organisation constrain the options available at another level. As Conway suggested, the organisational structure will influence the system structure. However, it is also true that the system structure can effect the organisational structure: 'Reverse Conway's Law' (Hvatum & Kelly, 2005).

Figure 1 shows that we can think of these different levels as partially constraining each other. The end state of one applying one pattern – the *consequences* – sets up the conditions – the *context* and *forces* – for the next. Applying one pattern generates the conditions for the next: thus, patterns are often found in recurring sequences.

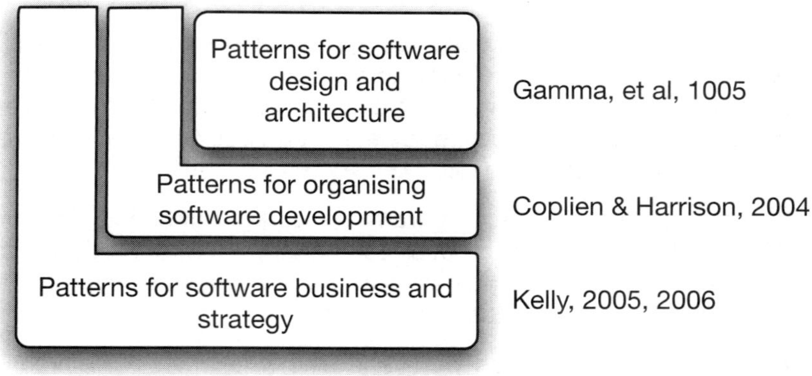

Figure 1. Patterns at one level are partially constrained by patterns at other levels

Tactics, in contrast with strategy, are often regarded as less important. So it is that some patterns may appear to be relatively unimportant. However, when viewed from a different perspective – perhaps a later date – these details can take on significant and even strategic importance. There are no firm boundaries between what is tactical and what is strategic; details considered tactical today may be strategic in future. One should not apply the labels 'strategic', 'tactical' or 'implementation' too quickly.

Why capture patterns?

Much tacit knowledge already exists in the minds of experts. In the case of business these experts are the managers, entrepreneurs and consultants who make business work. They have little need of explicit pattern documentation because the patterns are in their heads.

While this knowledge remains locked inside expert's heads it remains inaccessible to the people who live in the society they create. Modern society is increasingly governed by the business paradigm and the implicit patterns of that paradigm. For society and businesses to be successful this gap needs to be closed, a situation similar to architecture:

> *'So long as the people of society are separated from the language which is being used to shape their buildings, the buildings cannot be alive.'*
>
> *(Alexander, 1979, p. 241)*

There is a parallel between the construction of physical buildings and the construction of enterprises – an activity tellingly referred to as 'building a business'. Turning tacit knowledge into explicit pattern documents is an important step in sharing this knowledge. By sharing we close the gap between people and business, thereby improving the quality of life and opportunities for all.

Architectural 'patterns do not come only from the work of architects and planners' (Alexander, 1979, p. 199), and similarly business patterns do not need to come only from business experts. It is not just business experts who innovate; your local shop or café can be as innovative as a business consultant.

Explicitly documenting patterns has additional benefits beyond communication. Documented, patterns can be communicated, shared, analysed for improvements, alternatives or anomalies. The documentation process itself focuses attention on the act of design, it highlights the forces leading to the choice of a design and its consequences (both positive and negative.)

Patterns do not stop at design, they delve into the 'How do we build this?' question. And patterns beget patterns: patterns are generative in nature.

Audience

The patterns in this book are intended to codify some common business practices in a pattern language, so that they may be better understood, communicated and used. The patterns given here are intended for those interested in how corporate strategies are created and may be applied. This includes existing managers, future managers and entrepreneurs.

In particular, it is hoped that those on the receiving end – software engineers, testers, etc. – of such strategies and tactics will find the patterns informative and useful. Understanding what a company is attempting, why it is acting and the implications can be benefit everyone in the organisation. When company strategy is more widely understood, coordination should be easier.

The patterns presented here may be read and applied outside the domain of software companies. They may be applied to technology companies in general, and to non-technology companies in some instances. The domain and context of the patterns has been confined to software companies for two reasons. Firstly, this is the domain the author knows and in which he has experience. Secondly, limiting the domain helps to maintain the brevity of the patterns. Despite these deliberate limitations, the author believes many of the patterns may be applied in contexts outside the software domain.

A Story Book

Together these patterns form a story about how software companies do business. This story attempts to make sense of a diverse and changing field, a field which is not only confusing to newcomers, but is often confusing to those who have worked in it for years. What is *not* said in a story can be as important as what *is* said. Readers are left to fill in the blanks and incorporate their own experience and views, to make these stories their own.

While this author has striven for objectivity and universality, the patterns presented in this book are inevitably a reflection of his views, observations and understanding. Examples and references are included to support these views, but every example can be interpreted in many ways. More detailed analysis would certainly have enhanced objectivity, and may well have offered new insights and knowledge. But in doing so the stories would have lost their narrative.

Despite the wealth of good information to be found in academic journals on business and management, few practising managers or businessmen read these journals. For better or worse the academic form, the presentation style, the reference to past work and writing style make these journals unreadable for most people. While this author has observed some conventions, and wherever possible provided references, he has placed readability and story-telling above academic rigour.

In research terms the patterns in this book are based on the author's first-hand experience, supplemented with qualitative research. Much of the qualitative research is summarised in the boxed items between the patterns, the vignettes that open the patterns and the examples that complete the patterns. In most cases this research has not be conducted with academic rigour, but the author's views and intuition will hopefully compensate for this.

The patterns in this book aim to convey knowledge and understanding, but they are first and foremost stories. I intend these stories to be read, and hopes they will inform and inspire action in the reader.

Limits of the Book

Like any book, this book has its limits. Several have become increasingly apparent as final editing and preparation have approached, and deserve to be acknowledged.

The first limitation has already been mentioned: academic rigour has taken a back seat to readability and story-telling. From its first words to the final printed copies this book, over eight years will have elapsed in its making. During this time things have changed. Were work to begin on it tomorrow, it would be very different.

In particular, two major forces have emerged and continue to emerge in the world of software companies. Open Source development is providing new options for new businesses and changing the competitive landscape for those that already exist. While this book does not, perhaps, pay specific attention to Open Source as a business model, most of the patterns are applicable to companies working with Open Source models. It is my fervent hope that we shall see a book of *Business Patterns for Open Source Companies* before long.

At a far earlier stage than the Open Source movement lies the Lean start-up movement (Ries, 2011, `www.startuplessonslearned.com`). While still yet in its early days, this movement represents one of the most interesting changes in business strategy for some years. New patterns will arise in this field; only as these ideas become more widely applied will new patterns start to become visible.

Finally, while the examples in this book are intended to illustrate and explain the strategies and tactics under discussion, they are also hostages to the future. For example, Nokia provides the known uses for several patterns. Initial drafts of this book had Nokia providing even more known uses and examples, but Nokia in 2011 is not the successful company it was in 2007 or 2003. Things change, leaders becomes losers, strategies don't work or prove difficult to implement, and those pesky competitors change the context. Some of the original Nokia examples have been removed and others have become counter-examples. Time alone will tell how many of these examples and patterns stand up and are truly *timeless.*

Book Structure and How to Read

This book contains two types of pattern. Firstly, Patterns with a capital 'P' – CUSTOMER CO-CREATED PRODUCT, LOCAL GUIDE, PERSONAL SERVICE and more. These form the bulk of the book and can be found from Chapter 6 onwards. These patterns are written up in a defined format with a name, problem statement, a solution and supporting sections.

Then there are patterns with a small 'p': these are informal patterns described in unstructured English narrative. These are unnamed, dispersed and embedded throughout the book. To write a book containing only formal patterns would make for a dull book, and would also take significantly longer to complete, because of the review process, and far longer to read.

The obvious way to read this book is to start at page 1 and read to the end. There is nothing wrong with this approach, but it is not the way I would imagine reading this book.

Certainly, start at page 1 and read chronologically until the end of Chapter 5. Treat the book like a hyperlinked website: the pattern names are the links; follow them as curiosity strikes. As you go, you will encounter the names of patterns – PATTERN NAMES ARE IN SMALL CAPITALS FONT. If the pattern interests you, break off, read the pattern, then continue from the point at which you departed. If, while reading a pattern, you encounter the name of another pattern that interests you, then break off and read that pattern.

Taken this way, by the time you reach the start of the formal patterns, you will have read a good few of them already. Continue reading chronologically, but confine yourself to the opening sections and sequence diagrams of each chapter. Only read the patterns as and when you are motivated to.

You will also find boxed items interspaced with the text. As with the patterns, read these as curiosity strikes and as you encounter the references. Boxed items and individual patterns should make this a good book for flicking through and reading sections as you choose.

The book ends with appendices. These are intended for those who want really to understand patterns and the philosophy and thinking behind the patterns in this book. They also provide suggestions for where business patterns might go next.

Finally, as you encounter a pattern you think is useful, perhaps one you recognise – maybe you have an 'aha! moment' as you recognise something you are doing – please share it with a friend, a colleague or a co-worker. That is how the language of patterns will spread and become even more useful.

Sequence Diagrams

Each pattern chapter opens with a sequence diagram showing how the patterns defined in the chapter fit together with others in the chapter and patterns from elsewhere.

Figure 2 provides a key to these diagrams.

Figure 2. Sequence diagram key

These sequences have a casual resemblance to *Strategy Maps* (Kaplan & Norton, 2004). This was never the intention: sequence diagrams are well established in the pattern community, and pattern sequences are discussed in Appendix A. That two communities can find similar techniques for describing strategy implies that there is some merit to drawing strategy visually.

Comments Please

All the patterns in this book, with one exception, have been through an extensive review cycle at EuroPLoP and VikingPLoP conferences. The author continues to welcome comments on the patterns, although obviously there is only limited opportunity to update them now.

In particular, the author would like to hear about further examples of these patterns and instances where they have been used as a guide to business. Please send comments to allan@allankelly.net.

2

Structure of the Software Industry

If we are to talk about software creators and the companies that create software, we need to define what we mean by a *software company.* Or rather, we need to differentiate between the many different types of organisations that create software.

For the purposes of this book, I define a software company as '*a company that derives the bulk of its revenues from the sale of software or services to produce software*'. In most of this book we will be discussing one particular type of software company, the *independent software vendor*, or ISV.

While this book and the patterns within it contain lessons for all types of software producer, the lessons are clearest for ISVs. This is simply because ISVs have the simplest software business model. That is, the company lives or dies by its ability to sell the software it produces. Other software business models are equally valid, but the relationship between creating software products and making money is more complicated.

Types of Companies

There are several types of software-producing organisation that occur again and again. While the sections that follow do not constitute a comprehensive list, they do cover the majority of organisations that produce software. One might call these descriptions *patterns* of software companies. Indeed they are patterns in the sense that the same form is created again and again for recurring reasons.

However, these business models are not intended to document such patterns in *pattern form*. How an organisation comes to be an ISV, rather than a corporate IT department, is largely path-dependent: it is based historical events and decisions. Companies do switch between models, companies are spun out, merged and reformed, but the forces involved do not constitute the problem–solution pairing used in pattern form. (For more discussion on pattern form, see Appendix A and Appendix B.)

Independent software vendors

An independent software vendor (ISV) is a company that creates software for sale to customers. Originally, *independent* meant separate from the hardware vendors (for example IBM, Sperry, Data General, DEC and so on) that originally ruled the computing landscape. Computers were sold with software, the same company creating the hardware and the software. This model survives to this day and is discussed below (see *Vendors and the Software Stack* on page 24).

The first ISV is considered to be CUC, founded in March 1955 by Elmer Kubie and John Seldon (Hoch et al, 1999). Today the best-known ISVs are among the most widely known companies in the world – companies such as Microsoft, Oracle, SAP, Intuit, Symantec and Computer Associates.

ISVs are famously easy to start up. There are few barriers to entering the market and very little capital is needed to start an ISV. Indeed, some ISVs have their origins in student projects. The cultural home of the ISV is the Highway 101 corridor between San Francisco and San Jose, better known as 'Silicon Valley'. ISV start-ups are also celebrated in novels, such as *Microsurfs* (Coupland, 1996) and *The First $20 Million is Always the Hardest* (Bronson, 1998).

To start an ISV, all one needs is an idea for a product and some programming talent. To be a *successful* ISV is a different matter. Once established, an ISV must erect barriers to prevent the entry of competitors – or at least erect sufficient barriers to prevent successful entry!

Almost anyone can start an ISV, and with a lot of luck (not unknown) they can create a commercially successful product and a successful company. However, most ISVs probably fold before they have any impact on the market. An ISV that does not wish to count on luck needs marketing, management and more besides.

The majority of ISVs' costs are wages. Software developers and associated staff are not cheap. On occasions they can be persuaded to work for little or no money, motivated by the chance to be part of a success story, to create a great product or by stock options. However, in the long run an ISV must hire developers and pay a competitive salary.

As a result there is usually a gap of months or even years between the point at which the ISV starts spending money to develop its product and the point at which it starts to earn revenue from sales. Many companies turn to venture capital funds or business angels to help them through this period. To receive funding, however, the company must sell part of itself. (For a good description of this process, see *Start Up* (Kaplan, 1995).

Until the high-speed Internet became widely available and reliable, ISVs had a very simple business model. They developed software, copies of the software product were created on tape, floppy disks or CDs, usually with a manual, and everything put in a box. The company then tried to sell as many boxes as possible.

If the software was aimed at the home user – business-to-consumer, or 'B2C' – then companies usually tried to sell as many copies as possible through retail channels. This implied a relatively low selling price, say less than $1,000 per copy.

Business-focused software – business to business, or 'B2B' – usually came with a higher price. This was in part a reflection of the ability of business customers to pay higher prices, and in part a reflection of the higher costs of selling to business customers. Selling to a business customer often required a salesperson or even a sales team; since employing such staff is expensive, the software had to be sold at a price high enough to justify the extra costs.

The software sold in the traditional ISV model is often referred to as 'COTS' – *common off-the-shelf software* – which might more accurately be called 'COTSS': software where all customers have a common product. Customer might walk into a store, pick a product from the shelf, buy it and use it as-is. The term *shrinkwrap* is often used in the same sense and refers to the plastic used to wrap boxes.

Then came the Internet. CDs were no longer needed, as people could download the software, but the model was basically the same. A few interactive applications, such as webmail, began to appear. These applications existed naturally on the Internet with a web browser-based interface.

Following the 'dot.com boom', companies started to deliver software over the Internet, so-called *software as a service*, or 'SaaS' for short. SalesForce.com is usually credited with being one of the first to deliver software in this way. We will return to SaaS in *Software as a Service* on page 20; it is sufficient here to say that SaaS companies are a natural continuation of the ISV model.

In-house / Corporate IT

ISVs may be the best-known face of the software industry, and they may produce most of the installed software worldwide, but they do not create the majority of software or employ the majority of software developers. Most software is produced by organisations for their own use. This is referred to as *in-house* software development, because it occurs within the organisation.

Name any major corporation and you can be sure that it creates some software for its own use. If its does not, it is most probably because they pay another organisation to do it for them – such *external service providers (ESPs)* are discussed below.

Companies such as Unilever, Citigroup and BMW need software to support their own operations. There are many reasons why they may choose to write their own software. The most obvious is simply that they cannot find suitable COTS packages. Software that is developed specifically for a company or group of companies is called *custom* or *bespoke* software. Like a bespoke suit, it is created for one customer; it might fit others, but it will never fit them as well.

Perhaps the most rational reason why companies may choose write their own software is that in doing so they will be able to create a capability that no other organisation has, and therefore achieve advantage in the market. For example, if Citigroup were to produce a superior system for bond trading, it might be able to make more money than its competitors.

Unfortunately, many companies begin to write their own software systems for somewhat less rational reasons. When software projects are begun – or even just continued – for less than clear reasons, the work is likely to encounter difficulties.

Downturns can be boom time

At the turn of the millennium Mark was working for a small software company in London that produced a 'repo' trading system for banks and other financial institutions. (A 'repo' is a 'repurchase agreement', a complex loan arrangement traded on financial markets.)

The software system itself had started life at one of the European banks and been spun out as a commercial entity in its own right. However, the company struggled to sell the system to other banks, because each bank thought its own internally developed system represented a competitive advantage over other banks.

For a while the company had just one customer, the European bank that originally created the system. Then the 2001–2 downturn hit and all banks needed to save money. Competitive advantage was less important and cost-saving more important. Suddenly the company could sell its system.

Unlike ISVs and the other dedicated software companies discussed here, in-house IT lacks a business model of its own. The company's business is not software development; it needs IT systems – and thus software – to undertake its main line of business. Some companies operate a central budget from which their IT departments must decide how much to spend on each activity. Other organisations use cross-charging systems. In both cases it is difficult to draw a direct line between expenditure and business benefit. Michael Gentle (Gentle, 2007) argues that in most companies the mechanisms used result in an imbalance between supply and demand: as a result, demand far exceeds the supply capacity.

One of the problems faced by internal IT projects and teams is determining the value of the work. When a new system is designed to support a new business activity or product it can be hard to assign value between the IT and non-IT elements of the project.

Further, there is an incentive for those who want the project to go ahead (whether in the IT department or elsewhere in the company) to overstate its benefits and understate its costs. One study found that 38% of managers openly admitted to overstating benefits to obtain funding (Ward, 2006).

Because these companies do not depend directly on the success of their software, they are much more able to survive software development failures than ISVs. If an ISV has a failed development project, the company itself may well fail. If a corporation has a software failure, they are quite likely to continue as before. Consequently there tend to be a lot of software developers working on failing projects in large corporations.

Companies that produce their own software experience times when they do not have the capacity to undertake all the project they wish to. On such occasions they may engage an outside organisation – an *external service provider* (ESP) – to help cope with periods of peak demand. They may also turn to an ESP when they need specialist skills. For example, a company implementing an SAP system may well hire an ESP to provide the specialist skills required. Some companies also turn to ESPs because they simply do not want to create their own software; in some cases they don't want any IT operations at all. So they contract with an ESP to outsource provision of IT. This is discussed further in the following sections.

In-house IT departments may also provide opportunities for ISVs, although in a more roundabout fashion. An IT department that needs to develop an application for its own use because there are no suitable COTS application available may not be alone in its need: if one corporate IT department needs a new type of application, do others? Is this need unique to other organisations?

There may also be opportunities for in-house applications to be spun off into ISVs. Royal Dutch Shell spun off their data warehousing application to form Kalido; Soloman Brothers sold an internal reporting tool to a small Anglo-US ISV, which rebranded the application as their own and continued its development for several years.

Open Source

Differentiation is made here between companies that base their business on closed-source products, such as Microsoft and Adobe, and those that use Open Source, such as Red Hat and Canonical. Broadly speaking, the models outlined in this chapter can be applied together with an Open Source approach.

However, exploiting Open Source for commercial use requires additional thought and variations on traditional business models. This is beyond the scope of this book, but is the subject of a growing body of patterns (Link, 2010; Weiss, 2009; Weiss, 2010; Hannebauer et al, 2010).

External Service Providers (ESPs)

An *external service provider* (ESP) is a software company that is concerned primarily with bespoke software development rather than COTS packages. ESPs that may also be referred to as *consultancies* aim to have the same specialist skills found in ISVs, but to deploy those skills in the creation of bespoke software systems for specific customers.

ESP services need not stop with development of the software. They frequently become involved with adjacent activities, such as business process redesign, leading to the development of the software and the change management programme to introduce the software. ESPs may not only design and develop the systems, they may then operate the systems they (or others) have built, and even the business units using the software systems.

In their purest form, ESPs build systems for their customers. From this beginning ESPs have expanded in two directions. Firstly, have enlarged their service offering: rather than just supplying the software, they may run the software on a day-to-day basis and undertake enhancement work for their customers. They may also take over the running and enhancement of systems developed by the client or other ESPs, and may even take over the running of the entire IT department in an outsourcing arrangement.

The second direction in which ESPs have expanded is to grow beyond the IT department. ESPs such as Accenture have been active at taking over entire business processes. If the model can work for IT, then why not for human resources? Why should the ESP be confined to coding the payroll application? Why not run the entire payroll process? And if they can run the payroll, why not all account payable processes?

One specific expansion needs to be singled out: business strategy. Although IT workers are well paid, and the words 'IT' and 'cheap' are seldom heard together,

ESPs often find that developing software applications – mainly programming – has a low profit margin. Partly in an effort to find higher-margin work, and partly because of the relationship between IT and business strategy, ESPs have attempted to build high-profile strategy consulting businesses. Such moves, by the likes Accenture, Cap Gemini, EDS (now part of Hewlett Packard) and others have a mixed record of success.

Another reason for IT ESPs to move into strategy consulting may seem more Machiavellian. Business strategy is usually the domain of senior managers and company boards. By involving themselves in strategy consulting, the ESPs gain access to senior managers and board-level executives. Thus the ESPs have access to key decision-makers who are responsible for deciding which projects to undertake and who will undertake them. With board-level access, ESPs are in a position to set the agenda and propose ideas to their client companies, and in so doing they can ensure that they are best positioned to pick up the resulting work.

Governments are among the biggest customers of ESPs. Indeed, many EPSs devote resources to identifying new IT projects they can sell to a government. They will make a case for developing new systems for some government activity, then persuade the government to undertake the work. Needless to say, the ESP that thought of the idea for the new system is in prime position to undertake the work when the government contracts out its development.

ESPs usually work on a time and materials basis: costs are billed to clients with a mark-up. Few organisations willingly take on fixed-price work, which is hardly surprising given the poor delivery record of IT projects as a whole. Even where fixed-price work is agreed, it is not uncommon to find items falling outside the original contract for which the ESP can charge extra.

Upstream migration of ESPs away from hands-on development and towards outsourcing and business strategy leads to a continual birth cycle of ESPs. As large ESPs move into business strategy, they subcontract the low-margin programming work to smaller ESPs: this creates opportunities for new ESPs that can survive on low-profit margins.

Like ISVs, very little is required to form an ESP. Any group of developers can band together and, provided they can find a customer, set themselves up as an ESP.

A start-up ESP faces a different set of cash-flow problems to a start-up ISV. An ISV must start spending money on product development long before it sees any revenue. The billing cycle of an ESP is usually a lot shorter, perhaps a month. Therefore an ESP can start to recognise revenue far sooner. However, the ESP sales cycle is normally long: several months is not unusual. ESPs must find customers, persuade them to do business, then negotiate a contract.

An ESP that delivers a successful project is likely to be invited to tender for more work and is quite likely to work again with the client. There is therefore an understandable tendency for ESPs to bid low for initial work with a client in the hope of winning a contract. Once won, the ESP can look to secure more work, either as extra work on the same project or as follow-on work.

Taken together, these forces place conflicting demands on ESPs and team members. As with any supplier-customer relationship, whether it be building a house or building a software system, there is conflict between the interests of the supplier and customer. Such problems add further to the complicated matters around IT generally and software development specifically.

Data processing bureaux

For the sake of completeness we must mention data bureaux, also called 'computer bureaux'. Data bureaux take data processing work from an organisation and run it on their own machines, and perhaps their own software.

The 1960s and early 1970s were the high point of data bureaux. At this time computers were not nearly so common as they are today; mainframes were expensive, but the benefits of automation were obvious. A company would, for example, pay a bureau to perform its payroll processing each month.

Bureaux still exist, and in some ways were the original IT outsourcing operators. They also have a similarity to the modern SaaS: the software and hardware are the bureau's responsibility.

Software as a Service

SaaS business are a direct extension of the ISV model, but have characterises similar to bureaux and outsource providers. Instead of packaging their software on CD, an SaaS company will install it in a data centre and provide customers with a web-based interface to access it.

Customers benefit from this because they save in operating costs. They do not need to buy new hardware to run the software, they do not need to install it on desktop PCs, nor do they need to install updates. Memory and hard disks might be cheap, but installing software and fixing problems is expensive.

SaaS companies benefit because their software is normally sold using a subscription model, which means recurring revenue, typically every month. Software is normally offered in virtual packages, while customers are billed for the number of users, and prices may vary depending on which features are available. Unlike shrink-wrapped products, there is no piracy, because the actual software never leaves the SaaS company's premises.

This improves the SaaS company's cash flow and makes it less dependent on the successful launch of a new version of the software to bring fresh revenue. Since the cash flow is regular, investors regard it as a better bet than software sold for one-time fees.

However there are downsides to the SaaS model. Obviously customers must have a reliable, and preferably fast, connection to the Internet. While this may be taken for granted in most Western countries, it is not universal. It also means that customer's data is held by the SaaS providers. If the customer decides to change supplier, they need to ensure the removal of their data from the provider.

These issues and others mean that not all applications are suitable to the SaaS model. For example, those requiring complex user interfaces may not adapt well to a web-based interface – although this may change as new interface technology becomes possible.

Embedded software

There is a further type of software producer that exhibits some characteristics of the ISV and of the in-house organisation. An increasing number of companies today sell products that depend on software for what they do. Such companies range from Pure, which designs and manufacturers digital radios, to Rolls-Royce, which designs, builds and maintains aero-engines. Neither technology would be possible today without some software.

Pure exists to sell radios, but software is integral to the product. Similarly, Rolls-Royce could not produce a modern jet engine without software. Like an ISV, the product depends on software, but like a corporate IT function the software is not the product. Specialist ESPs also exist, such as Absolute Software in the UK, which develop software to embed in products for companies that do not have their own development function.

The term *embedded software* is commonly used to describe software for small devices such as digital watches, children's toys or mobile phones. Such software needs to run in a restricted environment with limited amounts of processor power and memory. While these are the characteristics of much embedded software, they do not hold for all. The hallmark of embedded software is that it is an integral, and often invisible, part of a product.

In this book, the term 'embedded software' is understood to have wide definition: software contained in any product where the product would not be possible without the software, but where the software alone is not the only deliverable.

For example, software is embedded in the Boeing 777 airliner. The aeroplane would not be possible without fly-by-wire control for the pilot (and in-flight entertainment for the passengers). The software in a 777 is embedded in the sense that it is an integral part of the aeroplane – it is embedded in the aeroplane – not in the sense that it is operating in a constrained environment (although parts undoubtedly operate within severe constraints of one sort of another.)

The objective for producers of embedded software is similar to that of an ISV: to sell products. The more products sold, the more money is earned. But producers of embedded software also operate like in-house teams, because they are but one part of an organisation delivering a product or services. Again it is possible to outsource development of the software, but this may surrender control of a vital piece of the final product.

B2B and B2C

Two abbreviations that crop up again and again in discussion of software companies are 'B2B' and 'B2C'. B2B means 'business to business', and refers to companies that sell to other companies, such as SAP, Oracle and SalesForce.com. B2C refers to companies that sell to the general public, 'business to customer'. For example, games from companies such as Ubisoft and Electronic Arts overwhelmingly sell to end customers.

It is exceptional to find a individual customer who might want to buy a copy of an enterprise product such as a SAP system or open their own SalesForce account. However it is common to find B2C companies that also sell to other companies. Many products that can be useful to individuals at home can also be useful to businesses, for example Microsoft Word.

This presents companies with a problem, or an opportunity, depending on how you look at it. The problem is whether to:

- Offer a single product to all customers that offers economies, but risks undercharging commercial customers or overcharging home users (as described in HOMOGENOUS CUSTOMERS (page 136), or...
- To segment the customer base and offer different products to each market, in which case there needs to be some way of deterring buyers from simply buying the cheaper version, as described in SEGMENTED CUSTOMERS (page 141).

Outsource and Offshore

In the interests of clarity it is important that the terms *outsource* and *offshore* are clearly defined.

- An *outsourcing* arrangement takes place when a company decides to pay an ESP to undertake some aspect of its IT operations. This usually involves more than just writing an application, and typically involves more than one system.
- An *offshore* arrangement takes plan when a company decides to undertake some of its IT work in a different country, usually in pursuit of lower wage costs.

While the two terms are frequently used together, 'outsource' does not imply offshore and vice versa. Therefore it is wrong to use the terms interchangeably. Table 1 sets out some examples to different combinations of sourcing and location.

Table 1: Differentiating between outsourced and offshore

Offshore	HSBC develops software for its London office in Bangalore	Wipro in Hyderabad develops software for a client in New York
Onshore	Rolls-Royce develops software for its jet engines in Derby, UK	ThoughtWorks develops software for a client in the client's London offices
	In-house	*Outsourced*

A company need not outsource work to offshore it. The American GE company established its own unit in India to move business processes offshore. This unit eventually became an independent company, GECIS, handing outsourced business process for GE and other companies.

This highlights the question: *what is offshoring?* If a global bank such as HSBC decides to develop software for the UK market in its India offices, most people would consider it offshoring. But if a company decides to develop the same software in its California offices, they would not. Answering this question is beyond the scope of this book.

(In recent years the term *near-shoring* has also entered the vocabulary. This is usually used to denote IT work done in the same country as the end users, but in a lower-cost location. For example, one US investment bank develops software for its London office in Glasgow, and the London office of a Japanese telecoms company has software developed in Cornwall.)

While offshore outsourcing deals may make newspaper headlines, many outsourcing contracts not only keep work in the same country, but keep the same workers doing the same jobs. So normal is the transfer of workers that the European Union even has regulations to govern such transfers – known as the Transfer of Undertakings (Protection of Employment) Regulations, or 'TUPE'.

While the term 'offshoring' may be relatively new, the practice is not. During the 1980s and into the 1990s development of the IBM CICS application happened at Hursley Park because UK developers were cheaper than US developers for IBM.

Since the turn of the century a trend has developed for outsource operations to move offshore. Indian companies such as Wipro and Infosys have been at the fore of this movement. There is some logic here: companies often outsource in an effort to reduce costs. Offshoring can reduce costs, so it is natural that in seeking to reduce costs the two go together.

More recently companies like Wipro and Infosys have started to build up their staff in countries such as the UK and USA to manage and operate parts of outsourcing deals that cannot be offshored. This is both to negate political objections to work moving offshore and in preparation for the day when India is no longer cheaper. Some sources suggest that with current inflation rates, Indian and Chinese cost advantages will have disappeared by 2015 (Jones, 2008).

While companies continue to outsource and offshore work, there are also stories of companies bringing work back in-house and undoing offshoring deals. Whether this constitutes any kind of trend is hard to say. It is certainly true that not every outsourcing or offshoring deal works well. It is also true that things happen to companies to cause them to reconsider such deals. As more such deals are done it is only natural that more arrangements will be undone.

Vendors and the Software Stack

Originally the 'independent' in 'independent software vendor' meant that the company was independent of hardware vendors who also supplied software. Hardware vendors both understood the hardware better than anyone and had need of software to run on their products. After all, what use would an IBM/360 mainframe be without the OS/360 operating system?

Over time two things happened. Firstly hardware, with some exceptions, became standardised and commoditised. Standardisation meant that the same software could run on a Compaq PC as on an IBM PC. Commoditisation drove prices down, and customers frequently chose hardware on the basis of price. While hardware became common and commoditised, the software packages provided differentiation.

The second thing that happened was the creation of a *software stack*. In the same way that an operating system runs on hardware, applications run on an operating system. Some of these applications, databases for example, form an additional layer upon which more applications can be built. Such applications form another layer in the stack. Although the exact layers of the stack will vary from application to application, the idea remains the same. (The layered stack is an example of an extremely high level LAYERS pattern (Buschmann et al, 1996).

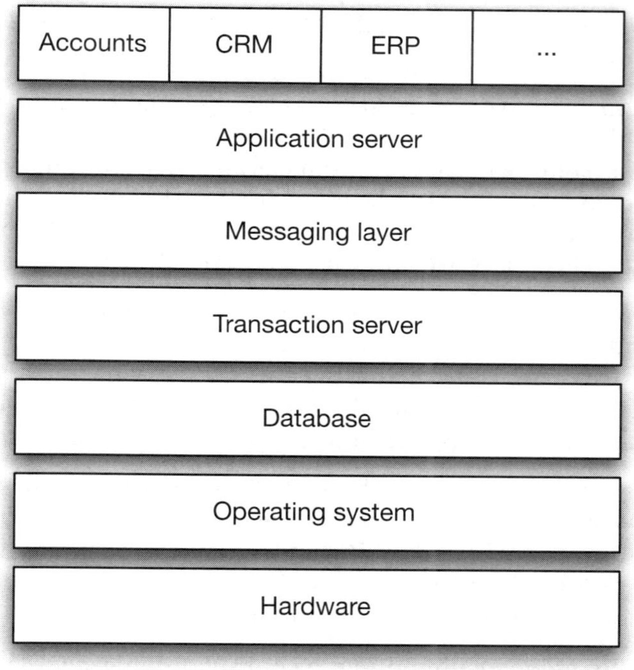

Figure 3. Example software stack

Hardware vendors still exist and in many cases still produce their own operating systems and applications, although this is more common in the mainframe market than in the PC and server market. Now however the hardware vendors are joined by software companies, ISVs, who are themselves vendors.

For example, Acer is a hardware vendor; Microsoft is the ISV when it supplying the Windows operating system for the Acer machine. This pattern repeats up the stack, with the topmost ISV playing the role of vendor to another ISP. For example, Microsoft plays vendor to Sybase for the Sybase database. Such relationships are an example of the COMPLEMENTOR, NOT COMPETITOR (page 309) pattern.

Although this stack has been relatively stable for the last 25 years or so, things are starting to change. As the mobile phone market converges with the PC market, *vertical companies* that integrate hardware, operating system and applications can once again demonstrate an advantage.

At the time of writing it is difficult to say whether the integrated model exemplified by Apple and Blackberry will triumph over the layered stack model exemplified by Nokia and Microsoft. Google has been following the stack model with its Android mobile operating system, but its recent purchase of Motorola's Mobility might mark the start of a change.

Many companies have chosen to tackle multiple slices of the stack. Indeed, Oracle and others aim to supply the entire software stack. With the purchase of Sun Microsystems, Oracle now produces an entire software and hardware stack: Oracle and ex-PeopleSoft applications run on BEA application servers, on top of an Oracle database running on Solaris on Sun hardware. (An example of the SAME CUSTOMERS, DIFFERENT PRODUCT (page 105) pattern.)

Oracle believe this will help its customers by allowing them to buy all their components in one place, and by ensuring that these components work well together. This arrangement also benefits Oracle, which can sell more products and lock their customers into their technology. The more pieces of the stack a customer needs to change, the less likely they are to change suppliers.

Until recently Oracle was a traditional ISV: although large, it was independent of any hardware vendor. As such it practiced COMPLEMENTOR, NOT COMPETITOR with the hardware and OS vendors. With the purchase of Sun Microsystems and the addition of Sun hardware and Solaris to the PRODUCT PORTFOLIO (page 296), Oracle is both complementor and competitor to the likes of IBM and HP.

Oracle is not alone in attempting to control multiple stack layers: Microsoft has long attempted to move up the stack by offering its own SQL Server database and range of business applications. In purchasing Sybase, SAP is attempting to move down the stack.

While such complementor and competitor relationships complicate the model, they are a fact of business life and competition. At almost every layer of the stack the vendor needs to sell product; the value of their product is enhanced when third parties can build on the product – to build a WHOLE PRODUCT (page 131). Companies such as Microsoft, Oracle and SAP need to manage difficult complementor and competitor relationships.

On the one hand vendors are trying to be open and welcome third-party developers, but on the other hand they also want to displace them. There is no simple answer to this conflict. Companies move between the two extremes; sometimes the whole industry seems to be heading in one direction and then in the other. Several of the patterns in this book discuss this conflict.

To complicate matters further, most vendors will offer some consulting services as well. At the most basic level this involves offering help when a product is new – see INITIAL HELP (page 248). This can be a source of additional revenue which customers value – hence LIFETIME SERVICES FOR PRODUCTS (page 252) and PROFESSIONAL SERVICES TEAM (page 258).

Some organisations, including the likes of Microsoft and SAP, go further and will take on the role of an ESP. Sometimes, as in the case of IBM Global Services, the ESP teams may use technology from competing vendors.

In 2008 Hewlett Packard, traditionally a hardware – and later software – vendor, bought the services company EDS for over $12 billion. This gives HP access to services revenue, additional opportunities to sell equipment and feedback on how to make better products (see the SERVICES FEEDBACK pattern on page 262.) Whether this results in a better deal for customers is debatable. Previously EDS would choose 'best of breed' products from the best-suited vendor. Undoubtedly now, whether deliberately or not, some EDS staff will feel compelled to advise HP solutions to customers.

Indeed, there is a long track record of hardware and software vendors buying services companies. The year after Hewlett P,ackard's purchase of EDS, Dell bought Perot Systems. These transactions came several years after IBM bought PricewaterhouseCoopers's 'Monday' consulting business. Earlier still, Compaq bought Digital (DEC) to acquire its services business. Examples of services companies buying vendors are fewer and further between.

The biggest technology companies frequently undertake multiple roles (ESP, ISV and so on) and thus occupy multiple layers of the stack at the same time. These companies claim to focus on the end result, resolution of customer problems, rather than the process that solves the problem. Only the customers of these companies can decide whether this is true. Certainly, in undertaking multiple roles, internal conflicts are inevitable.

The patterns in this book attempt to dissect these strategies and identify the common factors. Inevitably, new strategies and forces are constantly emerging and the landscape changing.

The ISV / ESP Divide

The ISV and ESP business models are traditionally the two dominant forms of organisation in the software industry. Yet the two models lead to markedly different structures, roles and incentives for managers and developers.

ESPs generally work to a *pull* model: customers come to them and request a specific piece of software. As a result there is only one customer for the software and ESPs tend to stay involved long after the sale is complete; indeed, they may work with the customer for the life of the software.

ISVs, on the other hand, typically work to a *push* model: they build the software, then attempt to sell as many copies as possible. A software sale may constitute the end of an ISV's relationship with a customer. In fact the ISV may actually view further customer contact as undesirable if it entails providing costly services such as technical support.

The pull model is desirable because it only creates what is needed: nothing more, and (hopefully) nothing less. Yet this makes the model difficult to scale, because each product is unique. The push model is desirable because the same product can be sold again and again: the model scales. The difficulty here is in building a product that is complete enough to sell, but not so over-engineered that the cost of building and ownership are too high.

While both ESPs and ISVs employ software coders, testers and project managers, ESPs tend to employ business analysts, while ISVs employ product managers. Both roles aim to discover what customers want and need and communicate this to the development teams, but their mode of operation is different:

- Business analysts work with a small group of customers, and/or users if those who buy the software are not those who use it. They look at the work activities the users undertake and the business processes. They may even analyse these and propose changes.
- Product managers also talk to customers and/or users, but they typically have a more diverse set of users. Rather than just talking to people who work for the customer, they need to find potential users at a variety of customers and understand their needs. Product managers also need to look at competitors' products and developing technologies to take a long-term view of future developments.

(Obviously, in companies that act as both ESP and ISV, both roles will be found in different areas.)

In short a business analyst's work is more tightly focused on specific customer/users and specific deliverables, while a product manager's role is to make sense of a variety of information from multiple sources.

In the ESP model, software requirements and specifications are often agreed before development work begins and are enshrined in a legally binding contract. Changes to these requirements are often a matter of conflict, and elaborate *change request controls* and *change review boards* are put in place to manage (or deter, depending on your point of view) modifications.

ISVs are not immune to changing requirements, but for them there are no legal barriers or client–supplier relationship to negotiate. Trade-off in terms of functionality and timescales is more clear-cut.

Most ESP projects are conducted on a time and materials basis. The longer an ESP spends on a project, the more they can expect to earn; similarly, the more people they employ to do the work, the greater the return. More people, for longer, means more revenue.

This can act as a disincentive to use existing code. If an ESP needs some special data structure that cannot be bought off the shelf, it is in the ESP's interest to implement the structure in code entirely even if the ESP has already done the same thing on another project. In doing so the ESP will charge for the same data structure twice, once each to two different customers.

The disincentive to reuse code is not entirely down to the fees to be earned writing it again. It is common for a client to own the intellectual property (IP) and software code at the end of a project. So even if an ESP has implemented the same functionality elsewhere, they may not be allowed to reuse the code.

This leads to another feature of the ESP model: companies, and individuals, specialise in certain customer domains. Consequently, individuals may find themselves building very similar systems for different customers year after year. Inevitably ESP employees (usually called 'consultants') take some of what they learn at one client to their subsequent clients. Intellectual property (that is, knowledge) in employees' heads moves from one client to the next even if the source code does not.

Such problems do not exist for ISVs that continue to own the intellectual property (IP) and code after a project ends. Indeed for an ISV the work is less of a project – which by definition has a start and end date – and more a product that will continue to be developed and sold for years. Therefore opportunities for code re-use are well worth taking.

The same factors also mean that there is a greater incentive for the ISV to keep its code base flexible, to refactor and improve difficult code, as time spent improving code now will pay back in time saved later. For an ESP though there may be little incentive to save time, neither is it certain that the ESP will still be working on the software the next time it needs modifications.

This is not to say that an ESP will duplicate work or avoid improving existing code; this is only to point out that incentives may exist. Because the ESP relationship is ongoing, customers need to feel they can trust their supplier in a way they may not when purchasing a single product from an ISV.

For both ISVs and ESPs staffing costs are the single biggest expenditure, and both types of software company need good staff. ISVs are not normally short of ideas for enhancing their product(s); however the amount of work they can undertake is limited by the number of staff they employ, which is in turn constrained by their revenue forecasts. Consequently ISV developers are seldom left without work.

ESPs have a different set of constraints. Again their revenue must – at least in the long run – cover their staffing costs, but there may be gaps in the work stream. Staff may be left with nothing to do for weeks or even months at a time. Staff waiting for assignments are said to be 'on the bench'. Such staff costs the ESP but does not bring in revenue; however, the ESP does not wish to let the staff go, because finding replacements is time-consuming and costly.

The list of differences between ISV and ESP models could go on. The key point is that while some skills (such as coding) transfer easily between the two models, the more managerial skills, such as determining requirements, project management and cost control, make it more difficult to transfer people between the two models.

Christensen: innovation and disruption

One of the more popular ideas in technology strategy in recent years is that of *disruptive technology*, or rather *disruptive innovation*. These terms were coined by Clayton Christensen in a series of articles and books (Christensen, 1997; Christensen & Bower, 1995; Christensen & Raynor, 2003).

Christensen states that the actual innovation is only part of the story. In order for an innovative product (or service) to be successful, it has to be marketed in such a way as to challenge the incumbents in the market. No matter how innovative the technology or novel the product, all new products compete against existing products for customers' money.

Existing market incumbents have a number of inbuilt advantages that favour them, and the status quo, over any new entrant. Simply launching a new and better product is unlikely to succeed.

Incumbents have revenues which many start-ups lack. They have an existing customer base, established partners, contracts and sales channels. Incumbents fit into an existing ecosystem of suppliers and customers that represent the existing market. They know the customers and the customers know them. Any change is likely to cause disruption for such customers.

For many of the companies – and individuals – change may not be an attractive prospect. It involves more work; it upsets existing relationships, supply chains, pricing schemes and operations, and entails risk. The idea that a better product will automatically sell is flawed, because so many customers have a vested interest in the current, albeit inferior, product.

The challenge for new entrants is to present their product in such a way that the benefits outweigh the risks and cost of change to customers. At the same time they need to ensure that incumbents do not feel threatened and deploy their advantages to squash the newcomer before they are established.

Therefore understanding the market and the needs of customers is essential in launching a new innovative product. Rather than innovating for innovation's sake, companies know where to focus their efforts. This is a topic picked up in other works, such as *Tuned In* (Stull et al, 2008).

Since knocking on the door of potential customers and saying "My product is better than the one you are using" is unlikely to persuade them to change, a more targeted approach is required. This solution starts by recognising that markets already exist. The long-term aim might be to create an entirely new market segment, but at first the need is to compete in an existing market against existing incumbents.

The next step is to segment potential customers and decide which segment to approach, and how. Christensen outlines two alternative approaches. One approach is to target those customers who are *underserved*: that is, customer who find that existing products do not exactly meet their needs. By making your product match their needs better, they will be more open to adopting your product.

The alternative approach is to target customers who are *over-served* by the existing product. These are customers who use the existing product but do not need all of its abilities, functionality or features, yet have to pay for these capabilities even though they are unnecessary. Targeting these customers means producing a more basic product and selling it at a lower cost.

In neither case is the technology itself disruptive, but in both cases the technology is presented in such a way as to disrupt the existing market status quo. The first approach disrupts by better serving customers, while the second disrupts by separating low-end customers.

There are clear parallels here with the targeted approach laid out in *Crossing the Chasm* (Moore, 1999) and Chapter 3, and in the generic strategies of Michael Porter (Porter, 1980). Christensen's first approach could be classified as a *differentiated niche* in Porter's taxonomy, and the second as a *low-cost strategy*.

Initially the segments served are likely to be so small that existing incumbents don't notice the loss of a few customers – they may even pleased to see non-core customers leave. Once the disruptive competitor does register on the incumbents' radar, they can find it difficult to compete because their existing customer base and strategies confine their actions. The existing market limits the action of the incumbent, while providing opportunities for the innovator. This condition has been labelled *tyranny of the served market* (Hamel & Prahalad, 1996).

Over time the new entrant expands the segment and adds additional segments, perhaps by expanding the capabilities of the product so that customers find it more useful, or by producing a series of products targeted at different types of customer. This incremental or piecemeal approach to growth is reminiscent of the pattern philosophy of Christopher Alexander.

For any company aiming at a disruptive approach a number of the business strategy patterns are directly applicable. Figure 4 shows a few of the patterns that might prove useful.

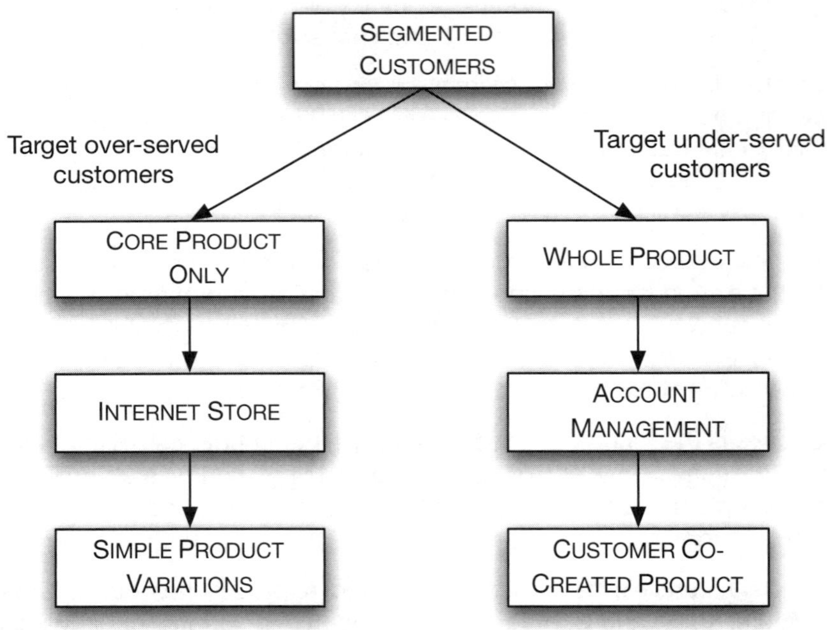

Figure 4. Pattern map to implementing Christensen's approaches

Closing Words

More, many more, types of software-producing organisations could be defined. Those described here cover the majority. Understanding the different types of software producers helps to explain the market and set a common language for the patterns that follow. Such understanding is also important for individuals as their career develops.

This book is concerned primarily with *software companies*: companies that produce software as a fundamental part of their business model. ISVs, ESPs, SaaS providers and producers of embedded software are the main focus. Of these the focus is especially sharp on ISVs. More than any other, these companies live or die by their ability to get the right products to market at the right price, at the right time and market them to customers.

The boundaries within these divisions are increasingly blurred. Is Microsoft an ISV or a vendor? Is Microsoft Consulting an ESP? Yet at the same time knowing the boundaries, and focusing within them, can help a company to greater success.

3

Software Company Lifecycle

Traditionally software development has been viewed as a project-based exercise. A project team builds a piece of software; one day that piece of software is 'finished', it is sold to customers and everyone lives happily ever after. But for a company that makes its living selling software, the product is never finished. If the product were ever to reach a stage where no changes were needed, the company would probably cease to exist (see *Peter's story* on page 236 for one possible example). New products and improvements to existing products are the lifeblood of ISVs and other software companies.

Thus, for ISVs, SaaS providers and others, the product model of development is better than the project model. Projects, by definition, have a defined start and end. Products, in contrast, continue – perhaps indefinitely, although work on the product might be divided into a series of projects.

When a company makes its living by selling software products, a project is only one chapter in the company and product history. The project view adds little to our understanding of how a successful company produces software products. When a product is successful, there will always be another development episode or project. Instead it is more informative to look at the company lifecycle.

While all companies are unique, the same patterns, problems and challenges emerge time and time again. Companies start up; they have to create a product, find customers, make sales and generally survive. Once established the company needs to grow. If it has taken venture capital, its investors will want to see rapid growth; few investors are satisfied with slow growth. Growth brings problems of its own. And inevitably, all companies face unexpected problems and setbacks along the way.

Many of the patterns later in this book address these issues. To set the context, we first need to look at the lifecycle of software companies.

Early Days

Most companies never make it past the conception stage: ideas stay in people's heads, business plans fail to be funded or people start but lack the energy to follow through. Even those plans that get past inception regularly flounder – products fail to make it to market, and those which do fail to sell.

In general, there are few laws to prevent starting a software company. Of course every country has laws against creating harmful products, laws against criminal activity and laws barring disreputable individuals, but there are no laws against starting a company with a poor product, ill-defined market or stupid managers. It is a matter of pride in countries like the USA and UK that new companies can be started very easily in a few days. However, while creating a new company might be as easy as falling off a log, building a successful company is far harder.

Market forces mean that most such companies will fail quickly. The more flaws in a companies, the quicker it will fail. The good ones are more likely to survive, but there are no guarantees.

Even among the companies that survive, there is no guarantee that they have actually done anything right. Sometimes success is pure luck – they opened an office in the right town, or just happened to be in the right place at the right time to make a sale. But most of the time companies survive because they have consciously done something – perhaps more than one thing – right. They may have a truly innovative product idea, they may have hired the right staff, and perhaps they have identified a genuine market need. Whichever it is, they get something sufficiently right to survive.

In the early days of a software company it has to do three things: build a product, find customers and establish the company (hire people, find an office and so on). A start-up has to launch itself and launch a product; established companies face far fewer challenges when launching a new product.

For a software company to survive it needs at least two essential factors: software developers and salespeople. Frequently it is two individuals who represent these two sides of its activities: one from sales and one from development.

In general, unless criminal intent is afoot or harmful products are to be produced, starting a company is like having a baby: there are no laws against it, but two consenting individuals are needed. Without someone to create the software there will be nothing to sell. And without someone to sell it, nothing will be sold. Many software start-up dreams fail for want of one or other of these factors.

Even if a company outsources software development or sells through distributors, it still needs both factors. They may be at arm's length, but they are still present. Somewhere in the company's value chain, it needs both.

Often one or other of these factors will be dominant. If the product really is innovative it is likely that the development side will be dominant. Consequently the company will grow with a strong engineering bias, respect for developers and a belief that technology holds the key to future success.

On the other hand, it is possible that the product is not very innovative; perhaps it is not even very good. But the salespeople are very good, the kind of people who can 'sell snow to Eskimos'. In this case the sales function will dominate company culture and development takes a back seat. As the company experiences initial success, these biases will become part of its culture. Unfortunately these biases may prove to be the seeds of future problems.

Provided the company can create a product and sell it, the company will grow. It is even likely that the company will grow fast. It is starting from a low base, so year-on-year sales will grow quickly. If the company has taken outside investment from venture capitalists or business angels, there will be significant pressure to grow sales rapidly.

With the company experiencing success and growth the product too will grow rapidly. The code base is small and therefore easy to understand, there is little or no legacy code to work around, features are relatively easy to describe and most of the original developers are still working on the code.

Growing

As the user base grows it becomes harder and harder to maintain its growth rate, simply because of the law of numbers. When the installed base is ten, adding one customer means 10% growth. If you start the year with ten customers and add one a month, at the end of the year you have more than doubled your customer base. But in the second year you have to acquire two new customers a month to repeat the same growth rate. Signing new customers doesn't get easier just because you have twice as many already.

Similarly the development team faces problems. As the code base grows it requires more effort to maintain as entropy sets in. New developers will be hired to cope with the increased maintenance burden and to speed up delivery of new features. These developers will need time to become proficient with the code base, and may never reach the level of understanding held by the original developers.

Meanwhile the original developers, who are accustomed to writing new code, now have to maintain existing code. Some developers excel in writing new code and dislike maintaining existing code in the extreme. As the development team grows all-round communication becomes more difficult, simply because there are more people.

About this time issues may start to emerge with existing code, particularly if it has been written in a hurry. Now that all the obvious features have been added to the product, new features are more involved, are bigger and take longer to implement. Both key functions, sales and development, start to respond more slowly. The challenges facing a company have changed. The company must still acquire new customers, but it also needs to keep existing customers happy; new products must be developed but the old product maintained. Company administration and communication also become more of an issue as the company grows.

More people, more departments, more locations: all these make management's task harder too. The original management might excel in innovation and risk-taking, but find managing an established company, with customers to support and growing staff numbers, more of a challenge.

At the same time divisions will emerge between the sales and development groups. Salespeople, keen for the next sale and commission, promise features that are not available, or promise ambitious dates for new versions. Developers rail against over-ambitious delivery dates and recoil at promises made by salespeople.

Enter marketing

In the early days of the company marketing is ignored. Marketing doesn't build products and doesn't sell them, but costs. Sales and development are essential but marketing isn't, so many companies start without marketing – but for a company to be really successful, marketing is essential.

At some point a company needs to embrace both *outbound* and *inbound* marketing. But because marketing is normally absent initially, by the time this happens the company has already created an engineering or a sales culture. Consequently it is difficult to embed marketing in the company.

Inbound and outbound marketing defined

Outbound marketing is the type of marketing most people think of when the world 'marketing' is used. It involves telling the market that a product exists, what it does, why they should buy it, where and how they can buy it. Outbound marketing is concerned with awareness, brand image, advertising, public relations and so on.

Inbound marketing aims to understand what potential customers want from a product and what will motivate them to spend money on a product. In contrast to outbound marketing, it is a listening exercise rather than a talking exercise. Inbound marketing may involve qualitative research (interviewing customers, observing customers, examining rivals) and/or quantitative research (surveys and other statistical analysis tools.)

Inbound marketing needs to occur before and during the creation of the product, while outbound marketing occurs when the product is ready for purchase. In small organisations the two functions often fall on the same individual or individuals. Larger organisations may appoint product managers to undertake inbound marketing and product marketing managers to handle outbound marketing.

Chapter 7 looks at marketing and patterns of marketing in more depth.

Specials

One issue is more likely than any other to set sales and developers at loggerheads: custom development, also called 'specials'. In the B2B market there will always be some customers who will want specific features and are prepared to pay for them. For a salesperson in search of a commission, or a company struggling with growth and cash flow, the prospect of a customer paying extra money for an additional feature is often too good to turn down.

Developers dislike custom features for good reasons. In most code bases a custom feature means a lot of extra work. It may mean a separate code branch, additional testing and a diversion from the agreed development path. Custom development diverts people from the main task in hand – building a better product – and creates confusion over what is best for all customers versus what is best for one customer. Then there are questions of ongoing support for any custom feature, and whether (and how) the feature can be made available to other customers.

Many if not most B2B ISVs hit this problem sooner or later. The cash is attractive, but usually custom features create more problems than they are worth. If nothing else, management loses time debating 'should we do this work?' Unfortunately, even when a company outlaws selling of such features, they all too often still get sold.

Doing such work is usually a bad idea for one simple reason: companies that are set up to create general products for many customers do not have the skills, process or understanding to do bespoke projects. Unless a company is prepared to set up a dedicated group to handle such work, it is better off avoiding it.

The Chasm

Marketing and selling technology is the subject of *Crossing the Chasm* (Moore, 1999), one of the best-known books about technology marketing.

Moore suggests that many technology companies never reach their full potential because selling technology to early adopters is very different to selling to mainstream customers. In fact, the difference is so massive as to constitute a chasm. Relatively few companies cross this chasm; most remain trapped selling an advanced technology product to a few technically savvy customers. Others fall into the chasm while attempting its crossing.

Most technology products, software included, follow a similar trajectory. This is called the *technology adoption lifecycle* – see Figure 5. Unfortunately those who are first to buy the product, *innovators* and *early adopters,* create problems for the seller at later stages.

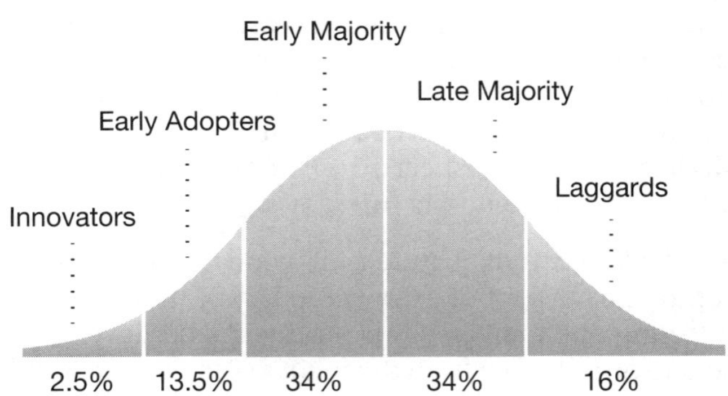

Figure 5. Technology adoption lifecycle model

Reproduced with permission of John Wiley & Sons, Ltd: Technology Adoption Life Cycle, *Crossing the Chasm*, Geoffrey Moor

Many software companies start out with the simple belief that 'if you build it they will come'. In some cases this works: the idea is so great or so useful that few can imagine the product before it is built, but once it is built everyone wants one. All that is required is a great technology and a belief in the technology. However, most products do not fall into this category.

A single-minded focus on technology may actually get in the way of selling more products: the innovators and early adopters who are first to buy the product actually fool the company's founders into believing that technology alone is the key to success.

When a new technology product first works it is amazing, like a dog walking on its hind legs. Technology oriented innovators will buy the product simply because the technology is cool. Next to buy it are the early adopters, people who see the value in the technology for themselves. These buyers are prepared to spend their own time and money making the technology work with their existing systems.

Combined, these two groups may represent a large market: just selling to these two can look a lot like success. Sales are plentiful and revenue rises. However, these two groups of buyers represent a very small part of the total market. The majority of the market falls into another two categories: *early majority* and *late majority*, and selling to these customers requires a different approach.

The *early majority* are very different customers to the innovators and early adopters. These buyers need to be shown the benefits the technology delivers; they are not impressed by technology itself, neither do they have the vision to see the product's potential. Rather than marketing technology or features, the seller now has to explain the benefits to their customers' business. These buyers are not interested in a dog walking on two legs – they want to know what the dog can do for them.

In addition, such customer are more risk-averse: they want proof that the product can deliver its claimed benefits. They want to see case studies of similar organisations that have realised these benefits. Nor are they prepared to spend their time making the product work for them, unlike the early adopters. They are not interested in the product or the technology, only the benefits.

The good news is this: this group is prepared to spend more money, because they can directly relate the product to benefits. But getting this money requires work. To sell to this group, the technology company needs to change how it operates, and especially how it markets and sells its products. This starts by focusing on a specific market niche, the smaller the better. Defining this niche will allow the company to define a market in which it is the market leader.

At the same time product development teams need to ensure that the product addresses the problems in this market exactly. Rather than being technology-led, the product and its teams need to be led by the problems in the market.

To address the problems in the market, the company needs to change its view of what it is selling. Rather than selling a technology *product*, it needs to sell a technology *solution*. This solution needs to address the whole problem, so if the customer requires training, this needs to be sold too. If customers need to integrate the new solution with existing systems, this needs to be included. Selling the solution means selling a *whole product*, one that includes everything needed for the customer to recognise the value from the product/solution. The pattern WHOLE PRODUCT (page 131) takes this concept into pattern form.

Once the seller has established its niche and demonstrated real leadership, it can look at expansion. Expansion comes from two sources. Firstly, from expanding the niche by including similar markets. For example, if the company has defined its niche as 'leading widget supplier in England', a natural expansion would be to 'leading widget supplier in Great Britain' and then to 'leading widget supplier in Europe'.

As well as expanding the niche, the seller gradually attacks additional, related niches. This is 'domino theory': capture one niche, then use it as a base to take the next niche, and so on.

After the early majority, the late majority group should come easily. These customers are broadly similar to the early majority, but tend to buy more mature products. Given time they will follow the early majority.

The final group of adopters who complete the cycle are the *laggards*, who only buy once the product is omnipresent. This group is so small it does not justify any additional effort.

Post Start-up Middle Age

All companies pass through a middle-age phase. For some it is a brief interlude between start-up growth and flotation or acquisition; other companies get past start-up but get stuck in middle age. Perhaps the company can't move on from early adopters to early majority, or perhaps the company doesn't even realise there is a chasm to cross. For one reason or another these companies are stuck searching for their breakthrough feature or sale. Without the breakthrough, they are unable to repeat the growth of their youth or establish the stability that would justify an ownership change.

To venture capital investors these companies are the *walking dead*. The companies have not fallen into bankruptcy; they generate cash, but not enough to justify the original investment. Without a breakthrough they cannot justify a public offering, and few, if any, other companies are interested in acquiring them. To close the company down would be to lose more money, but while the company continues to operate it absorbs venture capital management time and distracts from new investment.

Whether simply passing through or stuck, the challenges facing the middle-aged company are different to those facing the start-up. There is still a challenge to find new customers and keep existing customer happy, but the main challenge is to sell more to existing customers – the SAME CUSTOMERS, DIFFERENT PRODUCT (page 105) pattern. It is more efficient to sell to existing customers; selling more to these customers deepens the relationship, making them less likely to buy from competitors. Thus cash flow becomes more dependable and profitability increases.

Product-wise, the innovations that propelled these companies initially have started to age, and competitors have copied them by now. To continue growth, the company must innovate. However, repeating the original act of innovation is difficult: the original innovation may have been a one-off; the circumstances that led to it may no longer exist. The company must find the means to innovate internally.

In direct contrast to innovation, the company may also need to increase efficiency. Young companies sacrifice efficiency in the race to market; nobody pays much attention to operating efficiently simply because growth is so fast. Inefficient operations may be tolerated when sales are growing rapidly and managers' time is needed to expand the company by creating new relationships and hiring new employees.

When a company is growing, adding new products and services, staff released by improved efficiency can easily be absorbed elsewhere: there is no shortage of work to do. When a company is stuck or shrinking, efficiency improvements only result in cost savings when staff are laid off.

Investor Exit

Some companies are happy to reach the post start-up phase and become stable. They continue to sell the same product(s) with periodic updates. Mostly their existing customers buy the revised products; a few new customers come along and a few leave. Year after year the company essentially does the same thing.

This status quo may be acceptable if those running the company regard the business as a lifestyle choice. However, Anglo-Saxon capitalism, particularly in the high-tech sector, does not favour these companies. Technology change means that selling the same product year after year is not a long-term strategy. Innovation elsewhere in the industry may render the product useless. Alternatively, change elsewhere may mean that the product needs costly revision – for example porting to a different platform.

These forces make it hard for a company to reach a steady state. Those that do reach steady state have no need to change ownership, but for others, sooner or later, an ownership change is a fact of life. Many software companies take outside investment from private equity sources, typically business angels and venture capitalists. These investors want to see a return on their investment, usually within a few years – typically three to seven – and in order to realise their returns, the investment must be sold.

Some companies are able to avoid taking outside investment by *boot-strapping*. A combination of founders' own investments, perhaps by living cheaply, and revenue invested in expansion can allow a company to grow to a significant size without involving an outside investor. However, even here, it is likely that its founders will eventually want to sell their investment.

Whenever it happens, eventually a company changes hands. Well publicised flotations – or *initial public offerings* (IPOs) – of companies such as Google, eBay and Netscape make flotation the most well-known exit route. However, far more companies change hands – or to use the jargon, *investor exit* – as a result of a straight sale to another company.

Trade sales are happening all the time. Large software companies like Google, Microsoft and Oracle buy many companies a year. While big transactions, like Oracle's purchases of PeopleSoft or Sun, or Yahoo's purchase of Flickr, may be well-known at the time, many smaller companies change hands with little or no publicity. Sometimes the significance of a sale doesn't become clear until much later, such as Google's purchase of Android in 2005.

Big companies choose to buy small and not so small companies for a variety of reasons. The obvious motivation is to buy market share and revenue. Sometimes the objective is the resources of the target; for example Google's 2011 purchase of Motorola Mobility brought it a large number of patents, plus access to set-top box and cell phone handset design teams.

A less obvious but equally common reason that big companies buy small ones is simply innovation. New companies are often founded to exploit innovative ideas, and small companies are generally better at innovation than large ones. So big companies watch for new, small, innovative companies; they let angel and VC investors fund innovation, and if it looks promising, buy the company.

For the acquired, acquisition can bring big changes to a company. Once acquired a company may continue with little change as part of a division of a larger company, or it may be dismembered entirely. Parts may be merged or closed down. Jobs may be lost or created. Employees may be rewarded for staying, or may find that stock options make them millionaires who no longer need to work.

Flotation too can bring about big changes. The company is now public and held to a higher standard of reporting and behaviour. Rather than having to answer to founders and private investors, the company must answer to the sometimes odd demands of the stock market. Once listed, the company can simply buy innovation, just as Google, Microsoft and Oracle buy companies with technology they want. This can be an advantage to the company and fuel further growth. It can also be a distraction for senior managers, who now spend more time investigating deals, mergers and acquisitions than before.

Listed companies have a great advantage when it comes to buying others. Because their stock is publicly listed, it is liquid – that is, it is easy to convert stock into cash. Such companies can issue more of their own stock; their stock becomes a new currency with which to buy other companies.

Private companies also make acquisitions, but these are often costly, because the company has to borrow money or find a new investor to cover the costs. Takeover targets are reluctant to accept stock in return because, being privately owned, it is difficult to turn such stock into cash.

For the owners of a small private company, selling the company can be difficult. If they sell to another private company and receive stock, they effectively exchange their holding in one company for another. But if they sell to a publicly listed company they can, at any time they choose, exchange the stock they receive for hard cash via the stock market.

Death of a Software Company

Companies can fail at any time during their existence. However the younger a company is, the more likely it is to fail. Infant mortality is high: most companies under one year old fail. However, once a company is past its first year, survival chances improve remarkably.

Still, few companies survive forever. A study at Royal Dutch Shell found the average life expectancy of a multinational company to be between 40 and 50 years. Of the public American companies listed in the Fortune 500 index in 1970, one-third had disappeared by 1983 (De Geus, 1997).

Some companies succumbed to takeovers in their prime, like Siebel. Others are dismembered, with pieces being sold before a much-diminished rump is itself sold or fails. One of the largest examples of this happened in the car industry:

British Leyland, once the third-largest car manufacture in the world, was sold piece by piece until the remaining MG Rover collapsed.

Death comes to a software company when its sales do not cover its costs. Once a software product is developed and sold, companies can reduce costs and continue selling the product. Companies that have an installed user base, particularly when customers are paying regularly for support services, can stagger on for months or even years. This process can be especially prolonged when customers have data locked up in a proprietary data formats or on servers. Even when a product is too old to sell to new customers, existing customers may pay for technical support, bug fixes and minor upgrades, or simply continued use in the case of SaaS.

The larger a software package, and the larger the customer, the more difficult it is to switch. As a home user, changing the word processor I use is not painless, but is reasonably straightforward. However, if I am using an integrated application suite – word processor, spreadsheet, calendar, e-mail – then the task is somewhat larger and I am less likely to change. For a large corporation these switching costs are multiplied many times. A retail bank may have tens of thousands of users using the same word processor. Installing new software is the easy part: new software may require new hardware, support desks need retooling, staff need training and the ensuing drop in productivity cannot be ignored.

A failing software company can thus continue to extract revenue from its installed user base as long as it continues to exist, because the exit costs lock customers in. As long as costs are shrunk far enough, the company can continue. Since the majority of software companies' costs are staff-related, this means reducing staffing.

Technology companies rarely fall to direct competitors in a straight fight. Usually the victor changes the rules of the game. Microsoft did not displace Digital Research directly, they did so on the back of the rise of the IBM PC and its clones. Nor did Microsoft Word replace WordPerfect directly; it did so in combination with Windows and the integrated Office suit.

More recently Google and a resurgent Apple have eclipsed Microsoft, but not because these companies created direct, better, competitors to Windows and Office. By focusing on the web and portable products, Google and Apple have sidestepped Microsoft.

Death Throes

Software testers are often the first to be let go – that is, if the company ever hired any in the first place! Ironically, less testing can make customers more dependent on a company in the short run. New software releases will contain more bugs, meaning that customers require more support services and additional releases. Revenue may be boosted too if customers are prepared to pay for fixes.

Marketing staff are also among the early casualties of a shrinking company. Salespeople are needed to sell the product, but in the short term they can continue to use the same marketing resources. A shrinking company is likely to save money by attending fewer trade shows and exhibitions – again reducing the need for marketing staff.

As a company starts to conserve cash, some of its early start-up behaviours will return. Since there were no marketing executives or product managers in the beginning, they may now seem like expensive luxuries. After all, salespeople can do marketing, and developers know what the product needs… (To be fair, it is not just software companies that cut marketing and advertising budget when money is tight. There is a certain predictability in such cuts.)

As the cuts continue, administration staff will be hit. Since human resource staff are needed to administer the cuts, they may be safeguarded for a little while. They may also face the agony of laying off staff while knowing that they will be leaving too as soon as the task is done.

Companies often use early redundancy rounds to clear out developers who are considered difficult or ineffective, but on the whole development staff are not cut until later in the process. However, once redundancies start, developers are likely to start leaving of their own accord. In most countries, most of the time, there is a shortage of development staff, and those willing to look can usually find another position without too much trouble.

Similarly, once sales dry up, sales staff will start to leave. There is little benefit in laying off sales staff: since they are largely paid on commission there is little money to be saved by making them redundant. It is worth keeping the sales staff around while they make the occasional sale. But once the sales force realise that there is little prospect of new sales – and commissions – they will, like technical staff, vote with their feet and start to leave.

Gradually a vicious circle will develop as it becomes clear the company does not have money to invest in new and interesting products and projects. The more people who leave of their own accord, the more who will be encouraged to leave. Unless a company takes clear steps to stem the flow, this can become self-reinforcing: the more people who leave, the more leaving appeals to those who remain.

Such departures may save the company from making redundancy decisions, engaging in sometimes lengthy legal processes and severance pay, so action to stem losses may be slow in coming. The danger of course is that if the process goes too far, the company loses too many key staff and its decline cannot be halted.

In the short to medium term such cost reductions may be enough to forestall bankruptcy by bringing costs below revenues, even if there are no new sales. Such a situation can continue for years. Eventually, though, something gives – a major customer leaves, banks call in debts or what remains of the company is bought. Occasionally the loss of key developers can undermine a company; however, this is less often the case than developers believe. New developers can usually be hired, and while it may take them time to come up to speed, they can eventually keep maintenance releases coming.

In rare cases individuals who believe they are essential to the business may make demands and start issuing ultimatums. A company that gives in to such ultimatums is on a slippery slope: its management risks losing control, as individuals who find their threats acted upon will feel rewarded and are likely to repeat the exercise.

All these conditions create the vicious circle that makes recovery more and more difficult. A few companies do recover; somehow they find new sales. They may not develop new products, but they manage to breath new life into existing products, as carefully chosen improvements or by targeting particular market niches.

Walking Dead

Successful companies grow. Eventually the company is sold to another company or the company is floated on a stock market in an IPO (initial public offering). These are the lucky ones.

The unlucky ones cease trading eventually. The company may burn brightly for a while, it may look like a success, but like a firework it burns out and dies. Still, in a way these companies are lucky: their founders, investors and staff can draw a line under the experience and move on.

The really unlucky companies end up as walking dead. They sell products, bring in revenue, they may even turn a profit. But the profit they produce does not justify the investment made in the company. The walking dead present problems for everyone – especially venture capitalists, who want their investment back. While it trades and sells products, the company offers hope, but that is exactly what makes such companies so difficult to kill off. More investment may bring more success, or it might be throwing good money after bad.

The walking dead may be an embarrassment to their investors, who would rather be rid of such companies. But to close the company or sell it cheaply means recognising a loss on their accounts, and may reflect badly on its investor's image.

These companies are stuck in a no-man's land. They are successful, but not successful enough.

Closing Words

All companies are unique, but they face similar challenges. Over time the same problems and patterns play out at many different organisations. Software companies are no exception: each is unique, but all face a similar set of problems as they grow and mature. These problems and solutions are the raw materials from which the patterns in this book are created.

Many software companies start out with the simple belief that 'if you build it they will come'. Very occasionally this works: the idea is so great or useful that few can imagine the product before it is built, but once it is built, everyone wants one. All that is required is a great technology and a belief in the technology. Unfortunately most products do not fall into this category. A single-minded focus on technology may actually get in the way of selling more products.

If a software company is to succeed, it has to get a lot of things right. There are no guarantees, and too many companies fall into dysfunction, supported by customers who cannot afford to change suppliers and staffed by disgruntled employees.

4

Strategy

Strategy is both important and difficult to define. It is a guide to future activities but it is not a plan. It describes how a company can convert raw materials and knowledge into value for its shareholders and benefits to customers. Not only do different companies have different strategies, but the role and nature of strategy at companies differs.

Strategy is a forward-looking, over-arching, view of how the organisation would like to act in future. As such it implicitly contains a view of what the future will look like. Forward-looking strategy is deliberate: it sets out intention, objectives and plans.

Without a shared understanding between individuals of what the company strategy is and its intentions are, there is risk of no coordination between departments, teams and individuals: each runs in a different direction and there is little overall forward movement.

For technology companies strategy is particularly important. The software industry is fiercely competitive and significant sums of money can be earned and lost. Naive strategies may work in some industries, but the software industry is home to some very sharp strategic thinkers. Well thought-out and executed strategies can make the difference between a company that is constantly struggling for the next sale and one that is making its employees millionaires.

Yet strategy is not entirely forward-looking: strategy is also backward-looking. Not only does it explain what has happened before – *sense making* – but the experiences and lessons of the past themselves form the strategy. In this sense strategy is emergent: what has gone before creates the platform for what will happen in future.

Both emergent and intentional strategy have roles to play. Relying entirely on emergent strategy may be leaving things to chance a little too much. But believing that the future can be foreseen and creating all-encompassing plans seems a little simplistic.

Perhaps it is not so much the presence or cleverness of the strategy that is important, but the process of creating a strategy, forcing individuals – usually managers – to think through the future and possible responses to it. As US president General Dwight D. Eisenhower is reported to have said, "In preparing for battle, I have always found that plans are useless, but planning is indispensable".

Creating a strategy, by planning, a shared understanding is created. The future certainly will not unfold as expected, but the preparation and thinking prepare people for whatever might happen.

The patterns and discussions in this book are intended to play a part in this preparation and thinking. The patterns create a shared language, while the examples describe what has happened to similar companies in similar situations. As with software architecture and design, the shared language of patterns accelerates understanding and moves thinking up a level.

What is Strategy?

For some, strategy is a business model – it describes how the business makes money. For others strategy is about change – it is a means to move from where the company is now to somewhere better. For others it is about organisation, structure and maybe culture.

Harvard Professor Michael Porter has written 'Competitive strategy is about being different. It means deliberately choosing a different set of activities to deliver a unique mix of value.' (Porter, 1996). While Porter may be one of the best-known voices on corporate strategy, he is not the only one, and many others have a different take on strategy.

Porter's fellow Harvard Professor Robert Kaplan offers another definition: 'Strategy describes how an organisation intends to create sustained value for its shareholders.' (Kaplan & Norton, 2004).

Perhaps more down to earth is Jack Welch's suggestion: 'In real life, strategy is actually very straightforward. You pick a general direction and implement like hell.' (Welch & Welch, 2006).

For some, strategy is about creating the best match between inputs and outputs. For some it is focused on some aspect of the company: finance, human resources, technology, marketing, knowledge. There is some truth in all these definitions, because strategy differs from company to company and from time to time.

The Canadian Professor Henry Mintzberg examined several views of strategy in his book *The Rise and Fall of Strategic Planning* (Mintzberg, 1994):

- Strategy as a plan: a description of how an organisation will achieve its objectives.
- Strategy as a position: how the company and its products line up relative to competitors and customers in various markets.
- Strategy as perspective: the company's concept of business. Such perspectives may differ from person to person and over time.
- Strategy as a pattern, 'a consistent behaviour over time'.

Obviously the last of these four descriptions is of most interest in a book about strategy patterns. Before discussing this view in detail, the earlier three are worthy of some discussion.

To many strategy is self-evidently a plan, because it guides actions. Yet there is more to strategy than just a plan. Strategies can survive changing events in a way that plans cannot, and, as we will see, the sources of strategy stretch far beyond the planning process. (Anyone who believes that strategy is, or should be, a plan should read the Minztberg's book in full, as he presents the case against strategic planning.)

Much of the planning associated with strategy actually concerns position – price, competitors, customers and so on. Strategy decides where the companies want to be and planning is used to create a path to reach that position.

Viewing strategy as plan or as position assumes that strategy is explicit and tangible. However, viewing strategy as a perspective changes this, because perspective differs from individual to individual and over time. What is considered strategic today may not, in retrospect, appear strategic at all. Conversely, activities that may not merit the grandiose title of 'strategic' may later prove to have been so. Since it is not always possible to determine in advance what is strategic and what is not, strategy must be emergent in some degree.

Strategy means expensive

The economist John Kay suggests that 'strategy' is sometimes used as an excuse for spending lots of money: '"Strategy means expensive…. This is a strategic investment" should be translated as "We are going to lose a lot of money on this project". "This is a strategic acquisition" means "We are paying more for this company than it is worth"'. (Kay, 1998).

Marking activities as 'strategic' can make them seem grander than they really are and hide poor logic. Simply marking something as 'strategic' does not excuse managers from explaining their actions. Next time you hear someone explain a course of action as 'strategic', substitute the word 'expensive' and consider whether the action still makes sense.

Strategy, not Plans

As much as we might want strategy to be a plan, it cannot be. It may be a guide to actions, but it cannot be a detailed plan. Attempts to master plan strategy – strategic planning – are doomed to failure for a number of reasons[1]:

- Things change: it rains when it shouldn't and doesn't rain when it should, competitors launch products, customers reject new products and go crazy about others.
- Lack of perfect knowledge: ambiguity is rife in business: a well-run company might know its own sales figures, but it doesn't know the competitors' sales figures and can only ever estimate the possible total market.
- Errors: even the best plans contain errors.
- Plans have a tendency to extrapolate yesterday: using historic data may blind an organisation to changes in the market and underplay the effects of change.
- Implementation difficulties: moving from plan to implementation is no trivial exercise. Many plans, strategic and otherwise, have failed not because of any inherent problems with the plan, but because of difficulties putting the plan into action.
- Detailed planning is self-defeating: adding detail to a plan may help solve some of the problems listed here, but detail also make the plans bigger, meaning there is more scope for errors and a need for more effort to communicate the plan. In addition, adding extra detail increases the time it

[1] A fuller discussion of these issues can be found in *The Rise and Fall of Strategic Planning* (Mintzberg, 1994) and *Changing Software Development* (Kelly, 2008).

takes to create a plan, making it more likely that the plan will be out of date by the time it is completed.

- Plans are demotivating: perfect plans, without errors and inclusive of sufficient detail, can be very demotivating to those on their receiving end. The recipient is left without space for their own initiative, ideas or suggestions. Of course the perfect plan will already have accounted for these factors.

  Even more demotivating for employees is being asked to execute a plan they had no involvement in creating and which contains – at least in their eyes – errors.

- Learning is divorced from action: creating a plan is a learning exercise. When plans are created by one group and passed to a second for execution, much of what has been learned is not transferred – it is effectively lost. No plan, document or presentation could ever capture all the learning inside the planner's head, and even if it did, transfer would be very slow. Equally, the opportunity for feedback from implementers to planners is lost.
- Learning happens: the execution of a plan will lead to learning and experience, which may reveal better opportunities and courses of action than are contained in the plan. Again opportunities for feedback are lost.

The net result is that even if an organisation is pursuing a strategic plan, the end result will be different to that envisioned in the plan. The final outcome and strategy will be emergent to some degree. Accepting that strategy is in part emergent allows it to be embraced. Rather than trying to produce detailed plans in advance, companies can use strategy as a guide and use emergent behaviours to their advantage.

This is not to say that planning is pointless; indeed, planning can itself be a great learning exercise. Nor is it to say that plans are useless; the right plans at the right time in the right place can be a great asset. But planning and plans are not benign activities. Planning takes time and money; plans can be deceptive and can have a negative effect on those on the receiving end.

Strategy needs to be both forward-looking and backward-looking. In being forward-looking it sets objectives, paints visions and suggests routes to take. At the same time it needs to look backwards to build on what the organisation is good at, what it knows and the skills and experience of its employees. The challenge is to build on the skills, experience and assets of the past without being bound by it.

As learning occurs, as staff learn, and as new staff join, then new opportunities will arise and strategy emerges. Forward-looking strategy has a role to play in deciding which of these opportunities should be seized and which passed over. The resulting successes and failures will all contribute to the strategy that emerges.

Strategy as a Pattern

In characterising strategy as a pattern, Mintzberg does not make a connection with Christopher Alexander – who created the first architecture patterns in the 1970s. However, there is a clear parallel between the way in which Alexander sees architecture emerging from what has been shown to work and the way in which Mintzberg describes strategy as part intention, part design. Both writers see patterns as evolving from past events and actions. Patterns describe what did happen and inform what will happen.

This is where business strategy patterns fit in. Studying business strategy using the type of pattern thinking pioneered by Alexander and extended by the software community provides both insights into strategy and, perhaps more importantly, guidance to those who must steer companies.

Some patterns will be unique to a particular company; these are patterns of action and behaviour that only occur in the context of that company. Others will extend to companies with a similar context – most likely companies in the same industry, those who recruit from similar pools and those who face similar problems.

Still more patterns will apply more broadly because the act of being in business, of operating a profit-maximising organisation in a competitive market, itself creates a shared context. Whenever problems exist within a shared context, there are opportunities for shared patterns.

This does not imply that individuals and organisations are powerless when confronted with strategy. Strategy will be shaped by the events and actions of the past; context will impose limitations on the course of actions, and industry norms will point towards a common path. However, as long as those involved in decision-making are conscious of the constraints, options and existing patterns, they can make decisions to guide their actions.

Following any pattern involves a set of decisions and subsequent actions. Organisations may wander into some patterns by accident, but normally there will be a deliberate decision to do something as opposed to doing nothing. In some cases the best thing to do will be to break the patterns and do something different. As long as such decisions are taken consciously, this can make sense; it is when unconscious decisions fly in the face of normal practice that problems result.

Generative Patterns

'[These] patterns cover every range of scale in our surroundings: the largest patterns cover aspects of regional structure, middle range patterns cover the

shape and activity of buildings, and the smallest patterns deal with the actual physical materials and structures out of which the buildings must be made.'

(*Alexander, 1979, p. 309*)

Patterns are generative in nature. Using one pattern frequently leads to another known pattern, or sometimes it leads to a new solution. When the new solution has been used, tested and repeated often enough to prove its worth, it may be considered a pattern in its own.

Some patterns are written very broadly; implementing them will require several smaller, narrower patterns to be used. At other times the end result – the consequences – of applying the first pattern sets the conditions for another pattern, although which pattern will be applied is not clear until the results of the first have been seen.

Patterns are not a form of master planning; patterns set out a language and framework within which design, innovation and variation can occur. No two pattern instances will be the same; each will have its own variations. The experience and learning gained from implementing the first pattern will influence the choice of second pattern and lead to its own modifications.

Applying the patterns involves choices and decisions. Using patterns does not program a fixed course of actions. Deliberate acts of design are still required by humans: choices as to which pattern to implement, choices about how to implement a pattern, choices about which variations to apply or not. Even the choice to break from the patterns available and try something different. Making these choices is an act of design.

The result of conscious and unconscious variation means that no pattern sequence is preordained. Sometimes it is only possible to decide which pattern to apply next when the results of an earlier pattern are seen. As patterns are applied, learning happens, which feeds into the next set of decisions.

Both design, a deliberate choice of actions, and emergence are required to balance control and learning. The act of applying new learning requires deliberate choice and control; without control learning cannot be applied. But excessive control restricts learning. Fixing a design far into the future stops fresh learning from being incorporated.

Strategy is design which needs to encompass learning and control, although these two forces may be contradictory. Allowing for learning to occur and to influence the future course of actions means that only in retrospect is it possible to tell what really was strategic and what was not. Therefore the term 'strategic' should be applied with hesitation; that which is labelled 'strategic' might turn out to be merely tactical, while that which was minor detail turns out to be strategic.

The pattern form is well suited to studying strategy, because its generative nature allows for learning and emergence. Patterns have proved useful to software designers and, as this book sets out to show, will prove useful to business strategists.

Strategy means saying "No"

One of my personal rules of thumb is that strategy is about saying "No".

Strategy is not so much in what you decide to do – saying "Yes" is easy – but in the hard decisions about what you choose not to do. Anyone can start a company (the difficult bit is giving up paid employment) and do anything that is asked of them (the difficult bit is not selling yourself too cheaply).

Saying "Yes" is easy. But saying "Yes" is not a long-term strategy.

Strategy is about choosing not to do something so that you can focus on something else; it is about putting something beyond reach so that you stick to your chosen path and put something else first. To borrow the formation flying analogy from Chapter 1: formation flying dictates that you don't let a plane loop-the-loop whenever the pilot feels like it.

Of course every business would like to say "Yes" to every money-making scheme that presents itself, but that isn't strategy. That is opportunism, and while it might be good in the short term, it can lead to a very mixed-up business. Companies need to be able to recognise which opportunities make sense – will make money – and which they should turn down. They should also have the focus to say "No" to opportunities that might make money but which would not help position the company for the longer game.

Saying "No" is hard, not just because it means turning down opportunities to make money, but also because it means disappointing (potential) customers, and can mean disappointing your own staff.

It is only by saying "No" that companies can specialise and thus build unique capabilities. Of course saying "No" can become a knee-jerk reaction; saying "No" too often will close off all opportunities and prevent any specialisation. The trick is in deciding what to do and having the strength to stick to it.

Identifying Strategy

In some organisations the bias will be towards strategy that is decided and designed up front, while in others the strategy will be entirely the result of what happens and how people react. In other organisations the bias might be towards the 'let a hundred flowers bloom' approach, with many different groups running in different directions and running different experiments.

At other times the apparent absence of strategy might itself be a strategy. Shortly after taking on the CEO position at IBM, Louis Gerstner said "The last thing IBM needs right now is a vision." (Gerstner, 2003). In apparently rejecting any strategy, Gerstner was actually adopting a strategy of postponing any decision until more information was available.

Even in those organisations that openly advocate up-front strategy design and invest the resources to create strategies, there will be elements of emergent strategy. There are things that cannot be programmed in advance, such as how the competition will react, and opportunities that only become apparent as the strategy is rolled out.

Even if strategy can be planned in advance, there is still the thorny issue of implementation. Many strategies fail not because the strategy itself is flawed – although that too is common – but because implementing the strategy is difficult.

American management guru Tom Peters once described as 'wildly inflated' a poll in Fortune magazine that claimed that less than 10% of corporate strategies were actually implemented (Kiechel, 1984).

The former Soviet Union invested lots of resources in strategy and planning. The bureaucracy of Gosplan attempted to set out five-year plans. In the extreme the country attempted to control the weather in order to meet the plans. Despite this faith in planning, both Gosplan and the Soviet Union were failures[1].

Conversely, even those organisations that appear to have no preordained strategy will have something that guides their actions, even if it is not blessed with the name *strategy.* A small shopkeeper may not even know the meaning of the word 'strategy', but he knows that to be competitive with larger stores requires being open for longer hours and a location closer to customers' homes.

For some companies, such as those described in *Early Days* on page 36, the unspoken strategy is luck. They got lucky once, at the start, and future success depends on luck. This strategy may well work – until some competitor spots the opportunity and moves in.

One of the defining characteristics of strategy is that it has longevity. Strategy is defined, and whatever it says, it needs to be consistent over time. An organisation

---

[1] Gosplan's five-year plans also did much to stymie the Soviet computing industry; five year plans are not particularly helpful to an industry shackled to the 18-month cycles of Moore's Law.

that changes its stated strategy every week is not so much adopting 52 new strategies a year as adopting a strategy of weekly change.

Porter's generic strategies

One of the most influential writers on business strategy is Harvard Professor Michael Porter, who suggested there are a few 'generic strategies' (Porter, 1980). Of these, three are good and one is not so good. The strategies are inherently concerned with the product being offered. The assumption is that if the product can be cheap, or different enough relative to competitors, then it will sell.

The first generic strategy is *cost leadership*: simply be the cheapest provider of any given product or service. Companies like WalMart and RyanAir have experienced great success with this strategy.

Companies that do not adopt a cost leadership strategy need to differentiate themselves. So Porter's second generic strategy is *differentiation*: make your product different from the competition. Apple is a prime example of a company that does not compete on price, but rather on the difference of its products.

The third strategy outlined by Porter is to focus on a *niche market*. Rather than taking on the whole market, the company selects a niche. Within this niche Porter suggests the company focuses – perhaps unsurprisingly – on either cost leadership or differentiation.

Following the niche strategy entails following a very mini-version of one of the first two. The variation is that the focus is much smaller: the target is a subset of the entire market. Of course, this begs the question: *what is the market and what is the submarket?*

There is another strategy, *stuck in the middle*, which Porter advises against. Such products are not vastly different from competitors', but are not the cheapest either. Porter's view is that these companies will always lose out to competitors following either a low-cost or differentiated strategy.

Volkswagen offers another example. The company's VW cars are more expensive than those from General Motors and Ford, but do not offer the quality or differentiation of BMW or Mercedes. Volkswagen even produces cheaper versions of its own cars under the Skoda brand and more expensive versions under the Audi brand.

Perhaps the question that should be asked of Volkswagen, Sainsbury's and others is whether they are indeed 'stuck in the middle', or whether they have found some 'sweet spot'?

But there are a number of examples of companies that appear to be 'stuck in the middle' but are quite successful in what they do. Sainsbury's supermarkets in the UK do not compete on price: rivals such as WalMart/Asda and Netto under cut them. Nor do they compete on quality: rivals Waitrose and Marks & Spencer offer better quality.

The Porter patterns

In 2004 I rewrote Porter's generic strategies as a set of patterns (Kelly, 2004a). As patterns these strategies present a number of challenges. Consequently they are not included here, but are available to download from my website, `www.allankelly.net/patterns`.

When recast as patterns some interesting insights came to light. While Porter's strategies are useful for analysing a company's approach to market and for contrasting one company with another, they do not offer guidance on what a company should do. These generic strategies are so broad that it is not possible to offer specific advice on when to choose one strategy over another.

From a patterns perspective *stuck in the middle* seems a reasonable approach to balancing contradictory forces. While there are customers for whom price is not the overriding consideration, but who are not prepared to pay a premium, there will be a place for 'sweet spot' companies.

Porter also outlines *five forces* which, he claims, shape industries: *threat of new entrants, buyer power, threat of substitution, supplier power* and *competition.* In pattern terms, forces explain why the problem is difficult and influence the choice of solution. Yet these five forces do not help one choose between the three, or more, strategies. The choice of strategy is, possibly, arbitrary.

In the 2004 patterns I recast 'stuck in the middle' as SWEET SPOT. Such a strategy might not work in every context, but that only goes to show the importance of considering the context and forces before applying any strategy or pattern.

One new pattern did emerge during this analysis: ONE TRUE STRATEGY. It is better for a company to stick to one explicit strategy than to change strategy frequently, perhaps embarking on one strategy only to reverse course shortly afterwards.

Strategy Parallels Software Design

There are parallels between strategy design and the way we go about developing software:

- Both are highly abstract fields of endeavour.
- Both require implementation if they are to move beyond academic exercises.
- Both are flawed if they do not consider how implementation will occur, and poor implementation can undermine both.
- Both have a high failure rate, and in many companies the remains of a failed strategy or failed IT programme are all too evident to see.
- Both contain elements of planned, intentioned actions, and both need to allow for emergent properties as implementation unfolds.
- Simplistic views of both strategy and software design tend to degrade into planning and plans.

For business, strategy is design of business, and for software architecture, design is strategy of implementation.

For both strategy formation and software design to be successful there need to be feedback loops between up-front, system thinking and implementation. Given this, it is perhaps surprising that both fields are well-served by highly-paid experts – strategy consultants and software architects – who make a virtue of avoiding implementation.

There is an entire industry devoted to the creation of strategy tools (models and analysis techniques), and there is a similar industry selling tools for software design and architecture: CASE tools, analysis models and so on.

Preordained strategy, and strategic planning, had its heyday in the 1960s and 1970s. Since then it has been in decline. Similarly big up-front software design had its heyday sometime between 1980 and 1995. Since then it has been in decline, as the industry has sought adaptability and responsiveness to change over good up-front work with rigidly planned execution.

It is hardly surprising then that both domains have used the word *agile* to describe the new reaction-oriented approach. Agile businesses are ones that can change rapidly to meet customer needs and profit from doing so. Agile software development allows software teams to react likewise to their customer's needs.

As this chapter has argued, both strategy formation and software design are part forward-looking and control-oriented, and part-backward looking learning exercises, with results emerging over time.

That these parallels exist should not be a surprise if we consider Conway's Law again:

> *'...organizations which design systems (...) are constrained to produce designs which are copies of the communication structures of these organizations.'*
>
> *(Conway, 1968)*

Since organisational form and communication paths are often the subject of business strategy, it is hardly surprising that strategy and system design are entwined. What is less widely recognised is that the homomorphic force that brings this about can also run in reverse. Once a system is built, it can exert a force on the organisation to become structured in certain ways (Hvatum & Kelly, 2005).

In recent years some writers have picked up these parallels. McFarland asked *Should you build strategy like you build software?* (McFarland, 2008) and in *Closing the Gap between Strategy and Execution* Sull borrowed ideas from the software development community (Sull, 2007). Many of the ideas set out in *Changing Software Development* borrowed directly from themes found in business strategy literature and applied them to the software development arena (Kelly, 2008).

All these writers compare the process that brings about strategy with the process that brings about design. Since both activities are highly dependent on insight, innovation and flashes of inspiration, it may be that it is irrational to expect either to fit into a rational process. The case against rational software design was set out some time ago in *A rational design process: how and why to fake it* (Parnas & Clements, 1986; Hoffman & Weiss, 2001).

There is (at least) one tool in the software designer's armoury that has yet to find a parallel in the strategy debate: *refactoring*. Refactoring is the process of taking what exists and improving it over time through a myriad of small changes. It is a retrospective design that developers use to improve the maintainability of existing code.

Refactoring has always happened; however, it was usually conducted as an hidden exercise by slightly guilty developers who felt they should have 'got it right the first time'. With the publication of *Refactoring* (Fowler, 2000) this changed. By naming the activity and documenting it in a popular book it became a respectable part of the developer's armoury.

Similar things happen in business strategy and operations, but they are not blessed with respectability or a dedicated name. At best they hide as continual improvement and at worst as frequent reorganisations. Business strategists would do well to integrate the idea of refactoring into their thinking and language.

Delta model strategy

While Porter's generic strategies regard the product as the fundamental tool of strategy, Hax and Dean suggest that a product-based strategy is only one of three possible approaches. Although not specific to the technology sector, the 'Delta Model' does seem to explain the strategies of many software companies better than Porter's generic strategies (Hax & Wilde, 1999).

The Delta Model suggests three extreme strategies – arranged in a triangle shown in Figure 6. The first of these, *best product,* is a product-based approach. Companies following this strategy aim to have the best product – in terms of features, performance, cost or some other criteria – on the assumption that customers' purchasing decisions are based on product qualities.

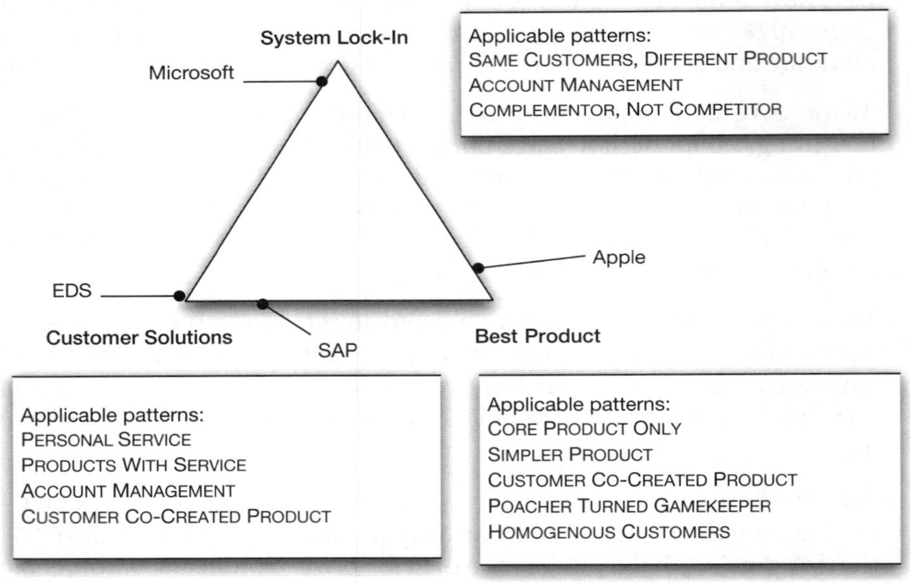

Figure 6. Delta Model and some applicable patterns

Original illustration in Hax & Wilde Sloan Management Review article Winter 1999 issue

Companies following a *customer solutions* strategy aim to meet customer needs as closely as possible. Such companies may offer services that fit the customers' needs for specialist help, or they may offer products that are well-suited to their context.

Historically the *lock-in* strategy has been widely used in the technology sector – consider IBM's traditional approach to mainframes, software and services. Here companies attempt to keep customers from changing to other suppliers by selling them a stream of products. The products interlock, and as the customer adopts more of the products it becomes more and more difficult to change supplier.

While *customer solutions* could map to either Porter's *differentiated or cost leader* strategy, and *customer solutions* would map easily to Porter's *focus* strategy, there is no obvious mapping from lock-in to Porter. This may be because with a lock-in strategy the vendor is trying to stop competition and limit buyer power.

Companies may adopt one of these strategies, or they may moderate it with elements of a second. For example, Apple's strategy for the Macintosh might be seen as a best product strategy. But when iPod, iTunes and iPhone integration are considered, elements of lock-In become visible.

Similarly, Microsoft may be regarded as an example of lock-in – Windows leads to Office, Office leads to Exchange and so on. Microsoft's offering of non-Windows products – whether for Linux or the Mac – might be an example of *customer solutions*, or it might be an attempt to extend lock-in further.

For each strategy outlined by the Delta Model there are a number of patterns in this book that may be useful. Some of these pattern might be applicable to more than one of the strategies.

These three strategies also bear a broad similarity to the three principle models for developing software. The *best product* strategy clearly corresponds to the ISV model in which companies (even Microsoft in this context) aim to offer the best product to multiple customers. *Customer solutions* corresponds to the ESP companies who focus on solving customers' problems. Finally, the *lock-In* strategy resembles the in-house corporate IT group that develops applications for captive customers.

Strategy for Software Creators

Strategy for software creators needs to balance a number of often opposing forces. Some of these forces are external to the company – customers and competitors being the obvious examples. Others are internal, such as how the company is organised and how products are developed. These are not isolated forces – they are entwined, as are the internal and external dimensions. To view one as more important than the other is wrong.

As suggested in Chapter 3, there are many ways for a software company to fail. In the short run one good decision may create success despite many bad decisions.

Yet in the long run forces need to be balanced if the company is to succeed; some of these are listed in Table 2.

Table 2: Forces to be addressed for long-term sustainability and success

Customer need	What is the problem or need customers have?
Technology	What will we use to resolve the customers' problem?
Sales	What is needed to make the customer part with money?
Marketing (outbound)	How can potential customers be made aware of your product and the advantages it offers?
Marketing (inbound)	How do you learn about the problems and needs customers have?
Operations	How can all these parts be brought together and made to work together?
Competition	Who else is doing this? Why will customers buy from us and not our competitors?
Product lifecycle	What stage is the product at in adoption terms? Who is buying it? What happens next?
Market lifecycle	What stage is the broader market at? What opportunities are arising? And which ones closing?
Financial	Can the problem be solved for a price customers can (and will) pay?
Personnel	How do we hire the right people? And how do we keep them?

The patterns and pattern sequences set out in this book are intended to help guide organisations faced with these challenges. The infinite variety of markets, companies and the people who make up those markets and companies means that no pattern language can contain all the answers. However the patterns described here should at least give you a starting point.

For software creators it is not always necessary to follow a unique strategy. The product the company creates will contain the unique proposition. In such cases a strategy may be devised from the patterns in this book.

In other cases the product itself will not be enough. In these cases some of the patterns in this book will prove useful, but you will need to invent new ways of marketing, selling or positioning the product. Still, the patterns here may well describe the behaviour of competitors.

Living companies

As with most business literature this book assumes that companies are (mostly) rational economic actors seeking to maximise profit – so-called *Anglo-Saxon capitalism*. Yet this hard-nosed view of corporate life does not offer a complete explanation of businesses.

One alternative view advanced in *The Living Company* (De Geus, 1997) suggests that we should view a company as a living entity. The company's main objective is not profit maximisation, but survival. Survival allows the company to continue in business, to develop another product, to serve customers again and to continue employing people.

A living company is as much a social community as it is an economic entity. The people who work for the company share an environment, a set of objectives and a set of restraints, and spend the greater part of their waking hours together. The senior managers of the company are but temporary custodians of the community and the culture.

The community shares memories, not just of office parties, but of ventures that worked and ventures that failed. These shared memories and experiences shape the identity of the company, and the identity in turn shapes the activities of the company. Companies that lack community, memories and identity find it hard to learn and grow.

For a company that aims to nurture its collective spirit and community, the pursuit of profit sometimes needs to take second, third or even fourth place. Companies need to allow for experimentation, they cannot relentlessly work their assets – especially their people – to the maximum. Some capability must be reserved for the unexpected and for gradual change.

To those solely focused on stakeholder value and profit, this may appear a waste of resources. For those looking to play a longer game, some resource must be invested in the future; profit maximisation is a short-term strategy.

Managing the community for the long term brings a different approach to management: in particular, the approach to the people in the organisation changes. Those focusing on the short term will tend to hire people who have the right skills today, people who can 'hit the ground running', and when profits turn down redundancies will be quick to follow.

Conversely, those managing for the long term will tend to hire people who fit into the community and share the values of the company. Giving employees the chance to grow as individuals is important. They need opportunities, experiences and space to learn and grown. Only when the employees learn will the company learn.

Some companies may consciously set out to become a living company, a community that shares a purpose and for which profit is a means to an end. The end is simply survival, the opportunity to continue in business. Other companies will embrace the profit-maximisation model; their management will run the company simply on economic grounds.

Businesses that actually decide to take one path or the other are probably the exception. Most companies unconsciously inhabit the middle ground. Some decisions are made on economic grounds, others on the basis of survival and longevity. Neither model is right or wrong: such distinctions are subjective and depend on one's own views and objectives. Rather than ask which is the 'right' model for a company, it is better to ask '*Does this view add to my understanding? Does this view help with decision-making?'*

For companies focused on the short term, striving to boost the next quarter's earnings, perhaps planning to sell the company, the economic view will be more relevant. For others, organisations that intend to survive and make regular if uninteresting dividend payments, the community view will be more useful.

Closing Words

There are many models that seek to describe companies and business life. Some of these models are presented in this book as boxed items or embedded within patterns. These models are only useful inasmuch as they further understanding and help resolve forces. The models are, in their own way, patterns.

The patterns presented in this book are, individually, excerpts of strategy. Some are larger than others, some seem immediately strategic, others will only seem strategic in hindsight.

In combination these patterns, sequences and models create whole strategies. Possible sequences are shown throughout the book; each one of these represents a strategy in its own right. Other strategies are possible by combining the patterns in different sequences or by adding unique elements to sequences.

Sometimes the right strategy is to ignore the patterns and sequences and instead forge your own unique path. While competitors stick to the patterns, there may be an advantage in doing something different. Before you embark on such a course, however, be clear why your proposed course is better for your customers than the existing patterns.

Finally, any strategy is only as good as the execution and implementation that follow through to deliver it. These patterns and sequences can help by providing a shared language and a starting point for action.

5

Funding the Start

There are perhaps as many ways of starting a business as their are businesses. Each business has its own story of the start. Forming the company is the easy part – a limited company is usually the place to start – but funding the company is more difficult.

The joint stock or limited company – an 'LLC' in the USA and 'Ltd' in the UK – must be one of the greatest inventions of the Victorian Age. The limited company is simple, straightforward, the starting point for all business activity. While the limited company might not be the perfect vehicle, it is usually an adequate starting point for entrepreneurial endeavours.

The exact rules differ from jurisdiction to jurisdiction, but in countries like the UK and US a new company can be created in a matter of days, or even hours. In the UK at least, no capital is needed for the new company; the only money that is needed is to pay the formation fees.

In other countries forming a company can take days or weeks. In some countries, like Germany, the company has historically been expected to be funded to the tune of several thousand Euros of initial capital. Such restrictions can lead to 'jurisdiction shopping': many American companies are registered in Delaware but operate and trade in other states, while German entrepreneurs frequently form British-registered limited companies because these are easier and cheaper to form than their local options.

Bootstrapping

One common problem for most new start-up companies is money. Most start with little or no capital. Fortunately a software business requires little capital to get going, enough to buy a few computers and a few software tools. Computers can be bought cheaply from many suppliers and many tools are available as Open Source (such as GNU C), or at discounted rates from vendors who want products created for their platforms (such as Microsoft tools).

Even the resources needed to make a software product available to the world have become cheaper. No longer is it necessary to cut CDs and physically ship them to customers. Virtual machines in data centres are getting cheaper all the time, and the likes of Amazon and Google offer metered capacity as it is needed.

However, software developers can burn vast amounts of capital in wages. Software takes time to write and developers need to eat. Not only that, but good developers can usually get highly paid jobs elsewhere without too much trouble.

Sometimes developers will work for free or for or stock options. This happens typically when the people creating the software are the company founders, and are in a position to work for nothing. Maybe they are young and have few expenses, or they have earned enough money from a previous job to take time out – as is described in the novel *Microserfs* (Coupland, 1996).

Whichever route is taken, the founders are effectively funding the company from their own resources. Crunch time comes when those resources run out: either there is a product to sell or the work must stop. This approach is referred to as *bootstrapping* – as in 'pulling yourself up by your boot laces'. In fact it is more of a race to create a product and generate revenue before money is needed.

Once a company starts to generate revenue, the revenue is fed back into the company. With no external shareholders to pay or loans to repay, profit can be reinvested. Even when the company can afford to pay wages, they may not be very high. Only when the company becomes cash-generating can the founders be repaid.

Bootstrapping has been shown to be successful and substantial business have been grown using their own resources. But for many bootstrapping doesn't go far enough. They have to look for additional funds. Bootstrap failures are also common. The revenue available from bootstrapping may not be enough to allow the company to develop products fast enough to compete. Rivals funded from external sources may expand faster, capturing customers and making it harder for a bootstrapped company to compete.

Bootstrapping can also make companies risk-averse: because finance is so limited, the implications of wasting it are significant. Such companies may engage in non-core activities that distract from the company focus.

Friends and Family

When bootstrapping is not enough or has been exhausted, founders may look to their immediate friends and family for funding. In return for a few shares (equity) people who know the founders best may invest a little money. However, friends and family don't usually invest great amounts of money. The developers, the founders, still have to live cheaply; the longer they can make the money last, the longer they have to create a product and make a sale.

Such friends and family are investors, but friends and family probably don't apply the same criteria of economic return as professionals: they are trusting more in the individuals than the product. Ultimately, professional investors are trusting individuals too, but professional investors don't know the founders so well, so the product serves as a proxy.

Banks

Banks have traditionally been a source of loans to business to help them to get started. However, for software companies banks are usually of little help in funding. When it comes to business loans, banks are generally risk-averse. All start-ups are risky endeavours, and software businesses more than others. Low barriers to entry, changing technology, dependence on key individuals and other factors all make start-up software businesses more risky than those in other industries.

Physical product companies, 'bricks and mortar' businesses, use borrowed money to buy assets; software companies use it to pay wages and other expenses. In the event of company failure a bank will attempt to seize assets to repay the loan. Since software companies don't have any assets to speak of, the bank's money is gone, so software companies represent more risk. Consequently banks are reluctant to lend to software technology businesses.

Once a software business is established, however, banks may be willing to lend to it. Even software companies accrue some physical assets – buildings, computers and so on – and source code itself can be used as an asset. When a regular revenue stream has been established – as with SaaS companies – this could be used as collateral for a loan.

Angels

After exhausting friends and family the next funding source is typically a 'business angel' – or just *angel.*

An angel is usually an individual who has been successful in business themselves and wishes to invest in early-stage companies. Investing early is very risky, but can offer the greatest return. By investing early the angel gets more equity for the money they do invest, so if the company is a success, they gain more.

Angels may bring more than just money. Many angels like to get involved with the business they invest in, perhaps in an advisory role, or perhaps more actively. This can bring valuable experience, contacts and insights to a new business, particularly when the founders have little such experience. However, not all founders are open to such involvement, and tensions can arise.

Venture Capital

Angels only go so far. If the company exhausts angel funding, the next stop is a venture capital company. Some of these companies are well-known, even legendary: Kleiner Perkins Caufield & Byers (KPCB) is perhaps the most famous, having invested in Sun, Amazon, Google and many others.

Each venture capital – or 'VC' – company has its own specialities and preferences. Some invest very early on, some late, some take an active role, some a passive and so on. Even within the VC there may be different specialities and preferences. Indeed, VCs don't have a single pot of money; instead they have multiple pots, called *funds.* The VC raises a fund, that is, they solicit investment from pension funds, asset managers, wealthy individuals and others. This continues until the fund reaches some predetermined ceiling. When the target ceiling is reached the company starts investing the fund money into companies itself.

A VC company may have several active funds at any one time, and each fund has its own criteria for investing and managing the investments. Each fund also has a life span, typically five years.

Those who invest in the fund expect to get their money back, with lots of growth, by the end of the fund's life. If a fund has a five-year life, the first year or two will be spent investing the money, the next year or two managing the investment, and the remaining time exiting the investments.

This means that VCs expect to exit (sell) any investment within a specific timeframe. Of course sometimes funds are rolled over and their life extended, or sometimes one fund will buy out another – either a fund from the same VC or, more likely, from another. The important thing to bear in mind is that one day the VC will want its money back.

VCs tend to invest in a series of rounds, named 'A', 'B' and so on, with each round being larger than the previous one. As a funded company matures, it will either achieve critical profit levels or require more investment. With maturity the risk of investing is less, but so too is the potential growth.

There is no limit to how many investment rounds a VC company may undertake; the only limiting factor is ability of the company and existing investors to persuade others to invest. As a rough guide, two rounds of funding would be normal, three occasionally, and sometimes more.

Venture capital can also be supplied by potential customers, or by technology companies wishing to support their own platform. For example, Intel has long invested in software companies that exploit the advanced features of their processors. Such investments may follow the usual rules of VC investments, or they may use different criteria depending on their objectives.

While any given funding round may provide X million dollars, it is unlikely to arrive in one single payment: it is more likely that it will be delivered in a series of *tranches* at set intervals. While these payments should be routine, they may be conditional on the funded company meeting deliveries or targets.

Private Equity

VC companies are examples of *private equity* investors, but not all private equity companies are VC companies. As the 'venture' in their title implies, venture capital companies fund new ventures. Many private equity investors want nothing to do with risky new ventures: instead they want to invest in established companies.

Kohlberg Kravis Roberts (KKR) may be the best-known private equity company, made (in)famous by the RJR Nabisco take-over, described in the best-selling book *Barbarians at the Gate* (Burrough & Helyar, 1991). Other big players include Blackstone, Silverlake and Carlyle.

The modus operandi of private equity (PE) companies is basically the same as for VC companies: raise a fund, invest the fund, exit the investments, return money with interest. However there is one particular difference: the companies' private equity targets have assets; offering these assets as collateral allows the PE company to lend money from the bank (leverage). Thus a small amount of investment money can be combined with large loans to buy big companies. Consequently, like a bank, private equity funds look at what assets a company has that can be offered as collateral in loans, or sold to return investments in the event of failure.

This debt strategy has been widely criticised for distorting business. Debts might not be repaid until the company is sold, or may be repaid over time; either way, interest has to be paid. This is paid not by the fund, but by the target company. Paying interest will cost, and as a result the target company's revenue will be depressed and it may look as if it is loss-making.

While early-stage software companies might not be able to attract PE investment, established companies might: established companies have assets and cash flow.

In these circumstances another difference between VC and PE companies becomes apparent: VC investors specialise in growing companies, while PE investors often specialise in extracting additional value without necessarily growing the target company. PE investors are sometimes called 'asset strippers', because they will sell profitable parts of a business. They make also work existing assets hard and reduce headcount in an effort to improve the return on their investment.

Investor Exit

Whoever invests in a business will expect to get their money back one day. This is called the 'exit'. Friends and family or banks loans might be repaid with interest, but when investments are made in return for equity (shares), this means that the equity has to be turned into cash.

While a stock market flotation – or *initial public offering* (IPO) – may be a legendary way of exiting – and making millionaires in the process – most start-up companies don't end in flotation. The majority of start-up companies end in failure and investors get little, if any, return on their investment.

Trade sales – mergers, acquisitions, takeovers – occur when the company is sold to another company, perhaps a competitor or complementor, or just a company that wishes to grow. The sale may be made for cash or for equity in the buyer. Provided the buyer is itself publicly listed (quoted), such equity can then be sold for cash.

Secondary sales occur when on investor sells to another investor. Say VC company A sells its investment to company B. This may occur because company A needs to close the fund, or because it can no longer see how to grow its investment.

There are in addition a host of ways in which a company can be sold to its employees, typically managers:

- MBO – *management buy-out,* in which the managers of the company buy the company, perhaps using PE money or loans.
- MBI – *management buy-in,* in which another team of managers buys the company, again using PE investment or loans.
- MWO – *management work-out,* in which a management team buys the company and repays the investors gradually over time from the company's revenues.

The thing to remember when planning the start is to plan the end. When asking people to put money into a company, they need to be told how they will get their money out. This doesn't have to be a rock-solid plan, but it does need to be realistic. In fact, its probably better to offer several different scenarios whereby the original investment will be returned with interest.

Funding Timing

While a few companies can leap to big-money funding – the start-up Google being one of the few that did – most use a combination of the funding sources outlined above at different times in their development. (See *The Search* (Battelle, 2006) for a good discussion of Google's funding.)

Figure 7 shows the general timing and size of each funding round. Early-stage investments – own funds, friends and family and even angel funding – tend to be small sums, say, less than $1 million – although obviously this changes with time and individual circumstances.

Later stages, predominantly venture capital, tend to start with much larger sums, say a minimum of $5m. Subsequent funding rounds tend to be bigger than previous rounds, but this is not always the case. Most VC companies don't invest the smaller 'seed' amounts, simply because the costs of making an investment outweigh the expected return that would be gained.

One funding source not shown on the diagram is IPO, or flotation. Companies can, and do, sometimes float on the stock market while still experiencing rapid growth and before reaching break-even. Netscape is perhaps the most famous example of this. By breaking the norm and floating to raise funds to become profitable, Netscape set the scene for the 'dot.com bubble' at the turn of the century.

During the bubble it became almost normal for companies to shun later rounds of VC funding and instead turn to the stock market for growth funding. Since the busting of the bubble the markets have reverted to the previous norm: compa-

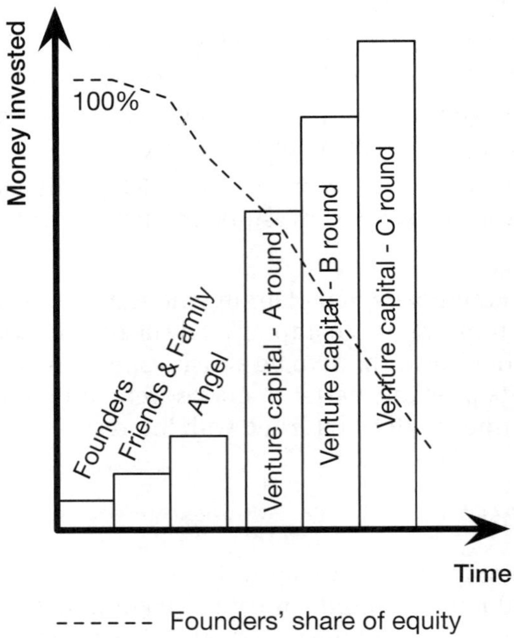

Figure 7. Alternative funding sources relative to one another

nies usually only float when youthful growth has become regular profit and investors need to exit.

In some places and at some times a 'funding gap' exists between what the very early-stage investors are willing to invest and what the VC companies will consider investing. For example, the top of the investment scale for angels may be well below the bottom of the scale for VCs.

In general, the earlier an investment comes, the more risk the investor is taking, while the greater the risk that is incurred, the greater the return expected. When equity is involved this frequently means that control of the company is split between founders and investors, or even ceded entirely to investors.

The longer a start-up company can wait before taking investment, the less the risk, therefore the less equity (and control) of the company is taken away from its founders. Of course, this additional time needs to be used wisely, to further research and/or develop the product and to make the early sales that validate the market. The more developed the product and the more proven the market, the less the risk.

At each round of investment the founders trade equity for cash. As a result their control of the company diminishes over time. In the beginning they may own 100% of the stock, but each time new stock is issued to new investors those who hold stock find that they own a smaller percentage. Gradually its founders lose the majority share in the company, and with majority they may also lose control of the company itself. Other investors may force the company to make decisions that its founders would not have done.

Angel and VC investors may initially be keen for a company's founders to retain more than 50% of its stock. This ensures that its founders still feel ownership and responsibility for the company. However, in later rounds, the founders will probably lose the majority stake and the control that comes with it.

However, all this is subject to change and circumstances. Inflation will ensure that the figures mentioned above will increase over time. Friends and family may have limited sums to invest, unless it is a very wealthy family. And the product or service you are offering might just be interesting enough to an investor for them to break the normal rules. However, far more start-ups will think their product and context qualifies as such a scenario than will ever be the case in reality.

Love–hate with Venture Capital

Technology entrepreneurs have something of a love–hate relationship with venture capitalists. On one hand, VCs have the money technology companies need, and many of the biggest names in the industry owe their success to VC backing. With VC backing a software start-up can stop living hand-to-mouth, always waiting on the next sale, and build for the long term – or at least the next three to five years.

On the other hand, VCs employ hard-nosed businessmen who want to make money. They care more for business plans than technological innovation. They set targets for their investments, make demands and set expectations, and when these are not met, wield the knife. Since they plan to exit in a three to five year timescale, companies tend to be run for short-term growth rather than long-term sustainability.

Although a little dated, Jerry Kaplan conveys much of this contradiction in his story of Go Corporation:

> *'Venture capitalists are masters of procrastination. Their standard practice is to keep all options open until the last possible moment, often abandoning some hapless entrepreneur at the altar after months of reassurances that there is just one final question before they will invest. The VCs know time is on their*

side: the less money the venture has, the more desperate it will be to make a deal…

The second and third rounds of financing are often the hardest. Although everyone involved would like to think that the process is rational, in practice it is as subjective as buying a house.'

(Kaplan, 1995)

Although ventures do occasionally get funded by VCs and angels without formal business plans, the overwhelming majority need business plans. A full discussion of business plans would take a book in its own right, indeed a quick perusal of any bookseller will reveal several dozen. However it is worth making a few points about business plans and what is expected.

Business plans need to contain some revenue and cost projections; the greater the degree these are based in research and customer understanding, the more legitimacy they will have. Almost inevitably business plans presented to VCs show a 'hockey stick' projection, as shown in Figure 8.

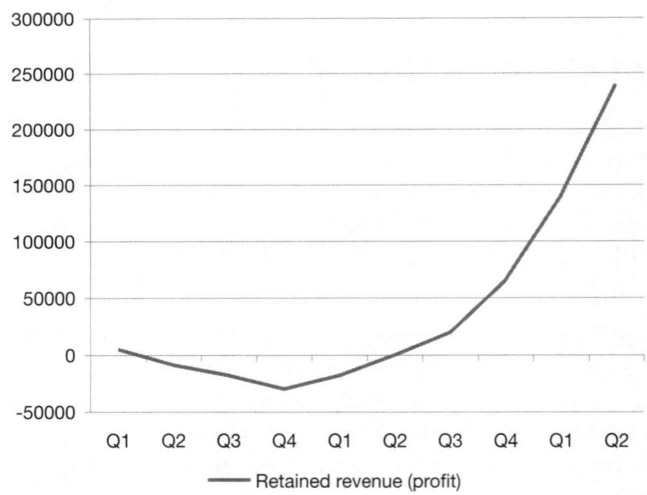

Figure 8. Hockey stick revenue projection

The hockey stick projection shows a company initially ambling along, maybe making a little money, maybe losing a little. Once an investment is made the company starts to spend money – hiring people, buying equipment and so on. As a result the company is spending more money than it has coming in (Q1–Q4). This continues while the company builds it product, market and business. Eventually this spending hits the bottom of the curve (Q4), sales start to increase and go on increasing. Expansion may continue, but now sales are more than covering the growth from Q4 onwards.

While many companies include such a projection in their business plan, few actually achieve it. Many, perhaps most, will never get the chance. Of those who do get investment funding, the money is the easy part: the difficult part is getting the sales and bringing in the revenue. Wielding the stick to ensure that this happens is what gives VCs their bad name.

The future funding needed to complete this plan – whether additional tranches of money already agreed or new financing rounds – may be conditional on specific targets. VCs know that some money will be lost throughout this process; they may not like it, but they ultimately accept it.

Some investment companies take a portfolio approach to offset the risk of losses. For example, they may invest in ten companies, of which they expect seven to go bust, losing them money. Two might be expected to break even, or be mildly profit- or loss-making, while one will be expected to be successful enough to cover all the losses and still show a healthy profit for the fund overall. The problem for the investors is that at the start of the process they don't know which of the ten companies will be the success.

Finally, the word 'profit' is itself something of a misnomer. Commonly profit is taken to be the difference between costs and revenue. This is more correctly referred to as *net revenue* or *free cash flow.* Profit is actually an accounting invention. A number of accounting techniques and local tax rules make profit highly subjective. For a start, should a company deduct debit interest when calculating profit? Since debt or interest can be offset against tax, it actually makes sense to have some debt in order to reduce tax.

Closing Words

This chapter has done little more than scrape the surface of the complex issue of funding a company through its early stages. Before involving any external investors into a company it is wise to consult experts, or at least those who have done this before.

Even before consulting experts, it is important to ask: *why bring in outside investors? What is the objective?* Certainly outside investors will ask this question, so if nothing else, it helps to know the answer.

Although software companies are expensive to operating in terms of wages that must be paid, they are not capital-intensive. There are few barriers to starting a software company, and they are regularly stated by individuals and teams with little more than their own funds.

Once started, the question often becomes *how big do we want to grow and how fast?* Certainly if you plan on being the next Google you will need some help. If on the other hand you are prepared to get rich slowly, then bootstrapping may well be the best course.

6

What to Build – Patterns about Products

The patterns in this chapter look at how to develop products that customers want, and the options available when deciding which products to create. Many of the patterns here show how product companies can create better products and improve their customer focus.

Technology companies often aim to create the best product possible. Armed with a technology, they seek problems that can be solved by it. Such companies are technically led and rich on innovation; they believe that the best product with the best technology wins. This approach is completely natural in companies that come into being to commercialise a piece of technology, and is typical of start-up enterprises.

Such companies are said to be *technology-led*, or *product-focused*. This approach stands in contrast to *customer-led* or *customer-focused* companies, in which the customers are the centre of attention. In customer-focused companies technology takes a back seat. The company tries to understand its customers, the problems they have and the constraints they work under, then seeks to apply technology to resolve these problems. It chooses the most applicable technology, whether it is cutting edge or well established.

However, it is difficult to be a customer-led company without customers. Until customers start paying money for products, actions are at best based on market research and at worst based on assumptions and opinions. When customers buy products – and even when they don't – they generate feedback about what the product is and should be. The money they spend is itself feedback about what

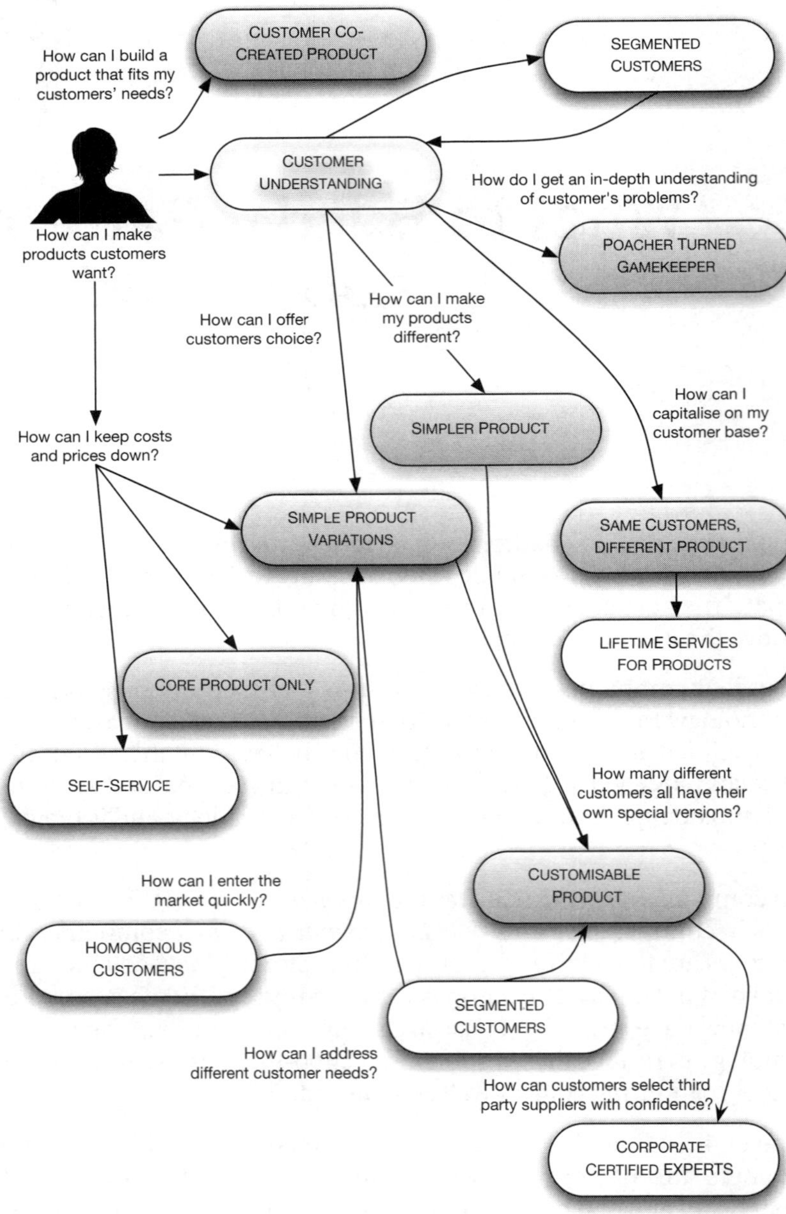

Figure 9. Product patterns map

they value, and what they don't. However, expenditure is a rather blunt form of feedback; it needs to be combined with customer understanding.

Once customers start buying a new difficulty can set in: obsession with an individual customers and/or the next sale. Excessive focus on one customer can drive out a more balanced approach that is better for long-term success. The solution is to take a *market focused* approach. Rather than focusing on one customer, companies look across the market at multiple potential customers, the common issues and problems and what their competition is doing. The market is normally more than one customer; when the entire market is one customer there is little point in creating a generic product, because there are no generic customers.

Being focused on an individual customer is not such a problem for a service or ESP company. Since each service delivery is unique to one customer, each delivery is a self-contained project, which should be completely focused on one customer alone.

When creating products and strategy, software companies need an approach that matches market and customer needs with new technology. 'Cool technology' may be cool, but if there are no customers for it, it is worthless. Technology and the skills to use that technology are important, but should not dominate.

Market need is the approximate combination of the needs of multiple (potential) customers. New products are the result of addressing this need with new technology – see Figure 10.

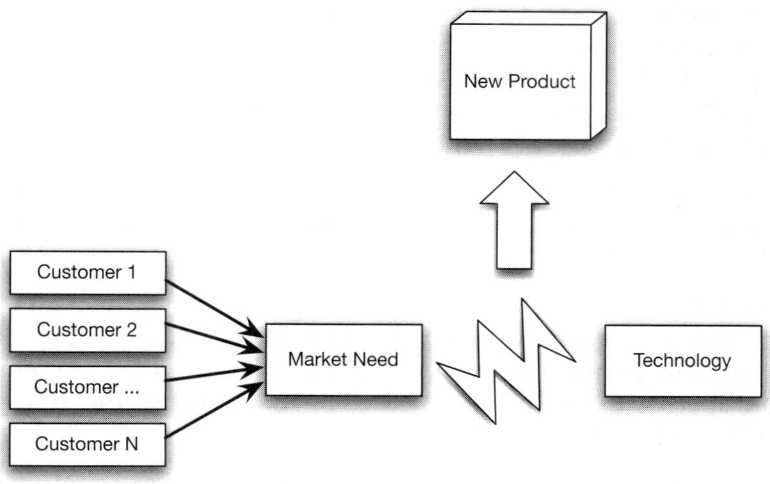

Figure 10. Combining market need with technology to create new products

A company that starts life focused on technology – as described in Chapter 3 – may find it hard to acquire a market focus as it grows, but this may be exactly what is needed if growth is to be maintained. Changing focus requires a shift in culture and structure. For example, switching from product to market focus means:

- Getting to know your customers in depth rather than finding the customers to match the product – use the CUSTOMER UNDERSTANDING (page 146) and SEGMENTED CUSTOMERS (page 141) patterns.
- Product changes need to be customer- and market-led, not innovation-led: innovation for the sake of innovation needs to be discouraged.
- Selling to the same customers again and again rather than selling new products to new customers – the SAME CUSTOMERS, DIFFERENT PRODUCT pattern (page 105). Consequently customer care and the after-sales experience are increasingly important.
- Supplementing your product offering with services and add-ons rather than creating new products – the PRODUCTS WITH SERVICES (page 242), INITIAL HELP (page 248) and LIFETIME SERVICES FOR PRODUCTS (page 252) patterns. Seek to solve the whole problem with a WHOLE PRODUCT (page 131), even if that means supplying services and third-party products – COMPLEMENTOR, NOT COMPETITOR (page 309) – with your own.
- Inbound marketing proceeds, rather than follows, research and engineering.

It is not always easy for companies with a history of focusing on the product to re-orientate their focus. Changing focus can be difficult and will require changes to practises and culture. You will need to get the customer's voice heard within your organisation. Staff will need to think less about 'cool technology' and more about customer needs. Back-office staff may not want to meet customers and technical staff may prefer to hide behind technology.

Reducing the focus on products carries the risk that you might miss some technology advance. Competitors may use new technology to produce a superior product, or redefine the market in novel ways.

The focus and the customer/product spectrum represents one dimension of strategic positioning. *The delta model* (Hax & Wilde, 1999, described in Chapter 4) proposes three dimensions of positioning: *customer solutions, best product* and *system lock-in*. In this model companies position themselves in relation to these three apices.

One example of customer focus is the SAME CUSTOMERS, DIFFERENT PRODUCT pattern (page 105) which suggests supplying more products to the same customers. Rather than engage in the time-consuming and expensive task of finding new customers, this pattern views existing customers as an asset. Selling to the same customers again is not only cheaper than finding new customers, but also deepens the relationship and helps ensure that it is ongoing – or, using the Delta Model view, a *lock-in*.

This is just one of four possible approaches to product development and sales. The matrix in Table 3 shows all four possibilities.

Table 3: Four views of customers and the product

	Same product	*Different product*
Same customer Approaches most applicable when selling to organisations where opportunities exist beyond initial users.	When products are consumed (razor blades, printer ink) this is always possible. When products last, such as software, ways need to be found to entice the customer to use more of the product.	Customer is the asset; find or develop new products to sell to the customer. See SAME CUSTOMERS, DIFFERENT PRODUCT (page 105).
Different customer Approaches more applicable when selling to a very large market.	Product is the asset view. Need to expand market or take market share from competitors. New sales channels can help find new customers, so consider the WHOLESALER (page 217), WHITE LABEL (page 208) and LOCAL GUIDE (page 200) patterns.	Diversification: a new product in a new market; inherently risky (such as tobacco companies diversifying into food). May be a brand extension, for example Caterpillar clothing.

Customisation, Platforms, Frameworks and Product Lines

Software is infinitely flexible, but it doesn't always make sense to take flexibility to the extreme – both for technical and marketing reasons.

The pattern CUSTOMISABLE PRODUCT (page 115) is about making modifications to a standard product so that it better meets specific customers' needs. As described, it is a solution to a specific problem with specific forces.

There are good reasons to argue against this approach; this author, in general, agrees with Cagan's argument against 'customer specials' (Cagan, 2008). However, specials are common practice and many companies do supply them; simply saying "don't do it" is not useful advice for many.

There are other forces that can lead to similar solutions. For example, WHOLE PRODUCT (page 131) advocates making the product fit not just a single customer's need exactly, but making a product that fits the needs of an entire industry, or market, perfectly.

Economics exerts powerful forces too: why design, manufacture and maintain a product for a niche market, when by targeting a larger market those costs can be spread over many more customers and sales? But in addressing bigger and bigger markets, the number of points of variation increases. This gives rise to more complexity, in the underlying code, in the customisations and in the marketing message to potential customers.

Attempting to manage these complexities has given rise to *product line engineering* and the idea of technology platforms on which applications can be built. Other commercial/engineering domains have pursed platform approaches, and there are lessons to be learned from them. For example, car manufactures build product lines for different car models: there is not just one type of Volkswagen Golf, but several: the popular hatchback (with two or four doors), an estate version and a saloon version (sometimes called Bora or Jetta).

But car manufacturers don't stop there. Increasingly, more than one product line of car is built on the same platform. Underlying the VW Golf is the PQ35 platform, which also serves for the Audi A3, Skoda Octavia and other cars in the VW stable – each of which has its own product line of saloons, hatchbacks and so on. Owners may then choose to customise their cars – a special paint job, a fancy spoiler or structural changes such as wheel chair access or foot steering for a disabled driver.

Some software companies have been successful in adopting this model, but history is littered with failed examples. The problem is that software development experiences diseconomies of scale: as scope increases, projects get bigger, requirements for different areas come into conflict, prioritisation gets more difficult, and as more people work on the development, the volume of interactions increases. As a result, costs rise disproportionately. A small, highly focused team will be able to develop a bespoke piece of software for a customer far faster than a large team developing a platform.

Building a platform of any shape or size is significantly more expensive than building a product, because it involves working at one or more steps removed from a usable product. More than one software company has found itself building a platform almost by accident, sometimes because the engineers decide it is a *good thing*. Software developers love building platforms and, without strong product management input, will create a bigger platform than needed. Since building platforms is more expensive, this can lengthen development and delay product release. But blocking developers' wishes can lead to discontented and frustrated staff.

Aside from code and test, there are other costs that need to be considered when embarking on a platform strategy. While it is necessary for a platform to be reusable, it is not sufficient. The easier it is to reuse the platform, the more it will be reused; this means supporting the ecosystem that uses the platform. Providing such support incurs costs: documentation needs to be written, training courses delivered and so on.

Some platforms – such as Volkswagen's – are intended for internal use by the company's own engineers. Others, like Microsoft Windows, are intended for external use by engineers outside the originating company. When the platform is intended for external use, more support is required, and consequently the costs will be higher.

Nor is it enough to offer a well-supported platform. There need to be incentives to encourage engineers to choose to develop on a platform. The platform needs to give them something they cannot get otherwise, or make their work much easier.

Offering a platform – even just an API – for external use implies a commitment to future support – few customers will want to buy the product if you refuse to support customisations in future versions. Supporting APIs can be expensive and restrict future options.

Even in the car industry there are some diseconomies of scale: one consequence of VW's extensive use of a few platforms is that introducing a new platform is very expensive and disruptive. When a new platform replaces PQ35, VW will need to redesign every car that uses the platform, retool multiple factories, and market launch many new cars before the full economies of scale are seen. Such high cyclical costs have resulted in moves to increase the number of future platforms VW uses.

Software development has had significant success with software frameworks that provide tools for developers working within the framework model. Microsoft's MFC was an early success in this field; the Open Source Hibernate framework is a more recent example. However, for every successful framework, there are multiple failures.

As well as technical considerations to steer developers towards product lines, platforms and framework, there are equally powerful marketing factors. Marketing a product as a platform entails creating an ecosystems of application developers before any benefit is seen. It may be better to market the product as an application in its own right, and only later reveal the platform's capabilities, as Apple did with the iPhone.

While the iPhone is usable as a phone straight out of the box, the SAP application suite is not. The entire SAP application suite is customisable and configurable through options, option tables and programming in ABAP (a Cobol-like language). This flexibility has allowed SAP to become the dominant enterprise application suite in ERP, CRM, finance and other business areas.

SAP's customisability is a double-edged sword: it is so customisable that it is virtually unusable in its uncustomised version. Customising SAP systems is a major development exercise in its own right, and provides opportunities for a VALUE ADDED RESELLER (page 203). Consequently there is a whole industry of SAP consultants, designers, developers and VARs.

Product line engineering, platform strategies and the development of product ecosystems are massive topics in their own right. Much has been written elsewhere about these topic, Dietmar Schütz, Markus Völter and others are developing patterns for product line engineering. Outside of the pattern form, *Platform Leadership* (Cusumano & Gawer, 2002) discusses the development platform ecosystems.

POACHER TURNED GAMEKEEPER

Figure 11. Those who used to work on the other side can be very useful

---

Former poachers know how poachers think, they know the poacher's techniques and motivations. They know where and when to look for poachers. They are effective at catching poachers.

Hiring someone from a customer's organisation can be a quick way to learn about the customer's problems and needs in depth.

Context You are a technology company making products and selling products to multiple companies with multiple employees each.

Problem *How do you get an in-depth understanding of your customer, their needs and the pressures they work under?*

Forces Creating successful products requires a deep understanding of your customer, the problems they face, how they use the current product and opportunities for new products. But you can only learn so much from observing and questioning the customer.

Acquiring an in-depth understanding can take a lot of time and effort, but in a competitive marketplace time to market is important. Spending time understanding the customer costs more money and delays work on the product.

Customers may be willing to help you develop your product, but they will have limits to how much time they can spend working with you; they have their own jobs to do. To really understand your customer and their needs, you need to live the customer's life. But you have your own life to live and your own job to do, creating products.

Some sources of information should not be used because they breach ethical and legal boundaries. To do so may make your company and you yourself liable to prosecution and damage your company's reputation.

Solution

Employ (ex)customers who have experience and knowledge of the application domain you are targeting. These people may be employed as subject matter experts, product managers or analysts, or hired on a consultancy basis for the duration of a project.

Your new employees will know the customer and their domain very well, but they may not understand your business or what is now expected of them. In their previous role they were not business analysts or product managers, so it is wrong to assume that they can take on such a role overnight. Arrange suitable training and mentoring so that they quickly master new skills and understand what they need to do.

For example, an expert hired from a telecoms company to work as a software product manager will know a lot about telecoms technology, issues and opportunities. However, they will not know much about software development and product management. It may be wise to pair them with an experienced employee while they learn the new role.

Once hired, take these people to see your other customers, so that they can generalise about the domain and identify common opportunities and differences. Have them brief your staff on how your customers work, where your product(s) fit in and what problems they find.

Do not expect your new hires to disclose confidential information; this would be unethical and possibly illegal, for example by breaching their contract with their former employer. Do not overstep the mark and breach ethical or commercial boundaries when hiring staff from corporate customers. Boeing made this mistake when it hired Darleen Druyun from the United States Air Force. Consequently Boeing's CFO was sacked, the CEO resigned and Druyun spent nine months in prison for corruption.

Consequences Customer knowledge and understanding now exist within your organisation. Such knowledge may cost a premium, so make sure that you make the best use of this experience and share insights. You have bought a snapshot taken from the moment your expert leaves their previous employer. Things will change with time: your customer will change and your new employee will see things differently.

You have bought yourself the in-depth knowledge and understanding of one individual from one corporate customer. Few customers will have identical environments and needs, so be careful not to extrapolate from one to many without other checks.

Some of the people keenest to work for your company will be champions for your product inside the customer organisation. Hiring them may remove your product's greatest advocate and open opportunities for competitors.

Hiring your customers' employees may upset your relationship. If you hire too many staff from the same customer, you may harm your commercial relationship.

Variations Hiring similar staff from corporations that are not currently customers can provide many similar benefits with fewer ethical dilemmas.

Related work SURROGATE CUSTOMER (Coplien & Harrison, 2004) suggests a role with 'someone who will try to think like a customer'. Someone who was once a customer will find this role easier to play.

Both CUSTOMER CO-CREATED PRODUCT (page 95) and this pattern aim at getting customer knowledge inside the development organisation. However, the two patterns take different approaches and may be considered alternatives.

This pattern is one means of achieving the *onsite customer* practise from *Extreme Programming* (Beck, 2000).

Examples

The author has worked for several companies where product managers, technical and commercial staff were recruited from customer organisations specifically because they had a depth of understanding about what the customer needed.

CUSTOMER CO-CREATED PRODUCT

Figure 12. The Boeing 777 is a customer co-created product

Photo by Solitude, user Demiss from WikiMedia (Creative Commons Attribution-Share Alike 2.0 Generic)

When designing the 777 airliner, Boeing wanted to create a plane that met customer needs. Under the banner of 'working together', eight customer airlines were invited to contribute to its design and participate in its development. United Airline's need to replace its DC-10 aircraft became a focus for the work, and engineers from United worked in Seattle with Boeing engineers and engineers from other airlines to create an aeroplane that met the airlines' needs.

Some have claimed that the 777 was the 'most customer-oriented aircraft yet'. Certainly in terms of sales the 777 has been very successful for Boeing.

Context You are developing a technically complicated product with many design choices.

Problem *How do you ensure that your product does what your customer(s) want?*

Forces You know the customer's general requirements and believe you have the ability to create a solution. But you lack domain knowledge and/or a true understanding of what the customer wants. There are many specific trade-off decisions to make that will require customer input.

The opportunity your product addresses is understood (more or less), but the solution is not so clear. In creating a solution you explore both the opportunity and the solution at the same time; consequently, your design choices multiply, and knowing what the customer wants becomes more difficult – *the devil is in the detail.*

Product development is risky. Even if you think you understand the customer's product needs and requirements, it is still possible to get things wrong. During the time it takes to create a product things will change. The more expensive the product development, the greater the need to reduce these risks.

Spending more time up front understanding customer needs would help reduce risk. But this will also delay the start of building the product and so delay future revenues. But without real understand of your customers, you are guessing.

New products should include new thinking, but if you rush to develop the product your past experience and knowledge will dominate, so the new product will not be so new.

Solution

Enrol one or more customers as partners in your development process. Give them an opportunity to influence the product design and implementation. Make the product development process a win-win situation for you and your customers.

Using a customer as a partner combines elements of bespoke product development and elements of generic product development. It is an opportunity to create a product that fits many customers' needs; it is also a challenge to avoid creating a product that fits only one customer's needs.

Talk to your partners – talk to them a lot, share problems and solutions, share documentation, share as much as possible. Have your people work at their sites and their people work at your sites. Show them mock-ups, prototypes and models of the product. Spend time discussing the models and working through usage patterns, operations scenarios and variations to models.

When selecting a partner, consider the practical aspects: *are you close enough geographically to meet regularly? Do you speak a common language, both figuratively and literally? Do your computer systems interconnect? Are your corporate cultures a good match?*

Such differences can halt cooperation before it even starts. You might decide to rule some potential partners out, or you may take measures to overcome the difficulty.

When customers and suppliers cooperate there is a need to respect each other's intellectual property (IP). Customers may be prepared to share some IP, but they may also want to restrict access to other IP, or ensure it is not made available to competitors. What IP may be used, and who owns the resulting IP, should be clearly agreed.

To partner with a customer you need to find a customer who is prepared to partner with you, and not just any customer will do. They will have a genuine need for your new product and see the advantage of working closely with you to shape the product and get early access. They need to be prepared to devote people, time and money to the project.

Customers who see the project as a route to get a cheaper product, or offload their own work, will not make good partners. Neither should you work with customers who might become competitors, although this might be difficult to foresee.

Consequences Working with customers results in a better understanding of the opportunity, solution and technical aspects. Your partner customer will benefit too. They will have early access to your new product and it will be a closer fit to their needs.

When working with a partner you can short-cut some of the up-front requirements and design because your customer is involved. Some of these decisions can be deferred, because you know you can ask the customer later. Other decisions can be made faster because the customer is readily available.

Informed and timely decision-making can reduce risk on the project and accelerate the development cycle. Both partners benefit from reduced risk, faster execution and a better product more closely aligned with the customer's needs.

However, joint development can also take longer, because more people are involved and need to share in the discussions. Reaching consensus can be difficult in large groups. If your corporate cultures and incentives are not aligned, cooperation may be fraught with disagreements and arguments. This in turn can poison the wider organisation.

Working with several partners at the same time may lead to conflicts when partners want different things.

Co-creating a product also means your partner's competitors may have access to the same product. If the product offers customers a competitive advantage, or contains confidential IP, they may prefer to develop their own custom solution even if this costs more.

Pricing a co-created product may be difficult. Offering the product for free or at a discount to partners may encourage some to join your programme, but such partners may not really value the product. At some point you need to know whether customers will pay cash for the product you are developing. If partners insist on some financial payment, offer royalties on product sales: this will align their interests with your own.

There is a risk that being too close to one customer during product development may result in a *customer special*: a product that is specific to one customer. Such products are often a diversion for ISVs which disrupt the roadmap.

Variations

IP may be protected by leaving holes in the system where customers can plug in their own IP modules. For example, if a customer has a particular optimisation algorithm they wish to use, the generic product may include a simple optimiser that can be swapped for another using *Patterns for Plug-Ins* (Marquardt, 2006).

Boeing's 'working together' philosophy also led to the creation of cross-functional teams of its own staff. Engineers would work together on one team rather than working as functional suppliers and customers to each other.

In June 2011 Chinese aircraft manufacturer Comac announced an agreement with RyanAir under which the airline would work with the manufacture on the development of the C919 aircraft. This is a variation in which the customer agrees to collaborate without actually committing to buy the end product.

Related work

This patterns echoes several of Christopher Alexander's patterns that suggest, or assume, that the end user is involved with the architecture, design and construction of their building, such as WEB OF PUBLIC TRANSPORT (Alexander, 1977). Another example of this approach is the ENGAGE CUSTOMERS pattern (Coplien & Harrison, 2004).

The Extreme Programming practice of *onsite customer* is a variation of this pattern.

The IN BED WITH THE ENEMY (Weiss, 2007) patterns also consider business partnerships, in this case partnerships with potential competitors.

Examples

A London-based telecoms software house worked with major customers in Europe and the USA to develop products later sold to many operators worldwide.

Military systems like the Eurofighter Typhoon are often developed by contractors together with national armed forces and later sold to third parties.

Simpler Product

Figure 13. Apple's original iPod was far simpler to use than its competitors when launched

Public domain from WikiMedia user Steve Sims

When Apple launched the iPod in 2001 it wasn't the first portable music player, nor was it the first portable digital music player, it wasn't even the first hard disk-based portable digital music player. Compared to its competitors in 2001, it was somewhat limited in its functionality.

But it was stylish and simple to use: somehow the two things seemed to go hand in hand. Not only was the iPod significantly simpler to use than competitors, it continued to get simpler. iTunes, and the iTunes store launched in 2003, simplified the process of getting music onto the player. The iPod shuffle removed virtually all controls from the player by embracing randomness.

You can still buy digital music players with more functionality than the iPod, but few do. The iPod has redefined what a digital music player should be.

Context You are planning to break into an existing market with a new product, perhaps using new technology.

Problem *What new product can you introduce to a market that is already served by products from established vendors?*

Forces Initially you need a foothold in the market. You need some revenue and some experience to refine your product. But entering a market against existing, well-resourced incumbents is difficult.

You have a product or technology, but it looks as if the market is already well served. Your technology may be superior to current products, but there are already several incumbents who produce good products; matching their products will take time and money.

The market incumbents produce similar products. They traditionally compete by adding new features and/or making their products faster. But customers are 'overserved' by products with features and capabilities that most customers don't need or use. New features add no value for overserved customers; instead, they detract from value, because they complicate the product further.

Although capable of doing what customers want, increasingly complex products become less usable and less elegant. Product complexity adds to the cost of ownership. Time must be spent learning the product, users need training, and even consultants to advise them. But customers expect these features, options and services. Without these features you are not a serious competitor, but adding them takes more time and money.

Solution

Create a product that is massively simpler to use then existing products and target a different set of customers. Target customers who value simplicity and usability, customers who do not need all the features of the existing products, who do have time to spend learning the product and who find the complexities of existing products off-putting.

Start by defining the problem your product is solving, and for whom. Apply CUSTOMER UNDERSTANDING (page 146) and SEGMENTED CUSTOMERS (page 141) to understand who your potential customers are and what they need.

Existing customers expect a fully featured product. Instead target customers who would benefit from the product but who do not buy current products because of complexity and/or cost. In this market segment you are competing against non-consumption.

When you understand your potential customers, address their needs exactly. Have your designers and engineers rethink the product and interface. Look at how customers are using the product and focus on what they are using it to achieve, rather than how they do it. Use personas to better understand your potential customers base and identify the most important customers/users (Cooper, 2004).

Look at existing products and try to eliminate options and extras. Apply the Pareto Principle to find the 20% of product that is used 80%

of the time: your chosen customers value simplicity over performance.

Look too at the services you provide to supplement your product (PRODUCTS WITH SERVICES, page 242). These services can indicate where customers have problems with your product: can you eliminate the need for training? What are the main issues raised with the help desk? The services too may be simplified to improve the customer experience.

Simpler products need not sell at a lower price than existing products; there may be a *simplicity premium* that allows you to sell your product for *more* than existing products. However this is not always the case: less functionality may still equate to lower price.

To reach this new market segment, choose a new distribution channel, one different to the current incumbents. If incumbents use direct sales, then try using indirect; if incumbents use indirect sales, then go direct using BRANDED SHOPS (page 172) and INTERNET STORE (page 177).

Consequences Avoiding competition, keeping the product simple and removing the need for support services reduces the cost, time and complexity of entering the market. This means that incumbents are unlikely to see you as a direct rival, thus giving you the time to increase revenue and build the company further.

By changing the basis of your product you disengage from incumbent rivals. You are now competing for different customers. Incumbents will find it hard to match your product because they are structured around existing customers and complex products. These companies have too much invested – financially and mentally – in the current way of doing things. They will fear undercutting their existing sales.

By targeting customers who do not currently buy, you sidestep current incumbents and their products. Incumbents are not your direct competitors, but they do help you position the product by showing how you are different.

Packaging new technology as a simpler product, and keeping it out of direct competition with market incumbents, provides time (and revenue) to develop the technology further. As the technology develops you can extend the initial product, or introduce new products, that compete more directly.

Your product is more accessible to customers because it does not require the same investment to start realising the benefits. Overall cost of ownership is reduced, because customers do not need training or advice on how to use the product. Your target customers are new to the product category and so do not expect additional support.

After your initial success there maybe a temptation to add features in future versions. Even customers who want simplicity may desire more features. To do so risks negating the initial advantage. You may find a way to include more features without increasing complexity. Alternatively you may introduce more products that reverse your original tradeoff.

In time you might find your simple product becoming complex. This would provide an opportunity for someone else to repeat this pattern with you in the role of incumbent.

Variations

Sometimes it is possible to hide complexity rather than remove it. Complex software products may offer *wizards* that guide users through a complex task. The wizard breaks a task into several discrete steps and only offers the most common options. If you find you are adding more and more wizards, it is time to look at a more radical simplification.

This pattern can also be applied to your company: be simple to do business with. Companies like JJ Bean in the USA and Marks & Spencer in the UK are famous for their liberal returns policies.

Related work

Existing incumbent companies may choose to use CORE PRODUCT ONLY (Kelly, 2005) as an alternative strategy. While they may strip back their existing product, making it genuinely simpler to use is often difficult. Additionally they will still have a high cost base which your technology (hopefully) avoids.

SIMPLER PRODUCT does not automatically imply CORE PRODUCE ONLY. For example, Apple's iPod is simple, but to keep it simple Apple offer additional services like iTunes and software for PC and Mac. A CORE PRODUCE ONLY strategy would leave these services for third parties: the loss of integration is likely to complicate the product.

The Innovators Solution (Christensen & Raynor, 2003) describes how companies can use innovative products to enter an existing market. Such products may have fewer features than existing products, but are targeted at a specific need. Combined with a lower price, this allows new entrants to compete with incumbents.

For more ideas on simplifying products, see *The Design of Everyday Things* (Norman, 1988) and *The Laws of Simplicity* (Maeda, 2006).

Tom Gilb encourages software companies to focus on the qualities that a software product needs to posses rather than the features. He argues that it is not functionality that makes a piece of software a winner, rather qualities like ease of use, performance and resilience (Gilb, 2005).

Examples

Blogging isn't anything new: an HTML editor is all that is needed to publish thoughts online. But Blogger and Typepad make blogging simpler than writing HTML. If Blogger isn't simple enough, BlogJet makes it even easier, and if that is too complex, try Twitter.

The original Google search box is another example of a simpler product. Unlike Yahoo the search screen is uncluttered: there is only really one thing you can do.

SAME CUSTOMERS, DIFFERENT PRODUCT

Figure 14. Sony sells more products to the same customers, from Walkman to e-Reader

Sony Reader by Rama from WikiMedia (Creative Commons Attribution-Share Alike 2.0 France); Sony Walkman by user Dub from Wikimedia (Creative Commons Attribution-Share Alike 3.0 Unported)

Once you have a relationship with your customers, they will trust you and your brand. You are in a good position to understand their needs and wants. Growing your market need not mean acquiring more customers (which can be expensive); growing your market may mean selling more products to your existing customers.

Modern consumers are faced with a bewildering number of brands and product variations. Choosing a trusted brand is one way to navigate the jungle.

Business customers find it easier to buy from suppliers they have worked with before, and the promise of compatible products is a big plus.

Context You are seeking to expand an established business that has a number of existing customers. The existing product line-up is limited; perhaps you are a SINGLE PRODUCT COMPANY (page 292).

Problem *How do you maximise your return from existing customers?*

Forces You already have a relationship with your existing customers. Satisfied customers have a positive impression of your company and your sales staff already have a relationship with them.

In contrast, new customers are expensive and time-consuming to obtain. But existing customer already have your product, so they are unlikely to buy it again.

In some markets there may only be a limited number of customers. Even when there are many potential customers, there may be a *long tail*, with a few big customers buying lots of products and many small customers buying a few products. But there may still be rich pickings in the long tail: neglecting smaller customers misses opportunities and risks opening the door to future competitors.

Established (and big) corporations often like dealing with newer (and smaller) companies because they often posses the innovations that established companies lack but which they need to remain competitive. But each external supplier costs the buyer money: the administration of creating entries in the purchase order system, checking contracts, hosting visiting sales people and due diligence to ensure the supplier is still going to exist next week.

On the other hand, it can be expensive and time-consuming to sell products to a new customer – you can't just walk up to the front door and knock. But once you have made the sale you need to move on to the next potential customer and repeat the whole process.

Solution

Expand your product offering so that you have more products to sell to your existing customers. Do this by focusing on the customer's needs rather than the product. This will benefit both you and the customer and deepen your relationship – you will sell more, they will get a better solution.

An existing relationship with a customer is an asset; selling more products to the same customer will generate more revenue from your asset. To better address a customer's need, you need to understand the customer. Fortunately an existing relationship is a great way to get to know the customer, their problems and how they can be helped. Using CUSTOMER UNDERSTANDING (page 146) will reveal ways to enhance your existing product and illustrate opportunities for new products.

Some sales will build directly on the products you have already sold: more licenses for the same software, upgrades to enhanced versions, new versions of existing software and add-on modules are all possible.

The next sale could be a service: support contracts, training and installation are highly applicable to existing products – this is described in PRODUCTS WITH SERVICES (page 242) and LIFETIME SERVICES FOR PRODUCTS (page 252)

Look also at what is used with your product. For example, software requires machines to run on: could you sell hardware too? Could you offer preprinted stationary and forms?

Products with similar characteristics to your existing products can be natural complements. A company selling antivirus software might also offer privacy or spam-detection applications.

Products need not be developed in-house: your relationship with the customer will allow you to endorse other suppliers. You could put your name on someone else's product – 'badge engineering' – or you may just resell another vendor's product. You may buy another company to add their products to your portfolio.

Partnership and distribution agreements can also provide additional products for your sales force. You might become a VALUE ADDED RESELLER (page 203) for another company, or provide a LOCAL GUIDE (page 200).

Individual customers may find a specially tailored version of the product better matches their needs. Similarly, special integration with legacy or third-party systems may enhance the customer's experience of your product and provide extra sales.

Be careful not to annoy your customer by over-selling or offering poor products. Just because you can make an extra sale does not mean you should. Selling a product the customer does not want, is unsuited to the task or of poor quality may sour your relationship with the customer.

Consequences Selling multiple products to the same customer will entrench your position, making it more difficult for competitors to displace your product – the start of a *lock-in* strategy. At the same time it will create more chances to learn about your customer and move the relationship forward.

Producing add-ons and enhancements for a product can provide useful revenue sources. However, if they are bundled with the product to sweeten a sale, they will generate no extra revenue.

With more products to sell you can concentrate your efforts on fewer, bigger, customers. This will be more cost-effective for both you and your customers.

Focusing on the customer rather than the product will help you serve the customer's needs better. Customers may welcome the opportunity to reduce the number of suppliers they deal with: buying is costly for them too.

Competitors might find it easier to enter your market through smaller customers who you neglect in favour of bigger ones. At first you may welcome this development, as it removes smaller customers and allows you to concentrate on the more profitable ones. However this might provide the market opening a new competitor needs to get started – *The Innovator's Solution* (Christensen & Raynor, 2003) suggests this approach for new entrants. Alternative distribution channels, or different versions of your product, can be used to address the smaller customers in the *long tail*.

Variations You might not sell a customer an entirely new product: you might make modifications to your existing product specifically for a single customer. Special versions of your product may result in improvements you can feed back into your main product line, or insights you can use in developing the next product. However, special versions also represent additional products you need to support and maintain in future. This can impose additional costs on the business.

Related work This pattern builds on ITS A RELATIONSHIP, NOT A SALE (Rising, 2002), which describes the ongoing relationship between a vendor and a purchaser.

ACCOUNT MANAGEMENT (page 187) and CUSTOMER CO-CREATED PRODUCT (page 95) may be used to help implement this pattern.

The lock-in strategy described in the Delta Model (Hax & Wilde, 1999, described in Chapter 4) is predicated on selling more products to the same customers and restricting the customer's ability to change supplier.

Research supports the view that repeat business from satisfied customers is cost-effective: 'A customer that generates £1,000 for a supplier in its first year is likely to generate a total profit of £50,000 if retained as a satisfied customer over 10 years.' (Doyle, 2002).

Examples

Large software companies like Oracle and Microsoft offer a range of products. Customers will often start the relationship by buying a key product, a database or operating system; over time the vendor moves to cross-sell additional products, such as an ERP system or office automation suite.

Many banks pursue a similar strategy: having sold a customer a mortgage or current (checking) account, they try to sell savings accounts, life insurance and so on.

Core Product Only

Figure 15. Renault/Dacia Logan

When Renault's Dacia subsidiary designed the Logan they designed it for low-cost sale, with an expected sales price of less than $6,000. Parts were 'borrowed' from existing Renault designs, and gadgets like electric windows and air-conditioning that had become standard in European cars were omitted. Despite that the car was to built to be rugged, to be sold and used in developing countries where roads might be potholed.

The car has been a surprising success for Renault, which even began selling it in developed markets like France. In such markets buyers often buy the car with lots of additional extras, like air-conditioning and electric windows, making the actual selling price far higher than the base.

Context You are following a *cost leadership* strategy (Porter, 1980) in an established market with established competitors offering well-known products, or you may be planning to enter a new market and compete with existing players.

Problem *How do you reduce costs to compete against established companies and products?*

Forces Competitors' products and services come as bundles: the core product is packaged and supplemented to make it more attractive and/or justify the pricing. But these additions are not essential to the product for many customers, yet add costs directly and indirectly, resulting in a higher price.

Competitors may be following a WHOLE PRODUCT (page 131) strategy, but in a new market, or a very mature one, customers may be competent in using the product and making it work for them,

Offering a low-priced product will cut your profit margin as well as your costs. But lower prices should lead to more customers and more sales.

Solution

Only sell the core product, don't bundle anything that is not absolutely necessary. Drive down costs by stripping out non-essential elements and pass these savings on to customers as lower prices. Look again at what you think is the standard product. *What extras are included? What is provided out of convention, not necessity?*

Many products come bundled with extras that are not strictly necessary, such as software packages with computers. For a company following a rigorous cost-leadership strategy, these extras drive up the price of the product.

Use SEGMENTED CUSTOMERS (page 141) to split up your target market. Identify the price-sensitive customers and understand what they would be prepared to give up in exchange for a lower price. Remember to look beyond those who currently buy; there are probably more potential customers who would like to buy but cannot afford the current price.

Identify too the over-served customers, those who do not need all the facilities and services that come with existing products. Would they be prepared to give these extras up in return for a cheaper product? Or maybe they would prefer a SIMPLER PRODUCT (page 100)?

Be careful not to strip the product down too far, lest customers bite back by giving your product a poor name. There are also legal limits to how far you can pursue this strategy. The budget airline RyanAir charged a wheelchair user an extra £18, but was taken to court and found guilty of discrimination. Apart from the £1,336 fine (and costs), the airline received much adverse publicity.

Look for opportunities to use SELF-SERVICE (page 268), so that the customer takes on tasks you would previously have needed staff for.

Find a low-cost distribution channel to sell your product through. VALUE ADDED RESELLER (page 203), INDEPENDENT RETAILER (page 213) and other middlemen will all add to the price. An INTERNET STORE (page 177) or BRANDED SHOPS (page 172) will help you control distribution and keep prices down, albeit at cost elsewhere.

Customers may still want some of the features and services you have removed from your product. This is an opportunity to sell extras for more money using SAME CUSTOMERS, DIFFERENT PRODUCT (page 105). Provide a menu of individually priced extras from which they can pick and choose. Rather than dilute your own focus on the core product, work with a WHITE LABEL (page 208) supplier so that you can share in the customer's additional spending.

Consequences In an established market incumbent players will probably have added features and services to their products to attract customers while maintaining high prices. Customers who do not value these additions now have an option to buy only the core product they desire.

Selling a reduced product should lead to lower production costs immediately. By passing savings directly to the customer, you can undercut rivals, differentiate your product and increase sales. This will attract existing customers of the incumbent suppliers and new customers who previously wanted but could not afford the incumbent's products.

In an *elastic* market, more sales at a lower price will lead to higher total revenues; in an *inelastic* market, revenues could be higher, with fewer sales at a higher price[1]. Either way, provided cost can be kept below selling price, there is profit to be made.

Of course, removing features from software doesn't make it physically smaller. But fewer features will reduce the amount of testing needed, reduce support issues and reduce the amount of documentation that must be written.

Stripping out extras may bring other benefits too: boxes can be smaller, saving on packaging and shipping. Less obvious benefits accrue too: smaller boxes mean that less warehouse space is required for storing products and fewer journeys are needed to move products. But there can be disadvantages: smaller boxes are less prominent on shelves and thus more easily overlooked.

---

[1] For a description of elastic and inelastic markets, see any good micro-economics text book, such as Begg, 2008 or Lipsey & Chrystal, 2007.

Removing additional features allows you to focus all your attention on the core product. This gives you time to find more cost savings and keep it operating well – it may be that good operations produce cost savings of their own. Budget airlines have some of the best punctuality records in the industry: not only is this good for customers, but it keeps costs down because exception processing is reduced.

Customers can choose complementary products themselves to add to your product, thus creating their own packages. So rather than purchase a complete home computer package, for example, they can buy a PC from one supplier, choose an operating system from another and an office automation package from a third. Greater customer control translates to greater customer satisfaction, as with SELF-SERVICE (page 268).

Other companies may offer additional services and products to complement yours. For example, PayPal complemented eBay by offering a useful service not provided by eBay.

Sometimes the extras are actually essential, for example batteries for remote controls, or local taxes on hotel rooms. Customers who have incurred extra hidden costs may not trust your company again.

Variations *Cost leadership* is not the only strategy that might lead to a CORE PRODUCT ONLY approach. Entering a new market with INNOVATIVE PRODUCTS (page 313) or EXPEDITIONARY MARKETING (page 153) might benefit from this approach too. Rather than build large infrastructure and support networks, it can be better to enter a market with a core product, see how the market responds, then decide how to grow.

Related work Christensen and Raynor (2003) discuss several examples of new entrants disrupting existing markets with core products. For example, Bloomberg originally entered the financial data market with a basic product, and added more features and services over time.

Examples Limited software products have a mixed history. Microsoft Works has never displaced the market leader, Microsoft Office, but then maybe it was never meant to. Linux is free but corporate buyers still prefer to buy packaged versions that come with support.

Low-cost core-only producers have transformed other industries beyond recognition. The airline industry has been turned upside down by South West Airlines in the USA and copy-cats like Air Asia, EasyJet and RyanAir elsewhere.

RyanAir flights are CORE PRODUCT ONLY: no food, no seat reservations and even fewer toilets than competitors. The company transports people from A to B within Europe. This keeps prices low but complicates products: to get the cheapest fares customers must book as early as possible. Passengers need to navigate their way to and from airports that are often far from the final destination and have fewer ground transport connections.

Although RyanAir offers core product only flights, their website offers a lot more. When customers book flights the company uses COMPLEMENTOR, NOT COMPETITOR (page 309) to offer hotels, cars and other extras from partners and earn itself additional revenue.

Simpler or core?

SIMPLER PRODUCT (page 100) and CORE PRODUCT ONLY are similar patterns but have different objectives. The difference in objective can be summed up in one word: price.

Simpler products can command a premium price because customers value simplicity. Think Apple – easier to use than Windows and more stylish, but at a higher price.

Restricted, core, products are attempts to cut down products and cut down price. Think about RyanAir: the price is low, the service is basic, but it isn't necessarily simpler. Indeed, getting the low price, getting the seat you want, or getting to your ultimate destination may be more complex.

Customisable Product

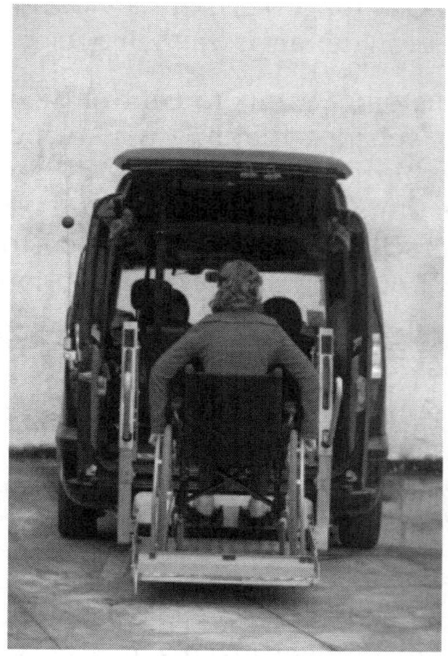

Figure 16. Cars get modified in all sorts of ways

Some companies set out to build platform products, some do it almost by accident. Nokia's Symbian operating system was always designed as a platform and initially attracted dedicated developers. Apple's iPhone was (almost) an accidental platform: according to some reports, Apple management resisted the idea for the App Store and did not see its potential.

Context You are an independent software vendor (ISV) with an existing software product in the market or near to release. A customer has approached you with a special request.

Problem *How do you incorporate customer-specific functionality without creating multiple product variations?*

Forces You have a generic product that is available to multiple customers, but some potential customers would like a special version with features and functionality specific to themselves.

The functionality requested is more than a few options in the program preferences, and the changes requested go beyond SIMPLE PRODUCT VARIATIONS (page 121), but are of no interest to other customers, or might even detract from their ownership experience.

The customer wants to control the intellectual property (IP) in the special version – they may wish to include their own IP in it, or to take ownership of the IP created by your team, or simply to restrict competitors' access to the IP and other changes. Consequently you cannot sell the changes to other customers and CUSTOMER CO-CREATED PRODUCT (page 95) is not an option.

You would like to carry out more customer customisation work, but when such work involves modifications to the core product source code. As the number of specials increases there is a combinatory explosion: *which modifications work with which others? Which combinations should be tested? How are priorities to be set? And how should you control the different source code bases?*

There are many ways in which engineering can produce multiple, similar but different version of a product: they could branch the product, use compiler macros, or use configuration options. But taking this route rapidly leads to a multiplicity of options, complicating development and testing and increasing the maintenance workload.

Incorporating these changes into your existing product will mean diverting your PRODUCT ROADMAP (page 302) to satisfy the needs of one customer, thus penalising customers of the generic product. But the customer in question is willing to pay good money for the special changes. For a start-up company the money on offer might be too good to turn down; for an established company, the money will add significantly to profit.

Solution

Allow customer-specific modifications and changes to exist separately from the generic product base. Make it possible to customise the product without changing the generic source code.

Set clear dividing lines between what is generic product work and what is customer-specific work. These lines need to exist on the PRODUCT ROADMAP (which is being diverted), in the organisation, in the management of the work and in the code base.

Initially it is best to have your own development team carry out customisation for customers using the new API, scripts and so on. They are the people who know most about how the product can be customised, and doing customisation will improve their understanding of how well the features work. They have a vested interest in keeping generic and customer-specific pieces cleanly separated, but on the flip side they know how hack it together too.

If customisation projects are happening regularly it is best to establish a dedicated team for this work and introduce more specific variation points into the code base (see *Customisation points* on page 118). This will allow core developers to continue working on the generic product without the disruption of special projects. More importantly, separate teams will create a division between special work and generic work. This will prevent special functionality appearing in the generic product and safeguard IP. Conway's Law (Coplien & Harrison, 2004) predicts that separate teams will create separate designs.

Over time some customer-specific features may migrate to the common product and some common features to customer-specific enhancements. Take care not to infringe IP when making customer-specific items common to all.

Consequences Separating the generic product from the special customisations allows the generic product to follow its own roadmap while the customised version meet specific customers' needs.

Creating a barrier to separate the generic product and the customer-specific customisations allows the two sides to develop and change at different speeds.

Code and customisations on the customer side of the barrier can be controlled and stored separately from the generic product. Since customisation work is isolated, it does not cause a combinatorial explosion of products or product configurations.

Customers only see their customised version. Neither they nor the core development team are encumbered with multiple special cases.

Providing customisation hooks is a major undertaking, and will need to be included on the PRODUCT ROADMAP (page 302) before the work is done. Once the hooks are provided, customisation work will not need to be included on the product roadmap and should not cause further diversions.

Variations CUSTOMISABLE PRODUCT is the first step towards creating a platform rather than a product. Platforms, like operating systems, exist to be customised for other uses. The line between a customisable product and a platform is particularly blurred when considering devices like the Apple iPhone and Microsoft XBox. Customers can download additional applications from an *app store*. This trend will become more prevalent as digital televisions become platforms and gain their own app stores.

Related work When customisation work becomes too much for your own resources to handle, or you want to encourage third parties to get involved, use CORPORATE CERTIFIED EXPERTS (page 272). Doing this will help create an ecosystem to develop around your product.

This patterns differs from SIMPLE PRODUCT VARIATIONS (page 121) and MASS CUSTOMIZATION (Pine, 1993) because it allows for far more – potentially unlimited – customisation.

When customers are willing to share enhancements and IP, CUSTOMER CO-CREATED PRODUCT (page 95) is an alternative pattern with lower costs. Providing customisation services to customers is a form of PRODUCTS WITH SERVICES (page 242).

Customer requests for special versions is a recurring theme in the ISV world and poses particular dilemmas for early-stage cash-starved companies.

Cagan strongly advises against agreeing to special versions of products that are not intended to be platforms (Cagan, 2008).

Examples Many well-known software products provide for customisation: Microsoft Excel, for example, provides a scripting language, a COM API that allows the application to be driven from another program and a plug-in API that allows users to install new functions. The Emacs editor goes even further by allowing users to add and even change the Lisp implementation of the program in which it is written.

Customisation points

Many of the techniques used to make products customisable are the same as used by designers of platforms, product lines and frameworks. Some are brute force – change the code and recompile, add an if statement or a compiler macro. Others are user accessible – configuration options, user preferences or macro-scripting languages.

Difficulties set in as increasing variations and options leads to massively increasing code complexity. There are a variety of mechanisms, or 'hooks', that can be used together or individually to provide additional customisability cleanly – see Figure 17.

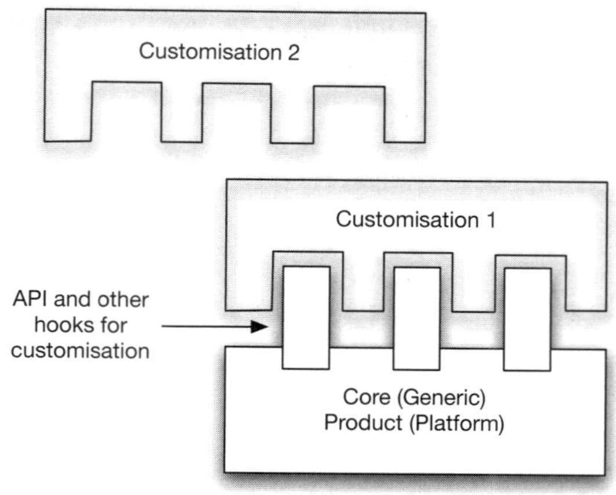

Figure 17. Customisations can connect to the core product through hooks

Options include:

- Allowing additional plug-in features and algorithms using *Patterns for Plug-Ins* (Marquardt, 2006).
- APIs that allow outside applications to drive the product or enhance functionality.
- Offering interfaces that allow external scripting languages to drive the product and use it as a toolbox.
- Building scripting languages into the product that can be used to build functionality or control workflow.

Retrofitting hooks and variation points to an application to allow customisations – let alone turning it into platform – is expensive and technically difficult. However, building a platform from the start is expensive and high-risk. Start-up and small companies tend to take the former approach, while well-resourced companies take the latter. While it would be nice to say one approach is superior, both approaches have benefits and disadvantages. The choice between one or the other probably has more to do with corporate cash flow than with architectural superiority.

As well as providing the hooks for customisation, documentation, examples and support for those customising the product need to be provided. Some degree of forward compatibility is also necessary, so that customisations can be used with future versions of the product.

While it is easy to add a function to an API, it is hard to remove one later. Once added, the customisation points will need to be supported in future versions: this will entail testing and documentation updates. Limiting additions to the minimum required and setting a clear retirement policy is needed.

Simple Product Variations

Figure 18. Like the iMacs of the late 1990s, Apple's iPad2 is available in multiple colours

After the initial success of the iMac, Apple launched a range of iMacs that differed only in colour. Economies of scale extended across all machines, so the production costs were the same for each machine, but the company had created several new products and differentiated themselves from competitors.

Apple has continued to repeat this trick with its consumer products – iPods and iPads come in a range of colours, and iPhones in black or white. Curiously the company no longer offers variations in Mac cases.

Context You want to differentiate your products while keeping prices down.

Problem *How do you increase variety and differentiation in your products without increasing costs?*

Forces You want your products to stand out as something different. But retaining economies of scale from mass production and commonality makes it difficult to offer anything other than a *one size fits all* product.

Customers like to be offered a choice and an opportunity to demonstrate individuality, but they are reluctant to pay higher prices.

Segmenting customers into different groups allows companies to charge different prices to different customers, increasing revenue. But creating multiple products is expensive and may not be justified by the segment size.

Solution

Offer a basic product with several simple variations; keeping the variations simple will keep them cheap. Variations might be cosmetic only (like Apple's coloured iPads) or they might focus on some aspect of the product, say hard disk size in a PC. Such variations retain economies of scale in production, so costs are contained, while customers get a choice.

Apple highlights consumer choice by openly displaying different coloured iPads next to each other. Other producers may wish to hide the fact that the same core product is being sold in different variations. This may involve putting a different brand on the same product, as Ford did with Mercury-badged models. You might use different sales channels for different products, as Hewlett Packard does with its HP and Compaq laptops.

Differentiating product variations by channel, feature set or brand will be necessary if you wish to price product variations differently.

Before implementing this pattern, make sure the variations really are cheap to offer: switching a factory paint shop between colours can time-consuming.

Consequences

Economies of scale can be maximised because the same basic product is being produced with the same parts. The variations offered to customers are cheap and add relatively little to the production costs.

Cosmetic differences offer customers choice and individuality, but have limited power to segment the market. Buyers are not stupid, and while they value the choice and variation, they are unlikely to spend a lot of extra money when differences are obviously cosmetic: Apple offers all iPads at the same price.

Production costs are not the only costs of supplying customers. While different colours may cost the same to produce, products must still be stocked, shipped and sold. Producing too much of the wrong variation may be costly: you may need to discount such products.

For physical products storage costs will increase too; retailers need to stock each variation to ensure they have the one a customer wants. However, online retailers and build-to-order manufacturers turn this to their advantage.

Marketing several products that are all basically the same will make the replacement cycle more expensive and difficult. Multiple products need to be retired at the same time and replacements introduced.

Too much variation can confuse customers and stop them from purchasing. The author was recently confused by the range of Canon Ixus cameras on offer: the subtleties of the differences made it almost impossible to decide which camera to buy. When customers are acting in a SELF-SERVICE (page 268) model, this can impact other customers' experience and company productivity (Tax et al, 2006).

Variations By adding a simple variation you may even be able to sell the same product again. Film companies release different cuts of films: Wikipedia lists seven different versions of the film *Blade Runner*, including an international version, director's cut and final cut, in addition to the version originally released in the USA.

Another variation used by the film industry is the inclusion of bonus material, such as theatrical trailers and actor profiles on special DVD releases.

Offering a product variation as a *limited edition* offers several opportunities: the limited edition may be the centre of an advertising or publicity campaign; creating an artificial shortage of the product can help support a higher price, or justify a short-term price reduction. Such editions may be restricted in quantity or by a time limit.

Related work Original equipment manufactures may combine SIMPLE PRODUCT VARIATIONS with WHITE LABEL (page 208) to provide similar products to different customers.

MASS CUSTOMIZATION (Pine, 1993) extends the idea of variations while maintain mass production and low prices. Such a strategy requires integration of ordering and production, a significant undertaking.

Examples ISVs offer different versions of the same product to different markets. Microsoft offers 'home', 'student' and 'professional' versions of Office. Microsoft's naming for each Office package explains who should buy which version, but sometimes it can be difficult to tell why one should by one version over another.

Altova used to offer 'home' and 'professional' versions of XML Spy, although why anyone would want to edit XML at home has always escaped this author. The company now markets 'standard', 'professional' and 'enterprise' editions, but one has to read the feature lists to know which version one might wish to buy.

Paradoxically, simple variations are not always as simple and cheap as they look. Historically, changing the colour of a car has been expensive, whether done at production or later. Daimler-Chrysler's smart division used coloured plastic panels rather than paint; this reduced the price of variation at production time and allowed owners to change car colour relatively cheaply – another point of differentiation. Recently manufacturers have adopted printer-style ink cartridges to make paint shops more flexible.

7 Marketing

Companies often start with a very simple view of their customers, either through design or ignorance. A HOMOGENOUS CUSTOMERS (page 136) strategy can help to keep costs down and simplify operations. Such a strategy may work well with a CORE PRODUCT ONLY (page 110) or SIMPLER PRODUCT (page 100) when the focus is on the product. When pursued out of ignorance (or arrogance), such a strategy may be a naive attempt to satisfy all the people all of the time.

Moving beyond a homogenous view of customers requires a better understanding of customers and the market as a whole. This means adopting CUSTOMER UNDERSTANDING (page 146) and SEGMENTED CUSTOMERS (page 141). These two patterns are complementary: better understanding of customers will allow segmentation, which will in turn allow a more complete understanding of customers. With segmentation, companies can focus on a limited number or even just one group of customers and attempt to serve it well.

The obvious but often ignored corollary of segmentation and intentional focus is the decision to forgo other segments and other potential customers. For example, if a company has a software product that can be beneficial to customers in the telecoms, media and other industries, it should decide to focus on just one segment, say telecoms, possibly with a secondary focus on media, but pass over opportunities outside these domains.

Unfortunately, the prospect of a sale, any sale, is often too much for a company to pass over – particularly a start-up. If the company is lucky it is just the sales team who are diverted by the bright lights, and the opportunity is lost. Unlucky

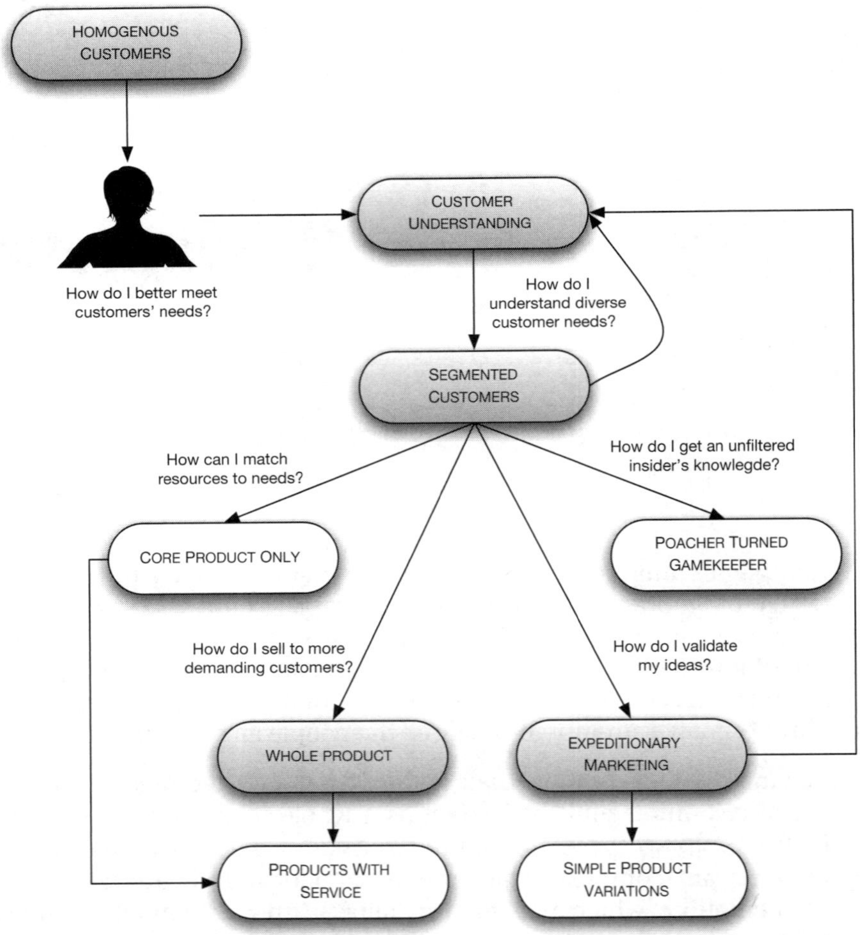

Figure 19. Pattern sequence for marketing patterns

companies win such non-core sales and find themselves suddenly pulled away from their strategic focus. The resulting product is all things to all men and the company continues to be pulled by the next big sale.

Discipline, not to mention cash flow, is required to maintain a strategy that says "No" to some opportunities in order to truly focus. Too often statements such as "We will focus on the media sector" are quickly followed up with "…and opportunistically in other sectors" or "Well of course, if the deal is big enough…" True strategy is marked as much – perhaps more – by what is not done as by what is done.

Of course, you might always decide that your strategy is optimistically to pursue any and all opportunities. In this case the company would need to be organised for high variability and rapid focus changes. Such a company might look quite a lot like an ESP-style company.

Saying "No" is easy to propose, but for a cash-strapped company, hard to follow. One way of reconciling diverse customer needs with a constrained resource base is to adopt a CORE PRODUCT ONLY (page 110) strategy. Defining the core product will benefit from understanding customers and what the common core is across multiple customer segments. Such a strategy may play well with a PRODUCTS WITH SERVICES (page 242) approach that customises the core product for each customer.

The WHOLE PRODUCT (page 131) strategy is somewhat different to the CORE PRODUCT ONLY strategy. Successfully delivering a whole product requires in-depth understanding of what a customer wants. This means identifying a segment and meeting the needs of that segment precisely. This is likely to mean changes to the generic product and services to solve the customer's problem exactly.

Product modifications for a specific segment serve both to meet customer needs better and to signal to the sector that your company is serious about their needs. As such they are, in part, an outbound marketing exercise (see page 39).

Understanding what potential and current customers want is a never-ending exercise, and one that must involve meeting customers. There is an almost never-ending stream of questions that can be asked of customers, but time with customers, and their patience, is limited. One option is to bring a potential customer in-house. Provided there is a customer willing to cooperate, CUSTOMER CO-CREATED PRODUCT (page 95) is one option; another is POACHER TURNED GAMEKEEPER (page 91).

Introducing a product to the market is a true test of customer understanding and segmentation. Until a customer is asked to part with money, everything is hypothesis and speculation. It is not just money that is received when a customer buys a product – so too is information: the information that someone, somewhere, thought the product was worth the money being asked for it. Nor should failure to sell be overlooked as a source of information.

The sooner this information is obtained, the greater the value it holds. The EXPEDITIONARY MARKETING pattern (page 153) seeks to gather information about the market through the introduction of products. Hopefully some of these products will be hits, but perhaps just as important is the information gathered in the exercise, information that can be fed back into the understanding of the customer and product development process.

Success with EXPEDITIONARY MARKETING depends on being able to accept product failure in the market. If the organisation cannot accept failure, or the cost of bringing a product to market is too great, then the strategy will fail. To succeed, the organisation needs to be able to fail fast and fail cheaply. Which naturally leads to the use of SIMPLE PRODUCT VARIATIONS (page 121) to map the market and validate assumptions.

The key factor in all these strategies is the need to understand customers. This is the domain of inbound marketing and it is important to understand the difference between inbound and outbound marketing. To summarise the earlier description (page 39):

- *Outbound marketing* is the one most people think of when they hear the word 'marketing'. It is about telling people your product is there. Outbound marketing most obviously includes advertising, but is also encompasses public relations, packaging, distribution channels and lots more.
- *Inbound marketing* is the less well-known sibling but, for a software company, is arguably more important. Inbound marketing is about understanding your customers, your market and your competitors. It is inbound marketing that finds out what a software product needs to accomplish and what features it needs to posses.

The Missing Link

As Chapter 3 described, for any software company to succeed, it must have a development group and a sales group. However, early success is entirely possible without a marketing group. Yet marketing is absolutely essential to the successful growth of a software company.

One study put sales and marketing costs as high as 37% of a software company's revenue. The same study suggested that these costs could account for 70% of all licence revenue (Watson et al, 2005). Marketing should not be an afterthought. Look at the most successful software companies: Microsoft, Oracle, Intuit and so on. Their success lies not in technical excellence, but in successful marketing. Windows beat the Macintosh because Microsoft out-marketed Apple. Few developers at the turn of the millennium believed Oracle to be technically the best database – at least in this author's experience – but Oracle dominates the post-millennium database market. Oracle, Microsoft and IBM have prospered as Sybase, Informix and other vendors have disappeared or been acquired.

Intuit's success is slightly different, and for this we need to understand that marketing has two sides: outbound and inbound. Intuit are acknowledged masters of this. The original Quicken package did not do anything that a savvy computer user could not accomplish with a spreadsheet. At the time of its launch there were already similar products on the market. Similarly, nobody needs to buy TurboTax. Tax authorities the world over, like the IRS and HM Revenue and Customs, provide plenty of documentation and advice on how to fill out a tax return. The key to Intuit's success is a deep understanding of what the customer wants to do. With this understanding, it creates products that make it easier to do things, and then makes it so easy that people will pay for it. Intuit product managers have been known to follow customers home, watch them install software and observe how they use it.

In the beginning a successful software company, by luck or good judgement, creates a product that fills a customer need. If the product does not fill a need, it is unlikely to sell and the company will cease to exist. But unless a company is prepared to rely on luck, it needs to learn how to identify and meet customer needs.

Knowing which customer needs to meet involves knowing who the customers are, what customers are trying to do, what restrictions they are working under, as well as knowing what competitors are offering, what technology offers and what future technology might offer. In other words, inbound marketing. However, inbound marketing is too often overlooked because outbound marketing dominates people's perception of what marketing is. The term 'marketing' usually describes just outbound marketing, and the job title 'Marketing Executive' relates to outbound marketing.

In a software company, inbound marketing usually goes by the title of 'product management' and is undertaken by people with job titles such as 'Product Manager' or 'Technical Product Manager'. In other industries, for example fast-moving consumer goods, Product Manager may be an outbound role. These managers are concerned with brand and product positioning; this can lead to confusion.

ESP software companies don't tend to have product managers. Instead they have business analysts. While product managers tend to be outward looking – facing customers, the market, competitors and new technology – business analysts are more inward looking: they consider specific conditions at specific customers. Both are charged with decided what needs to be done, but they do this quite differently.

What of Product Owner?

The Agile method Scrum (Schwaber, 2003; Schwaber & Beedle, 2002) describes a role called *Product Owner*. This role is often filled by product managers, but not always.

The Product Owner role is best though of as an alias. Normally the holder is a product manager (in ISV and similar companies) or a business analyst (in ESP companies and corporate IT departments). Scrum describes what the Product Owner does as part of the Scrum process, but not how that person knows what they know and how they work outside of Scrum.

Outside of Scrum – the stand-up meetings, planning meetings and so on – the Product Owner is analysing the software needs using the skills of a product manager or business analyst.

To complicate matters, SaaS products and companies for whom the web is the primary delivery channel need Product Owners who combine the skills of both product manager and business analyst.

WHOLE PRODUCT

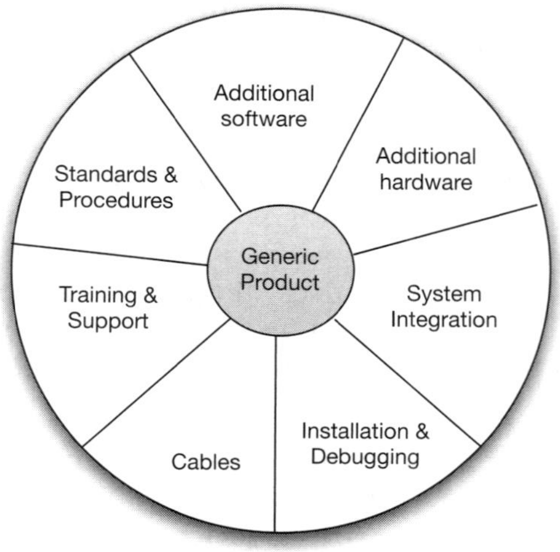

Figure 20. The whole product doughnut

Reproduced with permission of John Wiley & Sons, Ltd: *The Simplified Whole Product Model, Crossing the Chasm*, Geoffrey Moore

---

In the 1980s Silicon Graphics (SGI) set out to target the Hollywood post-production film-editing process. Rather than emphasise the raw power and all-round capabilities of their machines, SGI specifically presented their machines as 'video image editors'. They added features such as video device interface ports to their machines to make their product superior to competitors for this specific task.

Context Your first products are in the market and have sold well to early adopters. There is more to using the product than *plug-and-play*.

Problem *How do you ensure technical products solve customer problems and deliver value to customers?*

Forces New technology is cool in its own right; it may be used in many ways and produce many benefits. But using the technology to address real-world problems requires effort to make it useful. Some customers (early adopters) are prepared to buy the core technology and make it work for them. But many more potential customers are not prepared or able to put in this effort, so will not buy your technology.

You wish to expand your market beyond the technically-savvy early adopters, but your product is complicated and understanding the promise requires vision. There are few individuals who have the vision and skills to see what your product can be, and even fewer organisations that will invest the effort required to recognise the vision. Beyond the technically-savvy is a much bigger market: more sales and greater revenues.

The value of your product can only be recognised when it is used in conjunction with others – maybe specific hardware, or additional software – or when people are trained in the system. When the product is integrated with existing systems and processes are changed, the true benefit becomes clear. Each of these prerequisites puts obstacles in the way of sales and of customers seeing the full value of your product.

Competitors offer products that can match or even better your products in many tasks. Your competitors may even have advantages over you, they may have a respected brand name, or their technology may be better. At the very least your competitors have the advantage of being *incumbents*: in-market, with established products, sales and customers.

Some markets may not be aware of how your technology can improve their work. Even if they *are* aware, they currently need to bring together and integrate several technologies to realise the benefits.

Solution

Identify a market in which your technology can deliver benefits to customers, and seek to solve customer problems completely. Match your technology to your chosen market; move from the generic to the specific. Bundle your generic product with the additional products and services that are needed for customers to recognise the promised value from the product. Market the package to customers in your chosen market as a complete solution.

Continually seek to identify the obstacles that stop customers from maximising their use and benefit from your product. Remove each obstacle, either by changing the product or supplementing the offering with extra products or services.

Differentiate yourself from technology peers by addressing the needs of a specific market. If the product needs additional hardware, bundle the product with the necessary hardware. If additional software is needed to interface with other systems, supply the software. If integration services, training or support are needed, supply these – use

INITIAL HELP (page 248). You may choose to supply these products and services yourself, or you may enter into partnerships with others who can supply them.

Direct your marketing effort at your chosen market. Advertise to this industry, attend their shows, sponsor their industry awards – be part of that industry. Show how your technology is better than competitors' because you cater for the market needs and solve their problems without hassle.

Be clear about the problems your product solves, before adding or changing anything about the product. Ask: *will this help solve the customers' problems?* Rather than think of your product as a set of features, think of it as a single solution.

Creating a whole product and matching customer needs is not about selling more accessories and services around your product, it is about making sure your solution solves a customer's problem and that the customer recognises value from your product. Taking features out of your product – SIMPLER PRODUCT (page 100) – can help the customer reach these objectives too. Don't clutter your product with features, especially not features designed for a single customer or non-core markets.

Consequences

Your technology is applied to a specific problem in a specific market – sometimes called a *vertical market*. The core technology product is augmented in such a way that it fixes this problem completely: you sell a *whole product,* not a technology.

The technology is hidden, removed and sometimes simplified so that the product application represents a complete solution. The benefits of this solution are available far beyond the technology enthusiasts.

By focusing on the benefits and final product, you set out actively to remove all barriers between customers buying the product and seeing its benefits. The value of your whole product is clearly spelt out by defining the tasks it will perform and the benefits it will provide.

You will differentiate yourself from competitors with similar technology who do not focus on your chosen market. You will be able to point to similar technology from competitors and explain why they cannot deliver the benefits you do.

You differentiate yourself from incumbents with existing technology by the things your new technology allows you to deliver that their technology cannot. Rather than face incumbents head on, your segmentation and focus allows you to pick off customers who value the things your technology can deliver for them.

Being the first to bring new technology to a specific market will give you a head start. It will also give you a chance to define the market and product offering. Even if you do not have first-mover advantage in the market or with the technology, you can still define a niche in which you will serve customers better than any competitors.

Choosing your niche, and focusing your technology into a product for a specific market vertical, limits the size of your market. Instead of targeting a wide and shallow market, you are aiming narrow and deep. Once you have dominated one vertical market, you can repeat the exercise in another market adjacent to the first. It is easier to tackle one vertical market at a time than attack on a broad front.

As your product offering grows you will be able to justify a higher price. Fixing a specific problem in a market will help identify the value, and thus price, of your product. When your product offering contains recurring work, such as technical support or operations management, you will be able to charge regular fees. The fees are not only an additional source of revenue – they are more predictable. Such fees will add to your company's value because they are considered 'high quality' by financial analysts and investors.

Focusing on a specific market or market segment will mean passing over sales prospects in other area. This is necessary to create true focus, but may lead to some difficult decisions, particularly when the sale in prospect is big. Continuing to chase deals outside your core market will dilute your focus.

An established company adopting a whole product strategy will need to change its own structure and organisation. People working to support non-core markets may need to be redeployed, or even laid off. Existing customers in non-core markets also present a problem: whether it is better to continue supporting them or withdraw your product will depend on your exact relationship with the customers.

Providing services as part of a product offering can cause conflicts in product development and quality management. See the discussion in LIFETIME SERVICES FOR PRODUCTS (page 252).

Variations

It is preferable to stop selling the generic product on its own. This will help focus your marketing message, simplify pricing and remove the danger of competing with yourself. But withdrawing from markets, or not allowing customers to mix and match your product with other 'best of breed', may harm some of your prospects.

Related work A WHOLE PRODUCT (page 131) strategy is the opposite of a CORE PRODUCT ONLY approach (page 110). Both strategies may lead to SIMPLER PRODUCT (page 100) and PRODUCTS WITH SERVICES (page 242).

Lean Solutions (Womack & Jones, 2005) advises suppliers to 'solve my problem completely'. That is, provide solutions to a customer's entire problem, not to part of the problem. Such an approach would naturally lead to a WHOLE PRODUCT strategy.

Examples *Crossing the Chasm* (Moore, 1999) contains multiple examples, including Silicon Graphics, Intuit and Documentum, as well as a longer discussion of whole product strategy.

HOMOGENOUS CUSTOMERS

Figure 21. When all your customers look alike, so do your products

---

Microsoft MS-DOS was an early PC operating system. It ran on IBM-compatible computers based on the 80x86 line of CPUs. Home users and corporate customers all used the same software. It came in the same boxes with the same utilities and sold at the same price. At one time it was pre-installed on every PC, whether the customer wanted it or not.

MS-DOS' successor Windows continued a one-size-fits-all approach. Windows NT Client and Server started to split the product along technology lines, and today Windows is split along customer lines, with products such as Home, Premium and Pro.

Context You are establishing a new, possibly innovative, product in a new market. Your company is new and you have limited resources.

Problem *How do I enter a market quickly when I do not understand all the potential customers?*

Forces Not knowing who your customers are might well be a sign that you do not understand the market. Money spent developing a product to enter the market may be entirely wasted if you discover that there are no customers after all.

Your product may be innovative and difficult to copy, so you have little direct competition. But this also means it is difficult to validate the market and know who will buy your product, why they will buy and how much they will pay.

A good understanding of customers and the market would help product development and direct marketing. Without a good understanding, money may be wasted developing features you do not need and marketing to people who will not buy. But since the product and market are new, it is difficult to know who will buy your product until you enter the market. Further study may be useful, but would take time and money.

Getting to market fast will save money, allow you to generate revenue and stake out some market space. But your product might be incomplete and competitors may copy the product.

You may choose to wait, hold back your technology, watch the market and learn what potential customers want. But this approach takes time and costs money – if only lost revenue – and allows competitors to enter the market first.

Solution

Assume all customers are similar; do not attempt to differentiate or segment the market. Build and offer one product only. Get the product into the market as quickly as possible while keeping costs down. Treat all customers alike: their money is all alike.

Focus on your product rather than the customers. You might adopt a CORE PRODUCT ONLY (page 110) strategy, or you might target your product at a specific group of customers. Knowing many others will buy it too, for now sell them the product but deliberately ignore their specific needs.

Keep the first product basic; resist the temptation to add more features. More features take more time. Since you know little about your potential customers, any effort on additional features may be wasted. Extra features may actually deter some customers. Basic products may be supplemented later with services – see PRODUCTS WITH SERVICES (page 242) – to help meet customer needs. Such services will also bring in revenue and more information on customer needs.

Generalise your thinking about customers' needs and requirements: they are homogenous, after all. Talk to a cross-section of potential customers and extrapolate from their common needs. Avoid people who are too close to your product already (such as employees) and try to avoid copying competitors' products – yours needs to be different and you are unlikely to win a feature 'shoot-out' with incumbents.

As your product sells you can develop your knowledge of the market. You may choose to continue with a homogenous strategy to keep costs down, or you may prepare for SEGMENTED CUSTOMERS (page 141). Either way, seek to understand who your customer are and why they are buying your product.

Create tracking mechanisms to collect information about your customers. Use customer feedback and registration forms (online or postal), find customers and interview them, watch them use the product, ask about their experience and ideas. Use this information to inform further product development and marketing.

As your customer base grows, make more attempts to understand who your customers are. Send people to meet the buyers and users; find out what they are using the product for and how. You might market one product to all customers, but it still helps to understand who they are and why they buy.

Consequences By entering the market quickly you can start to learn about your customers. If you have entered the market before your competitors (called *first mover*) then your lead will not last indefinitely. The more successful you are, the faster competitors will try to copy you.

Once in the market your conviction will be tested. If the product sells you can start to examine who is buying it, what they are using it for and how they are using it. If your product is not selling, you will still be able to ask people why they have not bought your product and what they have bought instead.

Success with a standard product for all may make it harder to change your approach. Sales staff may not want to be told which customer segments to target. Technical staff may not like being told which features to develop and which to drop.

While it is easier for you to study your customers, your competitors can study them too. They will seek to understand your customers, your market advantage and look for opportunities to segment your customer base so that their products can compete more effectively.

Variations The original IBM PC came in two versions: one with a hard disk and one without. As the market developed, more variations appeared. Today a single PC manufacturer such as Dell can have laptops, desktops, servers, home, business, small business and student ranges, and within each range SIMPLE PRODUCT VARIATIONS (page 121) to make hundreds of products.

Related work

HOMOGENOUS CUSTOMERS runs counter to advice in other patterns to target a specific market niche. It is typically used in the early stages of company start-up or product development – hence its placement at the start of Figure 19 (page 126).

Once the product is in market, the company can use EXPEDITIONARY MARKETING (page 153) to iterate over product development. As the organisation builds CUSTOMER UNDERSTANDING (page 146), there will be a move towards SEGMENTED CUSTOMERS (page 141) as more information about the market and customers is gathered. The company can then adopt a targeted niche strategy.

Examples

Budget airlines have only one class, rather than First, Business and Economy. Most dispense with frequent-flyer programmes, and if they do offer preflight lounges, they are open to all (for an additional payment, of course).

Increasingly budget airlines allow customers to add *optional extras* to their standard offering for an extra charge. Seat reservations, boarding the plane first – *priority boarding* – and seats with extra legroom are all available for an extra fee.

Nokia and Apple

Differentiation and segmentation usually help to create extra barriers to entry in a market. Segmentation might even be seen as a sign of a mature market. But a homogenous strategy can still benefit a new entrant.

Nokia have consistently pursued a SEGMENTED CUSTOMERS (page 141) strategy. Dozens, if not hundreds, of different Nokia phones are available. Basic phones, smart phones, phones in between, phones for gamers, phones for music lovers, small phones and large phones – and the line-up differs in every market.

But Nokia has been out marketed by Apple with its single phone, the iPhone. Apple offers one version of its phone world-wide, to all customers in all markets. If you can't afford the top of the range iPhone, then tough – you can't have an Apple phone.

Apple does offer a few SIMPLE PRODUCT VARIATIONS (page 121) – white or black, the latest model or last year's model – but these are nothing compared to the variations Nokia and others offer. The only big change in Apple's strategy came with the introduction of a CDMA version of its phone alongside the GSM/UMTS version. Given that CDMA represents about half the entire US market, this is hardly niche marketing, yet Apple waited several years before adding this version.

SEGMENTED CUSTOMERS

Figure 22. Customers come in different shapes and sizes

Software products have multiple customers: different companies in different industries and different types of end users. Banks, airlines and hospitals may all use the same application. Within each group there will be different people and roles using the product for similar ends.

Consider a hospital: doctors, nurses, administrators and managers may all use your application to do different things. Nor should you forget the manager who authorised the purchase but who never uses the software.

Context You make a technically complex product that is used by a variety of different people with different objectives in mind.

Problem *Your customers all seem to want different things. How do you know what features to provide? What documentation to write? What services to offer?*

Forces Your product may be useful to different organisations, professions and individuals. But needs and usage patterns will vary between groups. Trying to satisfy everyone is worthy, but is likely to mean that nobody is completely satisfied. Potential customers are not equal: they differ in needs, scale and budgets.

Within a single organisation there are multiple user roles that will have different demands on your product. Users will have different requirements because they fulfil different roles and because they will have individual preferences.

Developing new products and enhancing existing ones involves making judgements and guesses about how your product will be used. Many scenarios (or *use cases*) you imagine sound reasonable, but may be unnecessary. Some scenarios will contradict each another. Analysing all use cases would be expensive and time-consuming.

Solution

Segment your customers into different groups and address the needs of each group separately. Groups are defined by discernable attributes and characteristics that allow you to differentiate one group from another. Working with definable groups avoids generalisations that do not describe any one group accurately.

You may choose not to meet the needs of some groups if doing so would compromise the needs of another. When resources are limited is it better to target resources than spread them thinly.

Start by identifying your groups: define the attributes of each group and what differentiates them from one another. Next determine the size of the groups, then prioritise those in which you are interested for further study. Over time you may want to subdivide groups or merge them together as your understanding grows.

Segmenting your customers will allow you to segment your market. As you decide which customer groups to serve, you will define your market position relative to your competitors. You are also deciding who you will *not* serve. In some cases you may need to extricate yourself from an existing group to pursue your new targets.

Once you understand your potential customers, their needs and how they are different from other groups, you can set about creating products to address their needs.

Consequences

The choice of who to serve reflects and informs your corporate priorities and strategy. Segmentation can help to avoid situations in which most attention is paid to the customer who shouts loudest. Strategy is as much, or even more, about what you will not do, who you will not serve, as it is about what you will do and who you will serve.

Those users you decide to serve will benefit, because they will get a product that fits their needs more specifically. A deliberate choice not to serve some groups allows you to serve others better.

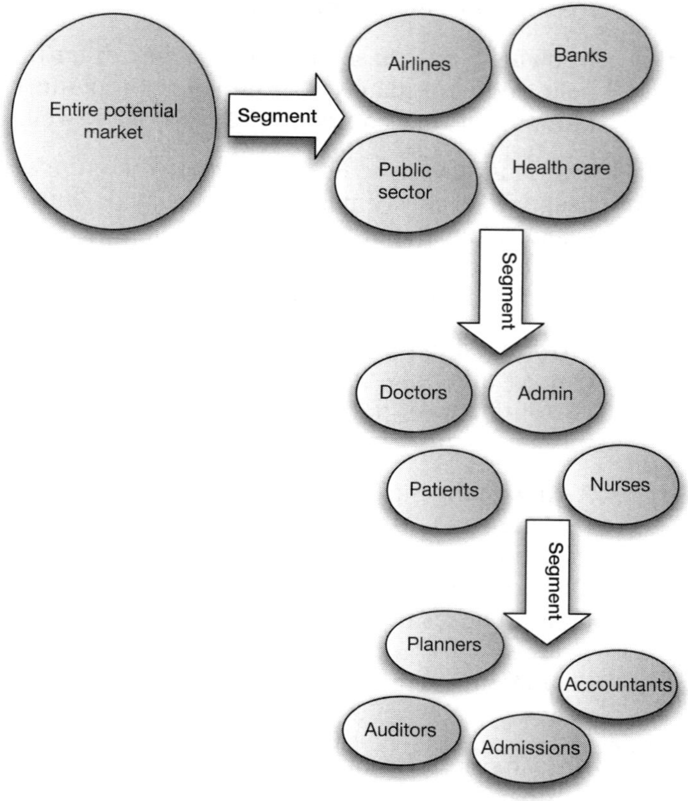

Figure 23. Break the market into ever-smaller segments

The groups you decide not to serve will benefit too if others decide to serve their needs specifically. In the short run it might be difficult to explain to customers and sales staff why you have decided to stop serving a particular group.

Targeting specific groups of customers and user roles will help you decide what products to build and what features they should have. This will take a lot of guesswork and 'what if' discussions out of the development process. Scenarios, features, user stories and use cases can refer to specific groups.

Subdividing your customer base will also help you to spot opportunities to serve customers better. Sometimes it is not necessary to offer a different product to different customer groups: all you need to do is emphasise different aspects of the same product. For example, SUV manufacturers might emphasise safety features to mothers, but off-road abilities to their husbands.

Knowing who you serve and how they differ from other groups will help to differentiate you from your competitors. You can also avoid groups that your competitors already serve well.

Segmenting your customers allows you to understand the needs and usage of each segment in more detail. With a little imagination, segmenting a market can go on almost indefinitely. Performing segmentation will increase your costs, but in the long term you will save money on marketing and sales effort.

Providing different products to different segments may allow you to charge different prices to different customers: some groups of customers have the resources to pay higher prices and can extract more value from your product.

Acting on the information may require some difficult decisions. Such decisions may be unpopular. For example, discontinuing service to particular customers or particular markets might cause bad feeling and arguments within your organisation. Such decisions and their consequences need to be understood and explained well.

Variations

Segmentation can also be applied to the pricing and distribution of a product.

An extreme form of segmentation is *micro-segmentation*, in which companies focus on even smaller groups.

Christensen provides another perspective on customer segmentation by suggesting that customers 'hire' a product to do a job. Therefore it is better to segment customers, not by attributes, but by the task they are seeking to accomplish (Christensen et al, 2007). Focusing attention on the outcome rather than the user or buyer may well produce different innovations and sales approaches.

Related work

CORPORATE CERTIFIED EXPERTS (Kelly, 2006) and SIMPLE PRODUCT VARIATIONS (Kelly, 2005) are both forms of customer segmentation.

HOMOGENOUS CUSTOMERS (page 136) describes a view of the market before segmentation and should be contrasted with this pattern.

The Inmates are Running the Asylum (Cooper, 2004) describes the creation of user personas that can be used to help design user interfaces. The same technique is used by groups such as product management and marketing departments to better understand customers.

Salt

Once salt was a cheap commodity. Everyone bought the same salt. Today we can buy table salt, cooking salt, sea salt, organic sea salt, rock salt, salt crystals, reduced sodium salt and more.

When a market is young or unsophisticated, one product can satisfy all needs. Having the basic product is worthwhile. Such an approach allows economies of scale to reduce costs and provide the product to many people who would otherwise not be able to afford it.

Yet this also creates opportunities for innovation and market segmentation. Understanding what is possible with the product – see SIMPLE PRODUCT VARIATIONS (page 121) – and the customers, as described in SEGMENTED CUSTOMERS, can reveal new opportunities for differentiation.

CUSTOMER UNDERSTANDING

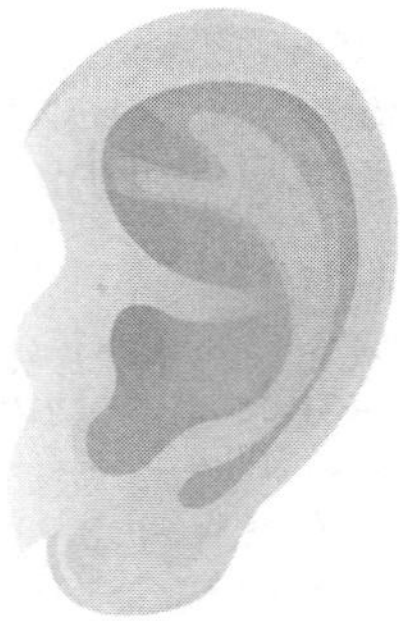

Figure 24. Understanding involves a lot of listening

Intuit's product managers are famous for putting customer understanding at the heart of their work. They are reported to have watched customers select and buy Quicken in computer stores. They then approach the customer, ask about their reasons for choosing Quicken, and on occasions accompany customers home and watch them install the product on their PC and observe how they used it.

Context You are developing a product and need to know what qualities and features the product needs and what it doesn't need. Maybe you are not using CUSTOMER CO-CREATED PRODUCT (page 95), or maybe you want to look beyond the lead customer.

Problem *How do you understand what your customers and the wider market want (and will pay for)?*

Forces Everyone has opinions and views on what a product should do, but desk-bound engineers and managers are not representative of real customers. This is especially true in start-ups, where past success may be based on founders' intuition rather than research, and inexperienced staff may be afraid to meet real customers.

Understanding customers in depth is difficult when they don't understand what the technology can do for them. Your engineers understand the technology, but customers don't. *If you build it, they will come...* maybe, or you will be left with a costly product nobody wants to buy, such as the Hewlett Packard TouchPad tablet. Technology is only useful if it can be applied to solve a problem or make life better.

You want to produce products customers want to buy, but finding potential customers, meeting them and discovering their problems takes time and money. It is easier to believe that if a company employs smart people, they will work out what customers want by themselves using logic and reason.

Customers are not homogenous in their needs or wants, and some customers have more buying power than others. But you want to create a product that will appeal to multiple customers – a market, not an individual.

Every salesperson will tell you that they know what the customer wants; sales people are often reluctant to let someone else deal with the customer. Sales people worry that non-sales staff may jeopardise a sale or relationship, and they worry that someone else might steal their customer (and their commission.) But, to create a product that meets the needs of the wider market, the views of individual customers must be balanced.

Solution

Meet and observe your customers – those who pay, those who use your products and those you would like to have. Interview them, observe them, question them, listen to them. Look at who they are and what their relationship is with your product. Seek to understand both your customer and their environment.

Understand customers as people; *what is the average age of your customers? Their education level? How long do they (would they?) spend with your product in an average day? What does their day look like?*

Observe how customers actually use the product, rather than how you expect them to use it. *Are there parts they never use? Do they use it for things you don't expect? Do they understand why they like (or dislike) the product? Can you apply Occam's Razor or the Pareto Principle?*

These may be obvious questions when selling consumer products, but they apply too when selling to corporations: organisations don't choose and use products, individuals do. Don't stop at company or group names: find those people who choose, use and benefit from your product in the organisation.

When selling to organisations, understand the culture and environment of the customer's company. Differentiate between economic buyers (those who choose your product and agree to purchase based on financial grounds), technical buyers (who evaluate it and choose it for technical abilities) and actual users, who may not have a direct voice in the purchase decision, but who use the product daily.

Meet with potential customers who evaluated your product but chose not to buy. Understand why they did not buy and what you might do in future to win them as customers. Repeat the exercise with those who did buy and undertake 'win/loss analysis'.

Find out what they think about your product and competitors', what their work and life entails and how it could be better: *why do they buy your product? Why do they use it? What problem does it solves for them? What constraints do they operate under?*

For business products there may well be a business driver, such as cost savings, greater efficiency or time to market, for using your product. For consumer products the benefits might be less tangible or easy to define: enjoyment, gossip, fashion.

Compare customer wants with their ability and willingness to pay. Many desirable features may simply be uneconomic to develop. Conversely, delivering specialist capabilities at a new price point may provide an advantage over competitors.

Understanding is not a single event. It requires constant attention: there are always more customers and potential customers to talk to, and those you have already talked to don't stand still. Visit them again; find out how their lives change and how your product changes it. Employ dedicated specialists to keep them under review.

Use qualitative techniques to understand customers and their motivations. When the customer base is large you might follow up with quantitative surveys. However, quantitative studies alone cannot lead to deep understanding of customers and their issues, because aggregate answers cannot show intentions and motivations.

Use SEGMENTED CUSTOMERS (page 141) to divide your customers into groups and consider each group individually. Examining each customer segment separately will deepen understanding, which will in turn inform segmentation (CUSTOMER UNDERSTANDING). When dealing with large organisational customers, consider the range of stakeholders within the organisation.

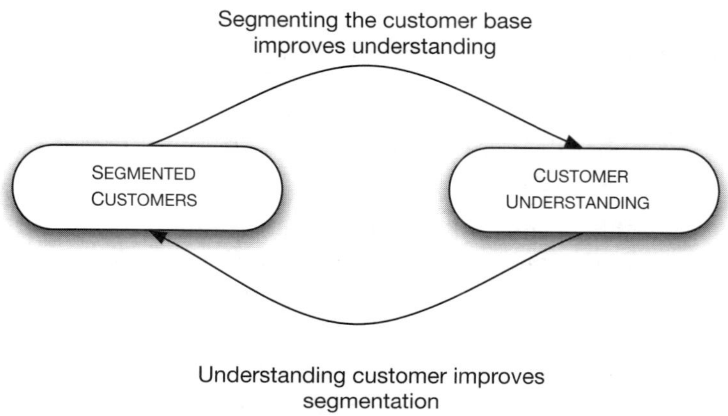

Figure 25. Segmentation improves understanding, which improves segmentation

When visiting customers who did not buy, tell them "I'm not here to change your decision, but I'd like to know why you chose our competitor, so that we can create a better product you might consider next time."

It can be difficult and time-consuming to meet customers, so stage events where customers come and meet you. This might be a 'meet the team' event inside your company, or a user conference with many different customers. You might even invite one of your customers to come and brief the team on the work they do and how they use your product.

Stay in contact with customers once you have met them, see how their needs change, and float ideas for product changes with them (though be careful not to commit yourself). Once you have met the a customer for the first time it is easier to talk openly on the telephone. You can stay in touch without the time and expense of a visit by using the phone.

Spend time thinking through what you want to know about customers and what you need to know to direct your product. Keep a list of standard questions that you can use to get beyond a customer's immediate issues and stock responses. After you meet a customer, review your meeting, document your findings and refine your questions for next time.

As your understanding of customers grows, create personas (Cooper, 2004) to help communicate your findings and share your understanding with the rest of your company.

Consequences In-depth understanding of customers, their attributes, needs and wants provides a solid base for reasoning about product development. Facts about what customers need, how they use products and what they are trying to achieve (should) trump views and opinions every time.

When you understand what customers need, you can apply your understanding of the technology available to create an innovative product. This will guide your product development and improve the chances of producing a star product.

Consequently your product will meet customers' needs better than competitors' products that are based on technology alone, or on the ability of a salesman to make a round peg fit a square hole.

By segmenting the customer base, product managers can decide which customers' wants and needs are considered first and foremost. Focusing on a limited number of customers helps to create the right product, but means that some customers' needs are left to one side. Trying to please all customers equally not only makes product development harder, but may result in a product which is ideal for no-one.

Sales people may object to others visiting 'their customers', because they seek to control the customer relationship and don't want customers poached (even internally). They may object because "I already know what the customer wants". However, what one customer wants might not be the thing the wider market wants, and this may create tension.

Product managers need to win the trust of sales staff by demonstrating that they do not want to steal the customer. Product managers tasked with understanding the customers are not paid on commission and will look beyond the next sale. They aim to create great products and leave selling to professional sales people.

It takes time and money to meet customers and understand the problems, constraints and opportunities they face. You also need the right skills to ask the questions and listen without putting words into the customers' mouths. In a technology-based company it can be difficult to see the value of people who are not actually coding.

Variations

POACHER TURNED GAMEKEEPER (page 91) provides another solution that can lead to a focus on a particular segment. SURROGATE CUSTOMER (Coplien & Harrison, 2004) offers other solutions to the same problem.

Many of the techniques noted above can be used to analyse competitors' products and their customers as well as your own.

Related work

The KNOW THE CUSTOMER pattern (Rising, 2002) contains similar advice. Other patterns in Rising's series can also be used to help – IT'S A RELATIONSHIP, NOT A SALE, BUILD TRUST, MIND YOUR MANNERS and LISTEN, LISTEN, LISTEN.

This pattern is the basis of the product manager role in independent software vendors and feeds the creation of the PRODUCT ROADMAP (page 302).

If you are using BRANDED SHOPS (page 172) or have good relations with an INDEPENDENT RETAILER (page 213), your product development staff may visit the stores, observe the sales process or even work in the store for a few days, to improve their customer understanding.

SALES/TECHNICAL DOUBLE ACT (page 192) can support this pattern by giving different viewpoints on customers and the individuals inside a company.

Many organisations start with HOMOGENOUS CUSTOMERS (page 136) implicitly, and after understanding their customers, arrive at SEGMENTED CUSTOMERS (page 141).

Techniques for increasing customer understanding are also discussed in *Tuned In* (Stull et al, 2008), *Inspired* (Cagan, 2008) and on product management training courses.

Examples

Visiting customers to understand their relationship and need for your product is an example of the Lean idea of *Gemba*. Gemba is a Japanese word meaning 'the place of current action'. Lean writers also refer to it as 'the place of truth' or 'where the work happens'. (Womack & Jones, 2005).

A product manager's tale

Allan was a product manager for a London software company. One of the biggest customers was a Nordic telecommunications company and he wanted to meet them. The first time he piggybacked on a visit by the SALES/TECHNICAL DOUBLE ACT (page 192). Every time the customer tried to talk about difficulties, the salesman talked and talked and talked. He saw difficulties as blocks to sales and didn't want anything to get in the way of a sale.

The meeting was pretty useless in terms of understanding the customer's needs, but it did allow Allan to meet a key customer. He cunningly found an opportunity to meet the customer a second time without sales staff being present. This time he focused the conversation on how his product helped the customer do their job, understanding how the customer worked, what their problems were, what they wanted to achieve and the obstacles in the way,

Getting to and from the two-hour meeting required two days out of the office, but the information gathered was pure gold. Many future product decisions were shaped by this meeting and others like it with more existing and potential customers.

Expeditionary Marketing

Figure 26. Exploration takes many forms

The clothes chain Zara (part of Inditex) almost invented the idea of 'fast fashion'. In preparation for a new fashion season, the company designs several 'platforms', but final design is delayed. Variations are test-marketed in selected stores, and those judged to be the most successful are rolled out across the international chain.

Context A new product has been developed but the exact configuration of the product has yet to be determined. Customers are unfamiliar with the product, so it is difficult to determine what their exact requirements will be.

Problem *How can you determine which features will be most attractive to the customer when customers are not familiar with your product or how they might use it?*

Forces With a new product concept it is difficult to determine exactly what the customer will want. Understanding of the market is incomplete: the exact configuration of a new product is unclear, but there is a vision of the new product and an understanding of its essential elements.

Development teams have a better understanding of what the technology can do than the customer. The team knows what is technically possible, but customers cannot imagine the products because they lack the knowledge of the technology and its application. So it is not possible to pin down the configuration, because customers lack experience of the product.

Mainstream market research techniques such as surveys and focus groups are useful for improving existing products, but can fail when the company is trying to come up with a truly innovative product.

Your basic product is easily reconfigured; each configuration may sell, but which one will sell the most?

Solution

Launch a product into the market at the first opportunity and quickly follow up with a range of variations. Watch customers' reaction, the variations they buy and how they use the product. Use this feedback to develop the next version of the product.

Once the product is in the market and selling, respond rapidly to customer signals and feedback from the initial products. Withdraw variations that don't sell and build on those that do sell. Incorporate further innovations and new technology.

When designing the initial product, build in options to vary the product. Use modular designs that can be changed easily and create SIMPLE PRODUCT VARIATIONS (page 121). Implement smaller, simpler features, and be ready to change or enhance the product.

Making use of existing off-the-shelf components will speed up development and reduce costs. However, the same components may constrain the designers into using existing solutions with little innovation.

Products in the marketplace are not only a source of revenue, but provide valuable information to help with future products. Even products that fail financially can provide valuable lessons – provided failure does not bring financial ruin to the company or embarrassment and shame to individuals and teams.

The organisation will need to adapt its development and product infrastructure to ensure that lessons learnt from one product are quickly fed into the next version. Reducing product development cycles and development costs will help to bring a new product to market quickly and economically, thereby providing for frequent, low-risk market incursions.

Maintaining a varied product line-up in the market can enhance learning opportunities, because customers have a greater choice. Developing several product variations simultaneously will provide for a diverse market offering and further enhance learning opportunities.

To help reduce development cycles and maximise learning opportunities, use multi-disciplinary teams made up of team members drawn from across the company, so as to leverage existing company resources and assets.

Consequences Quickly feeding the learning back into new products allows you to refine your products. As product developers become accustomed to working in this manner, they improve their pace of learning and develop intuition to help them work better.

Just because your company is creating a market does not mean your employees understand the market. Even when they are producing successful products, they may not have developed the deeper knowledge of how the market works and how customers think.

It is possible to make profit without truly understanding the market. Over time you will come to know who is buying the product and what features they want – CUSTOMER UNDERSTANDING (page 146). It is then time to start segmenting the market with different variations aimed at different customer groups.

Competitors will eventually follow you into the market you have created. Some of these may be 'fast followers' that are particularly able at copying designs and directly competitive products. While these companies may erode margins from products, they will always be playing catch-up.

Sometimes the market you expect to reach will not exist. Even after a series of product launches the market may not develop, or develop more slowly than you expect – indeed, there is never any guarantee that it will appear at all.

Variations EARLY AND REGULAR DELIVERY (Cockburn, 1998) described this pattern for software development.

Related work The term *expeditionary marketing* was originally described by Hamel and Prahalad (1991).

The EXPEDITIONARY MARKETING pattern complements INNOVATIVE PRODUCTS (page 313) because it helps companies to experiment with innovative products in a piecemeal fashion. EXPEDITIONARY MARKETING is a form of incremental product development – products are developed a little at a time and each change builds on the previous one. Excessive use of incremental development may hinder 'out of the box' thinking and the creation of radical product development, so EXPEDITIONARY MARKETING may conflict with INNOVATIVE PRODUCTS.

SIMPLE PRODUCT VARIATIONS (Kelly, 2005) describes one way of developing successor products.

Examples

Nokia produces a wide range of mobile phones, yet much of the underlying technology is common. Many phones are tailored to a particular market, both in technology and styling. New features may be tried out on one phone in one market, and if successful, rolled out across the range and other markets.

8

Distribution Model

Creating a product is only part of the story; the product needs to get into customers' hands. Stepping back a little, the product needs to be somewhere where potential customers will find it and can hand over their hard-earned cash in exchange for your product.

The nature of the product, the nature of your customer, price and a host of other factors – collectively called *position* – will affect the best place for your product to be seen and sold. Getting it to this place is referred to as a *route to market.*

Just getting a product in front of customers can be a big challenge. Getting it in front of the right customers at the right time and with the right presentation is an even bigger challenge. Getting it in front of customers at a time when they are unlikely to buy is a waste of your efforts. Get it in front of them when they have a real and pressing need, when you will be able to charge far more than if you presented it at a time when they can see the advantages but don't need to buy.

One of the first questions facing an entrepreneur is whether their product will be sold directly to customers or through an intermediary. Both approaches have advantages and disadvantages, and both are applicable when selling a high-tech product like software. Still, there is a decision to be made.

There are two sides to this problem: first is the sales process, and second is the physical delivery of the product. However, these two problems are intimately connected: the method of sale and the distribution of the product are not separate problems: they are the same question.

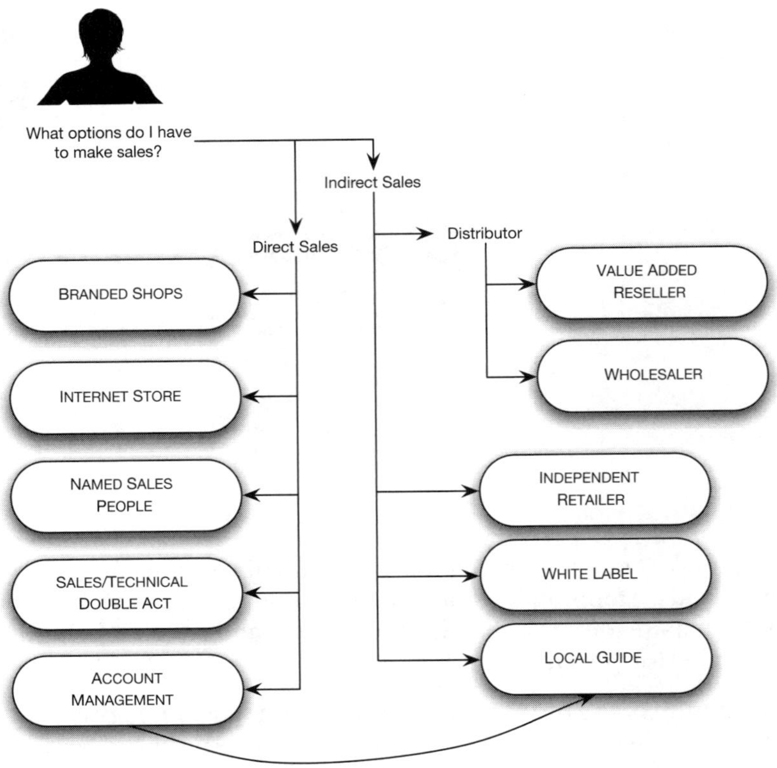

Figure 27. Map for distribution patterns

The patterns in Chapter 9 and Chapter 10 look at some of the many possible *sales channels*. Figure 27 shows the connections between the patterns, while the tables in the following chapters (Table 4 on page 171 and Table 5 on page 199) contrast the patterns with one another.

Innovative companies regularly invent new channels; some are successful, some not. Many of these new channels are variations and modifications to the patterns described. Each channel will have advantages and disadvantages, and each comes at a cost. A direct sales force might be able to command the highest prices for your product, but is also expensive to employ. A retail sales approach may generate a thousand times more sales at a fraction of the price.

Channels, both direct and indirect, form a company's *route to market*. This is a big topic; before describing any of the channel patterns, it is useful to set the context and background. This chapter sets some of the context for distribution, while the next two chapters describe the direct and indirect patterns in depth.

Each channel is subject to a multitude of forces – effectiveness, existing market structure, accessibility, timing and more. Unpacking each channel in detail would require patterns that are significantly longer than most of those in this group. Some forces, consequences and details of the solution are omitted for the sake of brevity and readability.

There are at least three views of each channel:

- The product producer
- The channel owner
- The customer

In keeping with the audience for this book, the patterns in the next two chapters are written from the perspective of the *product producer.*

Direct Sales

The simple answer to the question '*How can I get my software to customers so that they can buy it?*' is: create a website, upload the software, allow people to download it and charge them for doing so. This is shown in Figure 28 and described in INTERNET STORE (page 177). While this might be the most obvious way to distribute software, it is not necessarily the right one.

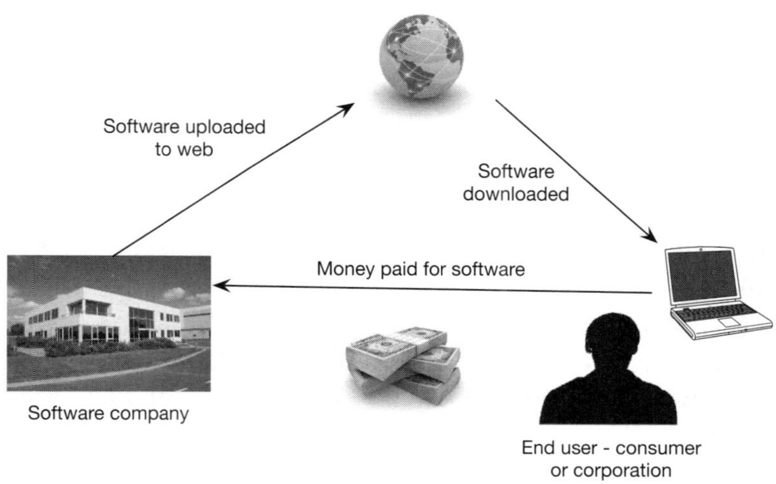

Figure 28. Software sold via the Internet

Traditionally much software has been burnt onto CD, packaged in boxes and sold at stores such as Best Buy and PC World, as shown in Figure 29. In such cases the software company persuades the store to carry their software; the store makes the sale and passes back some of the revenue to the software company. The patterns INDEPENDENT RETAILER (page 213) and WHOLESALER (page 217) discuss this model in more detail.

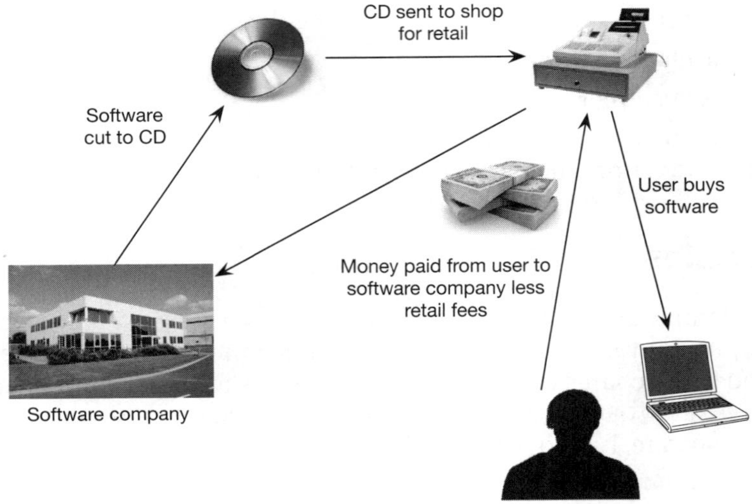

Figure 29. Software CDs sold over the counter

Both examples illustrate how the mechanism by which software – or any other product for that matter – is distributed physically is inherently tied up with the sales process. This is because, as the product passes from manufacturer to customer, money flows in the opposite direction, from customer to manufacturer. While there are slight modifications that might separate the two events – such as time-limited trials – delivery of the software and payment are part of the same event.

The distribution channel and sales model a company decides to use will depend on a number of factors. The most important of these are the value of the sale and the number of customers expected. While one might like to picture entrepreneurs sitting down and rationally calculating the best route to market, things are not always so rational. What economists call *path dependency* – or 'how you got here' – has a role to play too. Past experience with one or other distribution channels, contacts and simple opportunity all have a role to play in determining how a product is offered for sale.

The two examples described above are used typically to distribute commodity 'shrink-wrapped' software. Such software typically sells for less than $1,000 a copy and to many customers; these distribution models are used typically for business to consumer (B2C) transactions. The store-based model is also used by sellers of embedded software and pre-installed software.

Products such as digital radios or home PCs are sold in a store with the software already installed: there is no choice of software and no separate sale. Most people buying a digital radio just want a digital radio; they don't want to be bothered selecting a radio platform from one vendor and a radio application to run on it from another.

At higher prices there are typically fewer customers, if only because fewer customers can afford to buy the software. Unlike a car or a house, a software package is rarely a major decision for a individual or family. Above $1,000 most software is sold to other businesses, the business-to-business (B2B) market.

The more expensive the product, the more the customer wants to know about the product up front. When prices are measured in thousands or tens of thousands of dollars, customers want a lot of information before they buy. Very few buyers will spend $10,000 on software they just download from the Internet. To make these expensive sales, companies need to employ sales people. Figure 30 shows the direct sales model.

Sales forces are expensive to operate. Sales people are usually paid partly or entirely by commission. This may constitute 10% or more of the total sales price, pushing up the price. High-priced sales are seldom made in a single sales event; they may require multiple visits to the customer's site, perhaps accompanied by pre-sales consultants, product managers or others. This all pushes up the cost of a sale further.

It is not viable to sell low-priced software products through a direct sales channel because selling costs are high. To sell through a direct sales force, the product must be sold at a high price; consequently the product needs to be able to justify a high price. This does not mean that the product needs to be particularly big or complex, but it must do something that is at least hard to find elsewhere.

Of course there is nothing to stop a business customer purchasing software in the same way that a home consumer might, over the Internet or in the local store. In some cases this is practical; for example, a copy of Microsoft Excel is the same wherever it is bought. However, the business customer is unlikely to find much of the software they require in stores or for simple download – Best Buy does not stock SAP products, for example.

When a company's products are applicable to both home customers (under $1,000) and business customers (over $10,000) they are faced with a challenge.

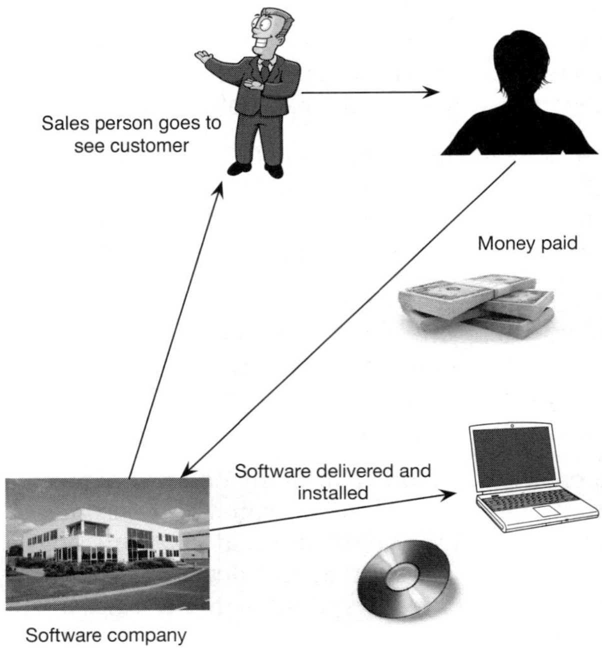

Figure 30. Direct sales

They may choose to sell to many customers at a low price, or to a few customers at a high price. Either way, some potential customers are left without the product and potential sales revenue is forgone.

One way around this dichotomy is to offer two sales options, one for the home customers and one for the business customers. To do this, some mechanism is needed to stop all customers simply buying the cheaper product. Selling through multiple channels can provide this mechanism. One channel targets business customers, the other targets home customers. This approach abounds in the hardware industry. For example, Dell markets their Inspiron laptop PCs to home users, but Latitude machines to business users. While home users can buy some Latitude machines online, most can only be bought by registered businesses. Hewlett Packard uses the HP and Compaq brands in a similar way.

This approach has been tried in the software industry but with much less success. While Microsoft sell 'home' and 'professional' editions of their operating systems, few software packages appear in multiple versions in multiple channels. Instead the same channels are used to sell versions with more features and higher prices.

Adding channels adds costs, particularly when the products in each channel need to be differentiated. Consequently, multiple-channel strategies are prone to disruption by one-size-fits-all type sellers, while one-size-fits-all strategists are in turn prone to disruption by those using multiple channels.

Distributors

Another way to reach customers is to employ distributors. This is particularly useful when the software company lacks the means and resources to reach the target customers. Sometimes distributors are used because there are simply too many potential customers, sometimes because sales require a local presence, and sometimes because it is not economic to sell directly.

Introducing distributors into the distribution chain can be a double-edged sword. Distributors bring benefits, but they also bring complications; they can reduce costs in some instances, but increase costs in other cases.

Adding an extra layer between company and customers will add additional intentions and objectives, and might reduce the information flow from customer to producer. Companies know less about their customer's buying habits, their wants and needs, but without a distributor there might not be any customers in the first place.

The simplest type of distributor is the distributor – see Figure 31. When selling software through stores a company may be happy to strike a deal with a big chain like WalMart, but dealing all the independent stores is time-consuming and impractical. It is far easier to deal with a wholesaler who takes the software package and resells it to multiple stores. The wholesaler can do this cost effectively because it deals with many software packages.

Software companies can minimise the need for a sales team altogether by appointing exclusive distributors. This is common in the games industry, where a small studio may code a game that is then branded and distributed by a much larger company.

Distributors also have a role to play in business-to-business (B2B) software sales. When selling to a business it can be difficult to identify the right people in a customer's organisation, and it can also be difficult to meet these people. In other words, making a sale is dependent on a salesperson's contacts and who they know.

When a software company does not have access to key decision-makers in a potential customer's organisation, it can use a distributor to make the contact. This is especially true when operating in a foreign country: here distributors may be allocated a specific geographic region or market.

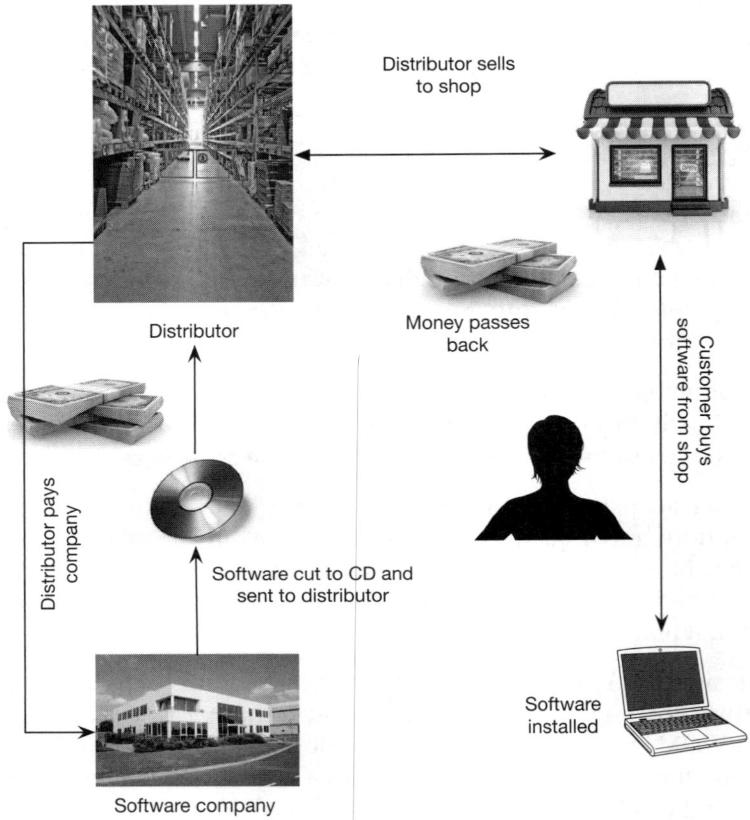

Figure 31. Distributor sales

It goes without saying that this sort of distributor is quite different to the wholesalers mentioned above. Business distributors may not even be in the software business; their role may be purely to make contacts. Although a sale may be arranged by a distributor, the software company may still need to provide sales people and marketing support.

Some distributors become very involved in the sale and support operations. They may even take over some of the value-adding activities from the original software company for their customers. Again this is particularly true when operating in a foreign country, especially one with a different language.

Value-added reseller are also used when a customer needs additional work to help it recognise the benefit of the product. For example, a new ERP system may need to be integrated with existing systems. A reseller may make the software sale and provide the additional work required.

The larger the role the distributor plays, the greater their fee. This is usually done in terms of a percentage of the sales revenue. The more responsibility a distributor takes on, the larger their cut. A distributor who makes a contact and nothing more may receive 10% of the sale price; one who makes the contact, makes the sale and provides follow-up support may take more than 50%.

Finally, distributors can play one more, distasteful, role. A distributor can be the conduit by which bribes are paid to ensure a sale. Including bribe money in a distributor's fee allows companies to keep their books 'clean' and places the payment at arm's length. While one cannot advocate this role, it is good to be aware that it happens.

Choosing a Distribution Model

There are many considerations to take into account when choosing a distribution model and channel. The market size, geographical spread and selling price will all be important considerations when deciding which distribution model to use.

A high selling price will support the cost of a direct sales team. However if the market is very big, it may still not be possible to build a big enough sales team, or, even if possible, it would take too long. In such circumstances it may make sense to segment the market and use distributors for some sales, while the direct sales force concentrates on the largest sales and customers.

For mass market products the selling price is unlikely to justify a direct sales force, but it might justify direct sales from a website. The traditional model of sales through stores or mail order is still viable and widely used. It is important to keep sales costs down in order to reach the mass market.

However, when a product cannot command a high price and the market is small, it may not be possible to produce and sell the product. Sometimes small, perhaps one-man, micro-ISVs can still turn a profit, but again selling price must be kept down. Under such conditions it might be more profitable to offer the software free of charge but sell advertising in or around the software. Removing the revenue stream also removes the sales costs.

Different Product, Different Channel

One reason to use multiple channels is to distribute similar but different products. Figure 32 shows how, having embarked on a strategy of multiple products, different channels – some direct, some indirect – are used to distribute the products. This approach is designed to prevent customers from choosing products that may be intended and priced for a different segment.

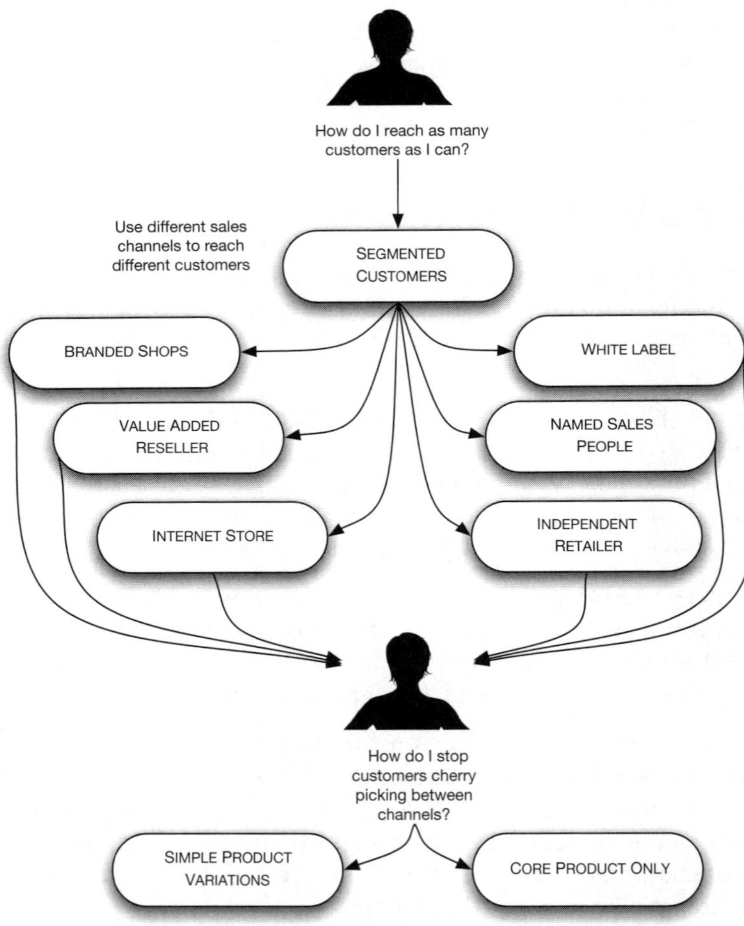

Figure 32. Use different products for different customers with different channels

However, this decision process may occur in the opposite direction too, as shown in Figure 33. A company intent on reaching as many customers as possible may embark on a multi-channel strategy. The different channels sell similar but different products at different prices.

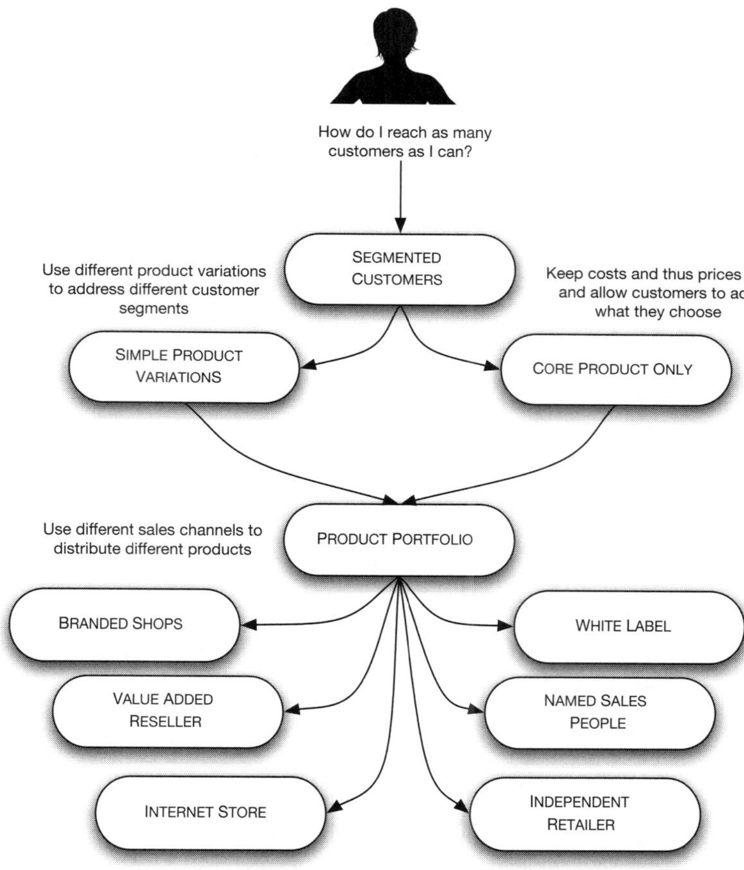

Figure 33. Selling through different channels leads to different products

For example, Hewlett Packard sells laptop PCs from its website and through independent retailers. If HP let customer surf between these channels, all channels would be driven to the lowest price: retailers would need to sell at the same price as online channels, and as a result they would not be able to make the profit they require, and might stop stocking HP laptops altogether. To prevent this HP offers product variations in each channel to further differentiate the offering and justify different prices. Whether different channels demand differentiation of products, or whether different products demand different distribution channels, may always be a question of perspective.

9

Patterns of Direct Distribution

All companies need to sell; if they don't sell, they don't last long. The patterns in this chapter look at how a company can go about distributing their products in order to make sales. Table 4 (page 171) contrasts the direct sales channels described as patterns in this chapter. This is not an exhaustive list of direct sales channels: innovative new sales models and distribution channels are regularly invented, although not all are successful. Successful models appear again and again.

There are many different types of sales model and correspondingly many different types of sales force. Some walk a shop floor, others sit in call centres and some knock door-to-door. For enterprise software, named sale people are the norm; for consumer products the Internet is a powerful medium, but retail sales, either direct or indirect, still dominate.

A company that manages its own sales controls the sales process and pays the not insubstantial costs, so it is important to ensure that the cost of making a sale can be covered by the price charged for the product.

It is seldom worth using a direct sales force to sell consumer products, as the value of the sales generally don't support the model. Real estate, cars and financial products are sold to consumers by NAMED SALES PEOPLE (page 182), but these are the exception rather than the rule. The number of products that are sold in this fashion has been declining in recent years, as customers become more knowledgeable and channels like the Internet provide other options.

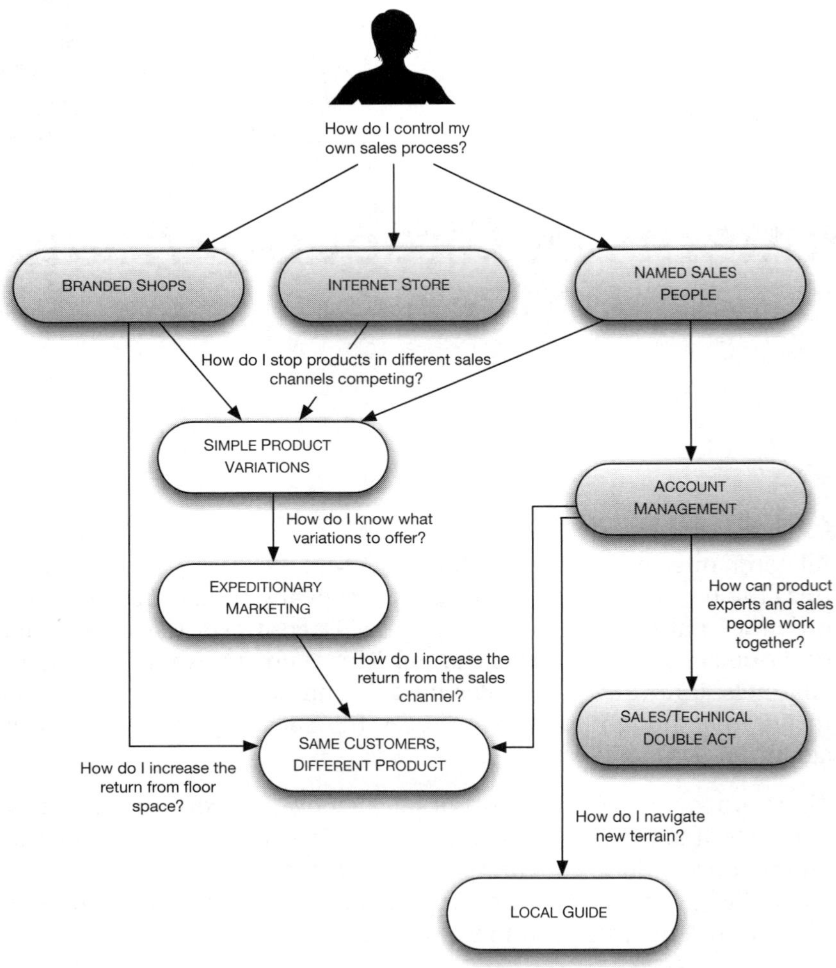

Figure 34. Pattern sequence for direct sales

Direct sales can still be made using online (INTERNET STORE, page 177) or captive retail outlets (BRANDED SHOPS, page 172). Whichever channel is chosen, there will be opportunities to sell additional products through the channel. Such products may come from your own company or another. A shop selling laptops might offer carrying cases from another company; an Internet site selling printers might suggest buying ink at the same time, or a salesman might sell additional modules for an application.

Table 4: Comparison of direct sales channels

	Advantages	Disadvantages	Examples
BRANDED SHOPS (page 172)	Complete control of sales process. No middlemen to share revenue with.	Expensive to operate. Require management time and attention. Slow to launch.	Nokia, Vodafone, Telstra.
INTERNET STORE (page 177)	Massive international audience. Quick to set up.	Customers spending tens of thousand of dollars will expect more than a download.	Grisoft (anti-virus), Coding Robots, (blogging tools).
NAMED SALES PEOPLE (page 182)	Good for high-value sales when customers expect attention.	Expensive to build and maintain. Takes time to set up.	Common for enterprise software such as Oracle, SAP, Autonomy.

In some cases channels are used exclusively. For example, small software companies often sell their products over the Internet and nowhere else; large software companies may only sell through NAMED SALES PEOPLE. At other times multiple channels are used for the same products: Apple will sell you a Mac over the Internet or through a store, and if you buy enough Macs you'll probably get your own account manager.

Sometimes multiple channels can be complementary: you visit the store, see the product, go home and then order the exact specification you want online. On other occasions channels compete: *why buy in-store when products are cheaper online?* One way to avoid competition is to distribute different products through different channels.

Branded Shops

Figure 35. The Apple store on Regent Street is the largest in the world

---

The Apple store on Regent Street in London says as much about the Apple lifestyle as it does about the products. Located alongside fashion brands such as Burberry, Armani, Jaeger, Hugh Boss, Banana Republic and Zara, the store feels more like a Starbucks than a computer shop.

The store sells Macs, iPods, iPhones and other Apple-related products from other companies. Customers can see and try products before they buy them; it is also a place to get Apple equipment repairs and to talk to experts at the Genius Bar. Physically it is less than 6,000 miles from the nearest Fry's Electronics, but style-wise it is over a million.

Context Your product is aimed at a mass market – the consumer (B2C) market, and possibly some business (B2B) customers, usually smaller businesses.

Problem *How do you sell directly to a consumer while controlling the experience?*

Forces There is more to selling the product than a simple transaction. Maybe the customer needs to buy a subscription, such as when buying a mobile phone. But if customers cannot buy your product easily they may well buy a competitor's product.

Third parties – middlemen – may still be useful in reaching some customers, but they will promote your brand along with other brands. Selling through a third party will reduce the revenue you receive; your will lose control of the sales process and control over how your brand is presented.

When you are selling a 'special' product – one with a prestigious brand name, one that involves a user in a change (such as moving from PC to Mac), or one that asserts their lifestyle and values (like buying Sony hi-fi) – then the sales experience is important: it is more than a transaction. Potential customers want to touch, feel and experience the product. The sales process is part of the experience.

Online sales are cost- and time-effective, but are transactional in nature: they work when the customer is secure in their decisions. It is hard to create that special feeling when selling through a third party. Brand managers have little control of customer experience when someone else is responsible for the sales environment.

Solution

Open your own shops under your own name with your own staff. Only sell your own products and those that complement your products. Make the sales environment and experience a lifestyle statement. Creating your own shops gives you control of the sales environment, the promotion of your products and the appearance of your brand.

Retailing is a very different business to technology product development, so hire people with retail experience to guide your retail strategy at a senior level. On the shop floor hire people who understand technology and can speak with customers. Make sure your staff are knowledgeable about your products.

Select sites that match your company image and the style you wish to project, even if these are not the cheapest available. Undertake some experiments in retailing before rolling the concept out *en masse*. Set up an initial experimental store: see what consumer reaction is and incorporate feedback before committing to expensive leases and staff.

It is unlikely that your own shops will replace other sales channels completely. Shops provide an additional channel and some image enhancement, so keep your other channels. Seek ways to extract synergies from the two. For example, this author visited his local

Apple shop to buy a cable. The cable was not in stock, but the assistant e-mailed him a link to the online store where he could buy the cable while they talked.

You will need to determine a pricing strategy for shops relative to other channels. If you want the shops to stand alone and demonstrate a profit in their own right, you will probably need to charge higher prices to justify the retail costs. So your product may sell at one price on the Internet and another over the counter.

Shops present opportunities for additional promotion and public relations. Inviting your loyal following to queue outside the store when you launch a new product can generate free coverage in the local and national press.

Consequences Controlling the physical sales experience allows the seller to generate emotional investment in the product, increasing the chances of a sale and creating more opportunities for *plus-one sales* (up-selling and cross-selling). You are able to create an image of exclusivity around your brand and control product positioning.

Providing an enveloping sales experience – physically and emotionally – is particularly advantageous when enrolling the customer in a brand identity and lifestyle. Simply by entering an Apple or Vodafone shop, the customer has started their product experience.

Allowing customers to handle a product and ask questions of knowledgeable staff helps them to appreciate the product and address their doubts and questions. Customers get good advice and are helped to select the right product for them without the confusion of competing brands. Your corporate relationship with the customer starts in the shop.

Investing in staff in the right place brings other benefits too: "Geek Squad is incredibly good at reducing return rates within stores... They can quickly identify a genuine fault, as opposed to user error or misunderstanding, resolve it on the spot and prevent products going through the return-and-repairs loop", according to the Chief Executive of Best Buy Europe. Investing in staff starts with a careful selection process. Apple, for example, takes great care over the staff it hires.

Running your own shops allows you to control the sales experience and process, and to position your brand. Having your brand displayed prominently in a public location will raise its profile and provide opportunities for additional sales and customer services.

Retail is a different business to technology and requires different skills and experience. There is no middleman with which to share the revenue or to discount your product against your wishes. But there are landlords, and prime locations don't come cheaply.

Owning and running your own stores is an expensive option and a major distraction for technology companies – as Gateway discovered to its cost. Expanding a chain of own-brand shops takes time if you are not to dilute the offering with second-rate locations, under-trained staff and poor stock control.

If prices are higher in the stores than online, customer may visit the stores, examine the products, then purchase online. The stores contribute to the purchase decision, but this does not show in the sales figures. Determining the cost effectiveness of mixed channels can be hard because they inevitably overlap.

Variations

Classic department stores have long rented space to brand names in cosmetics and clothing. In the UK, 3 – a mobile telephone operator– has copied this model. 3 initially sold through concessions within the existing stores of non-telecom retailer Superdrug: both are part of the Hutchinson conglomerate. This provided the company with a presence on the high street quickly and at a lower cost, although at the loss of some visibility, brand promotion and environment control. In time 3 opened its own shops and moved out of the pharmacies. While companies like 3 use BRANDED SHOPS early on to build brand awareness, others, such as Apple, start with an established brand they wish to expand.

BRANDED SHOPS can be used as an exclusive channel or a non-exclusive channel. As part of their offering prestige clothing brands sell exclusively through their own shops or carefully selected retailers that maintain the brand image. Most technology companies with shops usually take a non-exclusive approach, with independent retailers and online channels used in parallel.

Examples

Apple, Sony, Vodafone, AT&T and Lego have followed fashion brands such as Prada and Benetton. Other companies like BT in the UK have used BRANDED SHOPS in the past, but discontinued them. Telstra in Australia is, at the time of writing, experimenting with 'Telstra Life' shops.

There is more to successful retailing than an expensive store. In December 2009 Nokia announced closure of stores in New York,

Chicago and London, while retaining nine others. The London store is thought to have cost over $6.5m to refurbish, but did not perform as successfully as the Apple store, also on Regent Street. In retrospect the Nokia closure can be seen as a sign of problems to come. In 2011 Nokia announced that it would move from its own Symbian platform to Microsoft for future phones. The Nokia phones and stores could not complete with Apple phones and stores. No matter how good the retail experience, it cannot make an uncool product cool.

INTERNET STORE

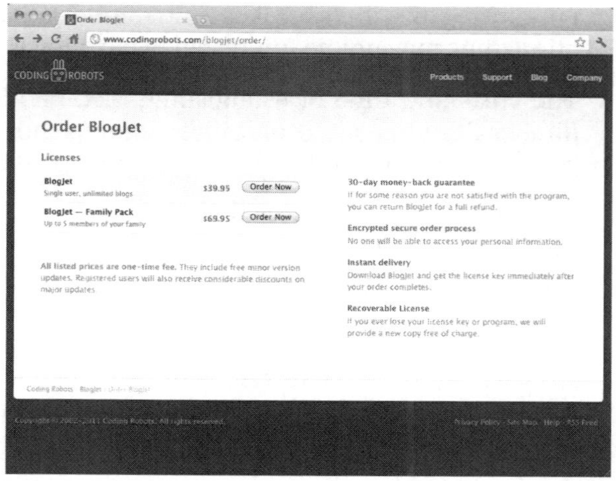

Figure 36. Coding Robots sales page for BlogJet

Permission to reproduce granted by Coding Robots, Dmitry Chestnykh

---

Coding Robots is based in Moscow but they sell worldwide via the Internet. Two Blue Cubes is based in South-East England and sells worldwide through the iPhone AppStore: the list could go on. The world is full of software companies that only sell their products online, and it doesn't matter where these companies or their customers are physically located.

Context Your potential market and customers are dispersed and your funds are limited. You don't haggle or negotiate with your customers: there is one price list and everyone pays the same, even if they pay in different currencies. Even if you could afford a direct sales force, there is no sensible place to base them.

Problem *How do you sell to a dispersed market while controlling costs (ideally minimising them) without a third party and with little infrastructure?*

Forces You want to sell your product directly to customers. But the potential market is dispersed throughout the world, so there are many complications and additional costs involves in getting products to every location.

A widely dispersed customer base will be expensive to address, but the selling price does not justify a large direct sales force; opening your own shops takes time, and is again expensive. Even finding and appointing distributors takes time – and if you are a new, small, operation, they may not be interested in carrying your products.

The costs and time of establishing BRANDED SHOPS (page 172) or a direct sales force are prohibitive. Signing shop leases and recruiting people takes time and entails commitments that reduce flexibility.

Selling online carries risks for the consumer. How do they know you are who you say you are? That you can be trusted with a credit card number? Or that your product does half the things you claim?

Solution

Sell your products from a website. Provide all the information the customer needs to make a decision and allow them to pay online. Use third-party payment and fulfilment providers to help reduce the risk and perception of fraud.

Case studies, data sheets, testimonials and videos can all be used to convince customers that your product meets their requirements. Offer customers time-limited trials and straightforward, no argument, easy to understand return and refund policies to reduce their purchase risk.

Even Internet sales require infrastructure: a website, shopping cart, payments system, download capacity and stock warehouses. As a software company you may be tempted to develop (and run) these yourself. Just because you *can* develop your own website does not mean you *should* develop one – a professional website designer may do a better job.

Today many good shopping cart and payment systems for online retailer are available. Systems such as Google Checkout, PayPal and WorldPay can be used with little development, are trusted by customers and have well known interfaces,

For products that can be digitised (software, music, films), once payment is made the product can be downloaded over the Internet and used immediately. For purchase of services, the customer may be provided with a token or e-ticket that can be exchanged at the point of consumption.

Physical products need to be delivered to customers: here too, the fulfilment and delivery process can be outsourced to specialists. In the extreme, *drop shipping* can be used. Here the seller only maintains the online presence; the WHOLESALER (page 217) operates a WHITE LABEL (page 208) fulfilment operation that will ship to your customers using your brand. You never need to handle the physical product yourself.

Before any sale is made customers need to find your site. Use outbound marketing to create an awareness and generate visits. Offline (traditional advertising, public relations and so on) and online marketing tools – banner ads, Google AdWords, social networking, Twitter and search engine optimisation – all have a part to play.

The anonymity of the process makes it hard to understand *why* your customers are buying your product. Without discussion it is difficult to know why they are buying. Monitoring site usage statistics can provide some useful information. You may also choose to contact some customers (and some 'almost customers') directly after the event and enquiry into their buying decisions.

To maximise understanding of your website, gather statistics – lots of statistics – and spend time analysing them. There are many questions to ask and improvements to make: *where do customers come from? Which adverts are successful? How do customers use the site? What is their path through the site? Why do they abandon shopping carts?*

Consequences The Internet provides a low-cost channel for sales, although marketing costs may be high.

Geographical location is not very important when purchasing on the Internet. Still, you will need to check local taxes and customs, and you can break local laws if you do not take account of customer locations. For example, eBay has had to limit sales of military paraphernalia in some countries.

Pricing on the Internet is transparent and there are few opportunities to differentiate your offering for particular customers. Potential buyers can see your price and compare it directly with competitors'.

There will still be infrastructure costs and transaction costs to pay. The more transactions you have through your site, the more attention you will need to pay to these factors. You also need to consider security; a breach of online security could damage your company's image.

Customers' risk is reduced when you use well-known branded service providers for transaction processing. No-quibble trials and returns reduce the risk of a poor purchase decision.

Internet sites can be set up, changed and withdrawn quickly. You can experiment with different offers and withdraw those that don't work. However, rapid changes or poorly prepared experiments may confuse customers.

Variations

Software companies first used the Internet to sell their products online, with customers either downloading the product or receiving media through the post. Increasingly, software companies rent their products over the Internet instead of selling them, using the *software as a service* model pioneered by SalesForce.com.

Application stores – *App Stores* – are the INDEPENDENT RETAILER (page 213) of the Internet. Rather than run your own website, payment and delivery mechanisms, Apple, Amazon and other App Store owners will do it for you. Customers can browse the App Store and choose the products they like, just as they do in a supermarket.

Related work

There is potential for the development of a pattern language about Internet retailing.

Examples

Software companies such as Adobe and Intuit sell large amounts of product over the Internet. Software can be selected, bought and delivered online with the click of a mouse.

EasyJet in Europe and South West Airlines in the USA sell tickets for future travel online. Provided that a service can be delivered separately from its purchase, other service companies can do likewise.

Mail order

The Internet has displaced mail order as the dominant direct marketing technique for the mass market. Today, while you can still have things delivered by mail, they are likely to be ordered on the Internet.

Before the Internet, companies would advertise their products in newspaper and magazines, on television or radio, or circulate their own catalogue. Mail order buyers would place their order by writing to the company, or perhaps by filling in a form and sending it, with payment, to the seller.

Mail order had many of the same attributes as Internet selling: the seller had complete control, there was no middleman and products were shipped directly to the customer. One complication was the lead times required by publications carrying advertising.

The big difference between mail order and Internet marketing is speed. On the Internet the order is placed once a form is completed; dispatch can happen the same day and delivery the next. Rather than printing and distributing a new catalogue a few times a year, products can be added, removed, highlighted and sidelined every day.

During the early personal computer boom companies like MITS in the US and Sinclair Research in the UK successfully established their computers using mail order. Sinclair continued to offer later machines such as the ZX Spectrum and QL by mail order, but most of the machines reached the mass market through an INDEPENDENT RETAILER (page 213).

Mail order survives as a supplement to Internet shopping and in some niche markets – particularly in clothing, where the likes of Boden and Littlewoods in the UK still offer mail-order catalogue shopping. Maplin Electronics still makes a printed catalogue available, but on the whole the technology industry has migrated to the web.

NAMED SALES PEOPLE

Figure 37. Everyone knows what a salesman looks like

Owen was a salesman. You rarely saw him in the office and he had frequent flyer miles coming of his ears. He sold telecoms software to some of the biggest operators in Europe. He wasn't alone: the company had another half dozen like him. The CEO would have liked more; they even recruited more, but those who couldn't sell didn't stay long.

Commission payments meant that when times were good they were very very good, and when times were bad… well, a good salesman knows how to sell himself above everything else. It is difficult to keep good salesmen at a company with products that don't sell.

Context Complex software products, particularly those which are innovative, such as enterprise software, require a more sophisticated sales approach than is possible with the Internet alone. When your product is highly specialised, technically advanced and/or very expensive, each sale becomes more complex.

Problem *How do I sell a complex (and expensive) product to corporate customers?*

Forces Sales to corporate customers with large price tags take time: potential customers need to be identified, contacts made and cultivated, demonstrations provided and business cases written. But the Internet is very transaction-oriented, so it is difficult to develop the necessary kind of relationship online. Big corporations don't go retail shopping for expensive software, so putting your product in a shop isn't going to work.

There is more to selling this type of product than simply showing the customer the product. The product may be new and novel; it may not be obvious what the product can do for the customer, let alone the value it can generate or money it can save.

Buying such a product involves more than just taking delivery. Existing systems and processes may need to change; old and new systems may need costly integration; jobs may be created or lost as a result of such decisions.

Committing to such a product may be a strategic decision for the company and may involve years of commitment. Then there are competitors, who would also like to make these sales.

Selling into a large company requires a proactive approach. Large companies have many mechanisms to stop employees spending the company's money and ensuring expenditure is approved and generates value. Corporate customers are also likely to have a number of suppliers chasing after their budget.

Solution

Employ your own sales force of specialists to sell your product to customers directly. Assign named individuals to named customers, link their remuneration to sales and allow them time to understand the customer.

By employing the sales force yourself, you can target the customers you think will benefit from your product. Selling is a person-to-person act; its about getting in front of the right people, having the right image and a good relationship. When you employ your own sales force you control – and take responsibility for – the relationship.

Over time the relationship between your staff and the customers will become as or even more important than any sales transaction, as described in IT'S A RELATIONSHIP, NOT A SALE (Rising, 2002). Your organisation will own the customer relationship, so there is no middleman to take a cut, control the information flow or take the customer to a different product.

The more a sales team focuses on its customers and market, the greater its chance of success. Help it do this by dividing up the prospects. Start dividing by sector, geography or deal size to meet your business objectives. Once divided, assign individuals to the divisions and customers in the divisions.

When you sell more than one product you will need to decide whether to divide the sales force between customers or products. Should one salesperson sell all your products to one customer, or will sales people specialise in particular products? If the latter, you need to avoid confusing customers who find themselves dealing with several different people at your company.

Different types of sales people may be appropriate at different points in the sales pipeline. Use call centre staff to identify and qualify leads, follow up with a SALES/TECHNICAL DOUBLE ACT (page 192) to meet the customer, make the case and have a single salesperson to close the sale. Use an ACCOUNT MANAGEMENT (page 187) specialist to follow up and secure future sales.

Employing your own sales force is expensive, so it only cost-effective for high-value products. When a market starts to commoditise, prices will be driven down and sales tactics will need to change to stay cost-effective. Migrate low-margin sales to the Internet, distributors or other low-cost channels, so that your sales force can focus on the relationship and high-end products.

Anecdotal evidence suggests that making a small sale to a big company can be as difficult as making a big sale, so don't shy away from big sales. When there are many open at once, focus on the biggest deal.

The job title 'Salesman' or 'Salesperson' can trigger immediate resistance in some people. Instead, you could give your sales people a euphemistic title such as 'Commercial Account Manager'.

Consequences When you control the entire sales process, you can give high-value customers individual attention to address their needs and concerns. You can decide which customers and contacts are worth pursuing and spending time on, and which should be passed over or directed to another sales channel.

The direct sales approach allows time for outlining the benefits of a product, the technology behind it and how companies can get the most value. The sales process includes discussion of corporate changes that result from product adoption.

When a purchase is a major or even strategic decision for a company – for example, adopting SAP – customers will need reassurance that your company will be around for the entire life of the product.

Customers may want to do due diligence on your company, to know about your cash flow, sales prospects, management team and investors.

Your sales people can help potential customers to navigate their internal controls and help them to show how your product delivers value above the price you are asking. They can also monitor competitors' progress with the same customers.

It is normal to reward sales staff with a significant commission on the sales they make, although they may get a very low base salary (or even none). Sales staff are often goal-directed individuals who are motivated by money. Such a reward structure can be at odds with the relationship approach to selling. Engineers may find the commission system distasteful, they may even have reason to dislike it, but it is a widespread and expected system in sales.

A sales force that is out meeting and listening to customers will be gathering information. Most of this will be sales information that needs to be fed into whatever system the company uses to manage sales. Other information may be helpful to product managers, development teams and top-level management. However, sales staff are unreliable reporters, as they are busy chasing sales. Relying on what sales staff report alone can be misleading, so cultivate multiple information sources.

Variations Some companies use NAMED SALES PEOPLE to both make the initial sales and undertake the follow-up ACCOUNT MANAGEMENT (page 187). Other companies let the sale people specialise in breaking new sales, while specialist account managers take over once the first sale is made.

Related work A direct sales force often works with a LOCAL GUIDE (page 200) or VALUE ADDED RESELLER (page 203) to help cultivate contacts and deliver complete solutions.

For really technical products, use SALES/TECHNICAL DOUBLE ACT (page 192) so that sales people can focus on selling and specialists can focus on pre-sales support and technical issues.

The sale should not be the end of the relationship. ACCOUNT MANAGEMENT (page 187) describes how to deepen the relationship and keep it active.

Once the customer owns your product, several more patterns can be brought into play to further the relationship and sales: SAME CUSTOMERS, DIFFERENT PRODUCT (page 105) and ACCOUNT MANAGEMENT can be used to generate further product sales, while PRODUCTS WITH SERVICES (page 242), INITIAL HELP (page 248) and LIFETIME SERVICES FOR PRODUCTS (page 252) can be used to help the customer get the most from the product.

Examples This approach is often used by producers of enterprise software such as Oracle and Microsoft. Smaller independent software vendors usually take this route when selling to corporates.

Sales overkill

The wrong sales approach can deter customers. You might actually want to do this as part of your filtering process, so that no time is wasted on customers who are unlikely to buy or are outside your target market.

This author was once tasked with evaluating two different software packages for detecting, and possibly fixing, memory leaks in an application. The first was a well-known product: you downloaded it, evaluated it, and if you liked it, put in a credit card number and bought it for $500.

The second package was less well-known but was highly recommended. To get a trial version I had to talk to a salesman. Right from the start he wanted to come and visit us. A trial could be arranged – not for the 30 days like the first product, but for three days, and we would need to have one of their technical consultants there to show me how to use it: no download and trial.

I stopped returning his calls and answering his e-mails. Eventually he got me on the phone. “What’s the problem?” he asked. “The trouble is”. I said, “I don’t know whether you are selling me a Honda or a Lexus. No matter how good the product, we’ve only got a Honda budget, and I think your selling a Lexus.”

Selecting the right sales approach is important. You can use multiple sales channels to reach different groups of customers: a direct sales force for high-end customers with deep pockets, and an Internet store for entry-level customers. Most probably you will need to differentiate the products sold by each channel, to deter customer from simply choosing the cheapest route.

Having multiple channels and products at different price levels also allows you to sell to customers who have little money today but may have more tomorrow. Closing the door on an unsuitable customer today may leave a bad impression: the same customer may be very desirable in a few years time.

ACCOUNT MANAGEMENT

Figure 38. Actively managing an account involves piecing together lots of information

---

Big customers who spend a lot of money with you can represent a big chunk of your income, so they are not 'just another sale'. When your product is important to their company, you are more than just a supplier and your relationship is about more than just products. There is value in the relationship itself, not just the sales.

Understanding your relationship will help you serve your customers better, secure future revenue and create opportunities to increase your profits.

Context You are selling technical products and services to corporate customers. SAME CUSTOMERS, DIFFERENT PRODUCT (page 105) suggests that you benefit most when you sell more products to your existing customers.

Problem *How do you avoid losing existing customers? How do you understand what customers really want?*

Forces Finding and selling to new customers is expensive, but by definition existing customers already have at least one of your products, so there is no obvious sale to be made.

Corporate customers face multiple opportunities and problems in their own business and market. Some of these issues may create opportunities for your products and services, but you need to know what these issues are.

Making a sale should create opportunities for further sales and support contracts. But your customers are your competitor's prospects; you still need to ensure that your customers remain your customers. You want them to buy more from you, but once you have made the sale you need some reason to stay in contact.

Sales staff are selected and rewarded on the basis of their ability to win sales, but managing an account over the long term requires more than just selling. Customers may be deterred from talking to people in your company if a salesman tries to make another sale every time they do so.

Solution

Treat customers as valued collaborators; continue to work with customers actively after a sale has closed. Appoint named account managers who can build a relationship with both the customer's enterprise and the individuals who work there.

Seek to understand how the customer is using your products, the challenges facing the customer and opportunities that exist for helping customers meet these challenges. Ask lots of questions: *how are they doing with the product? Was it what they expected? Do they need any help? Who else in the company does work like this?*

Managing a customer account goes beyond selling, and there is more to keeping customers happy than selling at a low price. It includes the post-sales experience – support services, training and customer follow-up. This is provided by a team, not an individual.

Rather than focus on the next sale, focus on keeping your customer happy. In the process find out what else they need and who else in the organisation may benefit from using your product. Continue to learn about your customers' needs and their problems. When the time is right, offer them your solutions.

Create a culture that encourages ongoing contact and dialogue with customers. Build continuity in the relationship; be responsive to the customers' needs and de-emphasise contact based purely on sales. Aim to stay involved over the long term and build a trusted relationship with customers.

Sales people may not be the right people to manage an ongoing relationship. While they may be good at opening doors, making first contact and closing a deal, they may lack the skills and motivation to maintain an ongoing relationship.

One option is to split the sales and account management roles. Once a sale is made, or even before, introduce an account manager who will continue the relationship and look after the customer. However, some sales people may resist handing over an account they have won. Alternatively, supplement your sales people with account managers who look after the account when there are no sales in prospect. Use SALES/TECHNICAL DOUBLE ACT (page 192) in both cases to split commercial and technical issues. Product managers can supplement account managers to increase the depth of customer understanding.

When recruiting account managers, look for people who will be interested in building a relationship rather than just making the next sale. Account managers who are simply sales staff working on commission may not be motivated to keep a relationship going when there is no sale in prospect. Balance remuneration so that staff can afford to build the relationship rather than just sell, sell, sell.

No one pattern or single set of actions can guarantee that your customers return to buy more from you. By building a relationship based on trust and continuing to learn about your customers, you should at least see problems before they occur and position yourself to find opportunities.

Consequences Selling additional products and services to existing customer can be cost-effective and information-rich. Technology change creates opportunities for everyone: customers, competitors and yourself.

Engaging with a customer on a regular basis will allow you to learn their future growth plans and requirements. Knowing customers' future needs can inform your own business decisions, leading to better products and benefiting both customer and supplier.

Competitors – especially new entrants – lack the customer assets you have. Investing in your customers will create a deeper relationship, thus making it more difficult for competitors to poach business.

An active account management programme will cost. Account managers will need to make visits to the customer and spend time understanding the customer. You will need to employ additional staff, and to pay salary, travel and entertainment expenses even when sales are not being made. Such expenses may be seen as easy savings when times are tough, but they represent investment in your relationship with customers and keep the prospect of future sales open.

Too much customer contact may annoy the customer and make them feel they are being constantly sold to. Having other points of contact, such as customer care and product managers, will help build trust and collect information without a sales motivation.

Related work This pattern can be used to help implement IT'S A RELATIONSHIP, NOT A SALE from *Customer Interaction Patterns* (Rising, 2000). BUILD TRUST and other patterns from the same language are also useful in this context.

LIFETIME SERVICES FOR PRODUCTS (page 252) describes how to continue services as additions to your product sale. Services such as technical support and training can generate continuing revenue over the lifetime of a product.

ACCOUNT MANAGEMENT can be used as part of CUSTOMER UNDERSTANDING (page 146); however, the two patterns have different objectives: CUSTOMER UNDERSTANDING seeks to understand customers so as to improve inbound marketing and product development, while ACCOUNT MANAGEMENT seeks to understand customers to secure additional sales and service. While similar questions are asked and ultimately a whole picture is constructed, there are potential conflicts in the objectives.

According to McKenzie (2001) a customer relationship is a conversation with exchanges. There is value in the relationship itself, not just the product/money exchanges. Customers who see value in the relationship will continue the conversation by buying more products. Active account management represents an investment in maintaining and increasing that value.

Examples A London software company supplied applications to most of the major players in the mobile telecoms market. The remaining sales prospects were small fry. New sales had to come from selling more products to existing big customers, so it was important to create positive sales and post-sales experiences. A hard sales approach might secure the immediate sale but damage the relationship and future prospects. Account management was handled by a SALES/TECHNICAL DOUBLE ACT (page 192), one for commercial issues (sales) and one for technical issues (everything else).

Another London software company, this time in the media sector, had its salesmen make an initial sale. They then handed accounts over to dedicated account managers. However, the handover was poorly defined, sales staff didn't like giving up customers, and the account managers lacked technical skills. In some cases it worked, in others it didn't.

SALES/TECHNICAL DOUBLE ACT

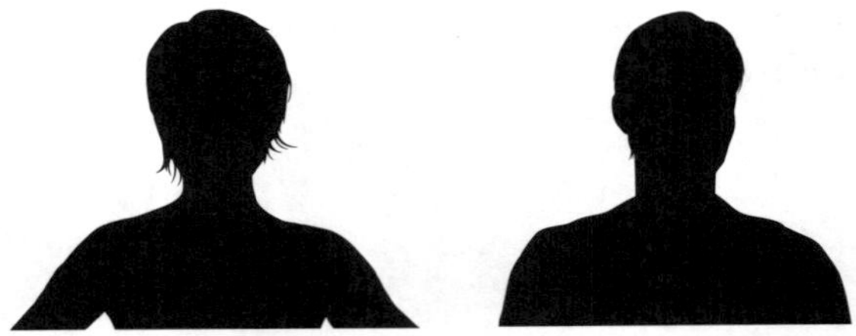

Figure 39. Two heads can be better than one

Allan was responsible for evaluating and selecting an enterprise search engine. Downloading and installing the trial software was easy, but then technical problems and questions arose.

When the search engine salesman called he brought a technical consultant with him. The consultant was knowledgeable about the things the salesman wasn't and could discuss technical issues in detail in a way that the salesman couldn't. Even after the sale the technical consultant kept in touch.

Context You are using ACCOUNT MANAGEMENT (page 187) to sell high-margin technical products to business customers.

Problem *How do you avoid overwhelming your account managers with commercial and technical issues, both before the sale and after?*

Forces Selling a technical product involves more than talking about technology; there are commercial issues to discuss, such as price and license duration. But technical people aren't usually good at commercial aspects, and sales people aren't usually proficient in technical aspects.

Even when you can find someone who can cover both the commercial and technical aspects of a product, there is often too much for one person to take in. Technical products often require in-depth technical knowledge as well as commercial knowledge.

Within customer organisations the people who make the technical decisions are often different from the people who make the decisions on expenditure. These groups may expect to deal with different levels of seniority and expertise in your organisation.

Discussing commercial and technical questions for a complex product takes a lot of time and energy. But you don't want to spend all your energy on these questions. At the same time as negotiating the deal you want to gain insights into your customer's business and how they want to use the product.

Solution

Have your customer account managers work in pairs: one handles the commercial aspects of the product, the other handles the technical aspects. This will allow you to hire the best possible sales people and technical people for your product. Individuals can focus on what they do best, rather than trying to master diverse skills.

Technical managers should come from a technical domain and should be trained in depth on the product. Some technical managers may come from internal groups such as development or support. Sales people may not need to understand the product in depth, but they should know the benefits and advantages of its application. Each group needs to respect the other and refer questions when appropriate.

Technical managers' involvement should be more than just pre-sales calls; their involvement should extend to pre-sales visits and beyond. As the technical manager wins the trust and confidence of customers' staff, your overall corporate relationship will deepen, you will better understand your customers and serve them better.

Technical managers may help clients with technical support issues, configuration, installation and training. Be careful not to overload the technical manager with too much work; most probably they will be working with several customers. With growth you may want to create dedicated groups to deal with specific issues and relieve pressure from technical managers, for example by using a technical support desk and a training team.

The sales-oriented commercial managers can concentrate on the financial and business aspects of the deal, such as pricing, terms and conditions, license renewals, support agreements and so on. They can take a strategic view and look for opportunities to sell more products.

Both managers should talk regularly about the customer, their current needs and their future needs. They should meet the customer regularly and conduct periodic account reviews that bring together everyone involved with managing the customer's account. Such reviews can help to identify sales prospects and future customer needs.

Consequences Customers will receive better commercial and technical service. You will gather more information, because different staff talk about different things to different people. Over time you will gain a more complete view of your customer. Customer employees will come to trust and share information with your representatives. Having two views of the customer will improve your understanding of the customer and the issues – particularly political ones – involved in a sale.

Using more than one person to manage the customer relationship allows people to specialise in what they are good at. It is easier to find dedicated individuals than to expect individuals to be proficient in very different fields.

Having more than one individual involved in a customer relationship acts as a safeguard against people leaving your company. Losing a salesperson can be unfortunate; if they take your customers with them, it can be a disaster. With two people managing the account you can provide continuity.

Where more than one person is involved in a sale the customers may become confused about who deals with which aspects. Even if customers wish to clarify the relationship, you might prefer to leave the boundaries vague. Blurring the lines may create opportunities for extra contact and information exchange. Still, be careful not to confuse your customers too much.

Having multiple account managers further increases the cost of managing a customer account. This is feasible for high-margin products; for low-margin products you might need to use service teams rather than individuals.

Variations When customer organisations are very large one account manager may not be enough to cover all contacts. Multiple account managers will allow responsibilities to be divided: different managers may deal with different customer divisions or geographical areas.

Related work SALES/TECHNICAL DOUBLE ACT can be used to help implement ACCOUNT MANAGEMENT (page 187) and CUSTOMER UNDERSTANDING (page 146).

Software developers sometimes use DEVELOPING IN PAIRS (Coplien & Harrison, 2004) to increase productivity. One developer reviews work as it is performed and helps with the decision process. This is a form of double act, but the developers have similar skills and periodically switch the roles of reviewer and coder.

Examples

Many organisations employ *pre-sales consultants* or *sales engineers* as technical contacts before the sale is made. This is a form of double act, but sometimes ends once the sale is made.

10

Patterns of Indirect Distribution

Direct selling might be the most obvious way of getting your product into the hands of customers, but it can also be time-consuming and expensive – not all products can sell at a price high enough to justify direct selling.

Indirect sales models seek to exploit the resources of others to get your product sold. In doing so you share the revenue with a partner, sometimes several partners. But it is not just revenue you forego in allowing others to sell your products: you forego contact with customers and have less control over the sales process.

There may be even more patterns of indirect distribution than there are of direct distribution. At one extreme is LOCAL GUIDE (page 200), which simply uses someone else to make contacts and smooth a selling process controlled by your own people. The other extreme is that of independent retailers who are supplied by a WHOLESALER (page 217).

Nor is there a black and white choice between direct and indirect sales. Different sales models and channels can be combined as long as they do not cannibalise sales from each other. One way around this problem is SIMPLE PRODUCT VARIATIONS (page 121), to create different products for different channels, as discussed in *Different Product, Different Channel* on page 166.

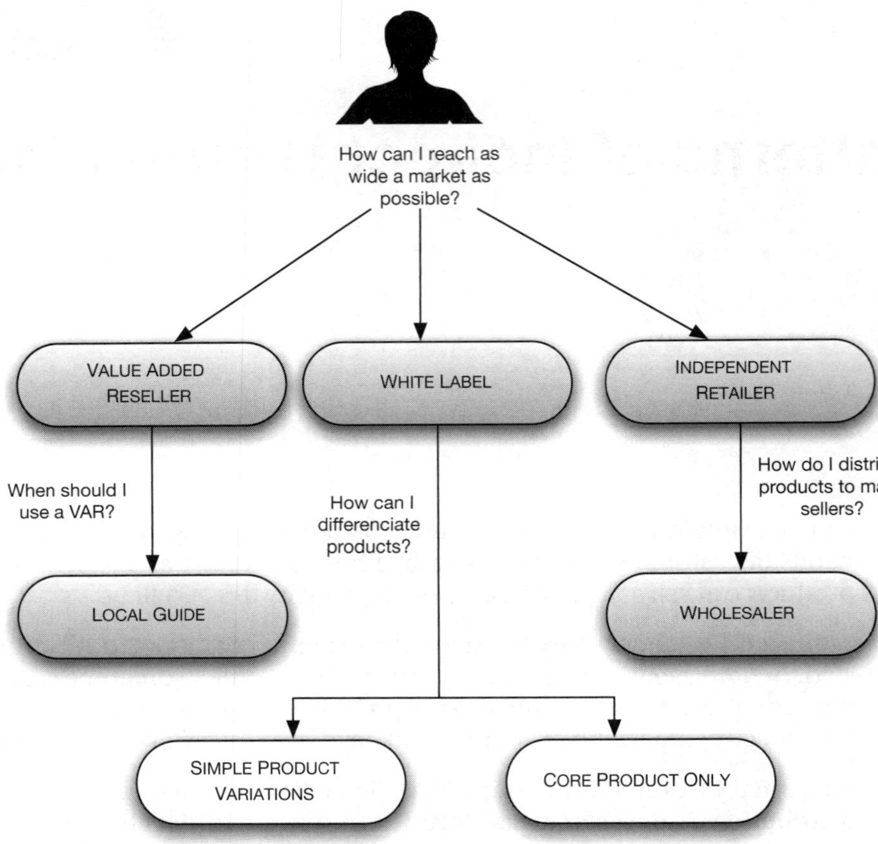

Figure 40. Sequence of patterns for indirect distribution

Table 5: Comparison of indirect sales channels

	Advantages	**Disadvantages**	**Notes**
INDEPENDENT RETAILER (page 213)	Retailer has record of selling products.	Little control of how product is presented, priced and sold.	Best Buy, Dixons Store Group and other high street retailers
WHITE LABEL (page 208)	Address additional market segments and opportunities. Leverage others' brands to sell more, while protecting your own from competitors.	Brand owner controls customer relationship and can change providers.	Virgin Mobile place their brand on services from T-Mobile, Sprint and other cell phone providers. PCs manufactured by Asustek Computer (Asus) are branded with many other companies names.
LOCAL GUIDE (page 200)	Has access to potential customers.	Takes cut of revenue for little added value.	Can be used in conjunction with NAMED SALES PEOPLE (page 182) or VALUE ADDED RESELLER (page 203).
VALUE ADDED RESELLER (page 203) (VAR)	VAR has customer relationships, sales force, professional services.	VAR controls customer relationship. VAR may have other objectives in a customer relationship.	Oracle have over 300 VARs[1]. All VARs are not equal; it is important to find one appropriate to your product.
WHOLESALER (page 217)	Reaches more independent retailers.	Even less control of sales. Little contact with final buyer.	Entertainment UK and Makro cash and carry.

[1] On 30 December 2008 Oracle's website listed 308 value added resellers worldwide. (`solutions.oracle.com/SHARED/PartnerCategory/ValueAddedReseller/Items`)

LOCAL GUIDE

Figure 41. Opening doors can be difficult

The Austrian distributor turned out to be one man. His office turned out to be a rented room in the Austrian equivalent of U-Stor-It. Yet he knew the right people and could get us in to talk to the people who needed our product – even if they didn't know it yet.

He did the introductions and left the selling to our salesman. But when we had done the deal and gone home he was still there to ensure everything went smoothly. It didn't matter that it was just him; it was about who he knew. His office didn't matter either, as he spent most of his time with clients.

Context You are using NAMED SALES PEOPLE (page 182) to reach corporate customers and you want to break into a new market or target a specific customer.

Problem *In a strange market, how do you get to meet the people at the companies you want to sell to? And how do you navigate the local practices and customs?*

Forces Making an initial contact inside one company can be difficult. Making multiple contacts inside multiple companies in a new market is an order of magnitude harder. But making contact is only the first step: you need to be taken seriously and you need potential customers to return your follow-up calls.

Local laws, customs and business practices differ from country to country. What is considered normal in one country may be illegal in another; what is illegal in one country may be essential in another. You can study a country and its markets for years, but without feet on the ground and local knowledge, you can still fall foul of local norms.

For example, you might be the most successful company Denmark has ever seen, you might know all the right people in Denmark, but replicating that success in the USA is going to be difficult, because you don't know the right people and the right way of going about business.

Solution

Engage a partner who can open the right doors for you, arrange meetings, give you credibility and advise on local presentation, practices and the norms of business. Local agents can help with this; in return they will expect a commission on your sales revenue.

Finding a good partner is not easy and needs to take time. Determine who your final customers could be and find out who already supplies them. Look for local companies who are in related businesses. These companies should already have the relationships that interest you. Former employees of your target customers provide another source of guides.

You need to be able to trust your partner, so meet them several times. Undertake due diligence on their financial affairs and make sure they know the right people and can get the right access.

The LOCAL GUIDE will have the contacts and presence to open doors and introduce you to the right people and get them to agree to meetings. Their knowledge and personal relationships mean that their calls are returned and that they are told how sentiment is shaping up inside the customer's organisation.

Your direct sales force still controls the sales process and you can walk away from a deal if it doesn't make sense. Once customers start using your product – and possibly before – your technical people can start to build a relationship with the customer so that you can understand their needs better.

Local guides may be called *distributors* or *value added resellers,* although they do little more than make the introductions and watch you sell. While they do not satisfy the descriptions given in the patterns of the same names, the names are used to explain their role to customers.

It is normal for such partners to receive a commission on each sale. They may actually transact the sale and pay you the residual amount. They may also receive a retainer's fee and fees from the customer for support services.

Consequences Effective partners will advise on local customs, laws and practices. They will help to close sales and protect you from locals who might take advantage of your naivety and inexperience in the market.

The commission earned by a middleman is hard to justify in terms of hours worked: instead, it is justified in terms of contacts, local knowledge and making deals happen. Having the door opened does not guarantee a sale, and it might be hard to justify recurring expenses when times are hard.

Intermediaries come with their own set of problems and issues. As your operation grows you may find that your guide cannot meet your needs. They may also pursue their own agendas that slow your sales process or lose sales. Be prepared to change agents if you find that your initial choice is not effective or is putting their own agenda first at your expense.

Variations While some 'middlemen' will remain involved in the sales process and take a hefty commission, there are simpler, transaction-based variations. Companies exist that will 'sell meetings' – you describe the type of company or executive you wish to meet and they will identify potential customers and arrange meetings for you. Fees will be levied for each meeting arranged successfully.

Local agents can also act as a useful conduit for paying bribes – especially if you want to obscure this fact in your accounts. (Not that this author condones such practices, but they occur.) While a third-party conduit may help to keep bribes off your books, the trained eye will spot the signs and you may still find yourself in legal trouble.

Guides are not only confined to geographical territories; they can help you with entry to new domains and sectors. For example, companies that wish to sell into the public sector may benefit from help in navigating government bureaucracy and expectations.

Related work In some countries, such as the United Arab Emirates, it might be a requirement of local law to work with a local partner.

VALUE ADDED RESELLER

Figure 42. Partner badges

Cisco, Oracle, SAP and many other technology companies operate value added reseller networks. Hewlett Packard describes its PartnerONE programme:

'Designed for simplicity, predictability and opportunity, the streamlined PartnerONE Program fully enables HP channel partners to win in the marketplace. HP has raised the bar. We stand behind our partners with more marketing and channel support…'

HP is looking to partner with companies that aggressively drive revenue growth by delivering HP products and solutions to mutual customers with appropriate skills and support. PartnerONE is open to resellers, solution providers, system integrators and ISVs doing business in the 50 United States.'

(HP website January 2009)

Context You have a product with many potential customers and/or many potential ways of being used. You have limited resources, and it makes sense to focus your efforts rather than chase after every possibility yourself.

Problem *How do you reach and support potential customers who have needs and requirements beyond your capability to deliver?*

Forces

Potential customers have money to spend and want your product, but you are not able to meet their entire needs with your product and company as it stands. Even in countries where you don't operate, there are potential customers; with a few modifications, the product might work well for customers you know nothing about.

Customers want a WHOLE PRODUCT (page 131), but you cannot provide such a product, or do not want to. But another company can create the WHOLE PRODUCT using your product, thereby generating a sale for you.

You can't do everything yourself; even when you do have sufficient resources, the more things you do, the less focus you have. In reality resources are always limited and there are competing demands for what is available. But without the sales people to visit customers, pre-sales staff to do demonstrations, professional services to carry out installations and others, you will miss sales.

These problems are most acute when a company is starting operations, because the need for customers is greatest and the resources most limited.

Success can magnify such problems. Without the people to make a sale, customers may buy from a competitor. Not only is the initial sale lost, so to is the follow-on work, and more importantly, your competitors' market share is increased at the expense of your own.

Even if you can increase staffing to meet demand, it may not be cost-effective to do so. There are some sales that are just too expensive to make. It seldom makes sense to make a loss on a sale.

Solution

Work with one or more partners who can reach the customers you cannot. Allow them to enhance the product as needed, embed it in their own product, sell their products with yours, or provide services in addition to the product.

In the simplest cases a reseller can address a market that you cannot reach easily, such as one in a different geographic region. Or they may address a segment of a market within an existing market: for example, you might already sell in the North American market, but you lack the contacts and knowledge to sell into government agencies. Although the term 'value added' is somewhat subjective, it is fair to say that any reseller who sells in a way that generates greater revenue is adding value.

VARs may add services that you cannot or do not wish to provide, such as an additional line of support, or support in the native language of customers. Some VARs will provide professional services to help customers use the product or integrate it into their existing systems, following the INITIAL HELP (page 248) and LIFETIME SERVICES FOR PRODUCTS (page 252) patterns.

Alternatively a VAR may add value by accelerating the sales process. They may act as a LOCAL GUIDE (page 200), or provide facilities and services you could yourself but which would take time to develop. True VARs will go beyond simply making contacts and helping you navigate a foreign land: they will play an active part in delivering the solution.

Some VARs may embed your product within theirs such that the final customer is unaware that your product has been sold too. In such conditions it might be better to consider the VAR as your customer, not the final user. The final user wants the VAR's product; yours is irrelevant – the VAR could switch from your product to one of your competitors' without their customers knowing or caring.

Sometime you will need to find VARs yourself; at other times VARs will find you. In either case you need to perform due diligence on the resellers to make sure they are who they say they are, that they are financially sound, honest and trustworthy. In many cases they will be representing your company and will be allowed to use your brand. Poor resellers may damage your brand.

Once you have agreed to work with a reseller, treat them as an extension of your own company. Invite their staff on your product training courses, support their support desk and agree an escalation procedure, loan them resources to master your products and procedures, give them access to your marketing materials and, if appropriate, let them use your brands and trademarks.

Consequences The additional resources and capabilities VAR partners bring are available to help meet customer needs that you cannot. The customer gets the product and service they want, you get another product sale, and the VAR makes a little money in the process.

A VAR may supplement your product with enhancements and services the customers need to get a WHOLE PRODUCT (page 131).

Your people and resources can be focused on your main goals. Customers receive the time and attention they need to buy and recognise value from your product via your proxy, the VAR.

Growing companies can leverage the resources of others to make sales and win customers. Established companies can benefit when faced with rapidly expanding markets (Doctorow, 2008). Vendors and VARs agree to avoid competing with one another. As technology changes, software vendors expand and VARs resell, additional products partners can come into competition. Vendors may, on occasion, decide to eliminate their VAR network to enhance their own revenue and profit.

Each extra sale your product wins thanks to the VAR is a sale your competitors are denied. Thus your market share has grown at the expense of your competitors, and you can look forward to future support revenue.

VARs can be an effective way of extending your sales and service team without incurring cost. However, it is often the VAR who owns the customer relationship. If the VAR decides to resell a competitor's product the customer may switch to the VAR.

Using VARs creates an additional layer between your company and its staff and the customer. It is thus more difficult to understand the customer's needs, incorporate their feedback into your product development and involve the customer in your initiatives. VARs may not be keen on following your price cuts, selling your new products or pushing your brand inside the customer's company.

Variations *System integrators* specialise in making different technical products work together. Such an integrator may or may not be a VAR. In some cases the integrator may specialise in particular produces, for example Oracle Financials, and be licensed to sell that product. This does not apply to all system integrators.

Related work In acting as a VAR companies are following COMPLEMENTOR, NOT COMPETITOR (page 309). Sometimes a VAR is a LOCAL GUIDE (page 200), and sometimes the term 'value added reseller' is used to explain the guide's role even though they do little more than make introductions.

Examples While the most obvious use of VARs is to help a company grow fast, even the biggest software companies such as Microsoft, IBM, Oracle and others continue to use VARs or have a VAR programme of one sort or another. VARs form a vital part of the ecosystem and allow established players to extend their reach and keep competitors at bay.

Quadratron UK was a successful VAR for Quadratron USA during the 1980s and into the 1990s – so successful in fact that the UK company took over development of the product. However, having been set up as a VAR, it lacked the skills and experience to create a successor product successfully.

White Label

Figure 43. A white label allows someone else to write in their name

---

Many holidays begin at the airport, so why wouldn't someone start their holiday planning at the airport website? And since airports are in the business of travel and holidays, why wouldn't they sell flights and travel packages?

But running a travel website is quite different from running an airport, and most airports pass over the opportunity: it's not core business. BAA, owners of Heathrow airport, solved the problem by putting their name and brand on top of another company's holiday planning product. If you book a flight via the website `www.heathrowairport.com` it looks like BAA – but take a look at the HTML source code and you'll find out who really manages the booking.

Context There are times when your own brand gets in the way. Maybe you don't have a brand (yet), or maybe someone else's brand can capture sales that yours cannot.

Problem *How do you take advantage of other companies' sales opportunities, brands and channels to sell your products?*

Forces You have developed a technology or product but have no brand of your own under which to market it. Building your own brand takes time and can be expensive.

You might already have an existing brand and some channels in place, and have the capacity to produce more product, thus earning more revenue and exploiting economies of scale. But selling the extra capacity through your own channels would result in marginal returns. The costs of making the extra sales (lower prices, more advertising, expanded sales network) might outweigh the extra revenue.

In any company with multiple products, some are less strategic than others. Non-strategic products may bring in good money, but need capital and management time.

Solution

Put a white label on your product and technology so that your partner can write their own name on the product and sell your product as their own. Choose partners who have sales opportunities they can exploit with your technology. The partner can sell under their own brand and maintain their relationship with final customers, while reducing their costs and time to market.

Your product and organisation need to be built for rebranding. Your product will need to be configurable so that another company's name, logo, colour scheme and contact details appear in place of yours. Payment processing, call centre support and correspondence all need to be rebranded.

Staff who operate the product or provide service on behalf of the customer will need to represent the brand used for each sale. You will need billing and reporting systems that can distinguish between your own sales and those of your partner and apportion the revenue appropriately.

In such an agreement you are an *original equipment manufacturer* (OEM). (Others may describe such an arrangement with the slightly derogatory terms *badge engineers* and *badge engineering*.) As such you may allow more than one partner to sell your products under their own brand.

Customers will be largely unaware that different products are the same underneath. Indeed, the differently branded versions of the product may well compete with one another in the same market. Alternatively, you avoid competition between partners by separating partners by market, say one for France and another for India.

Contracts need to be negotiated, administered and fees paid. This all adds to the cost of partnering, so remember to factor these costs into your profit calculations.

Consequences When you have an established brand you benefit from additional channels for your product. The different brands and positioning can capture different customer segments.

For a company without a successful brand, a WHITE LABEL product sold through partners can provide an effective route to market. However you will lose some control of the sales process.

When someone else brands and markets your product, you gain additional sales and revenue from sales opportunities you are not able to exploit yourself. This allows you to focus elsewhere – perhaps on the technology, or on achieving economies of scale.

Placing another brand on some of your products allows you to gain sales you would otherwise miss. You can sell at different price points, or with different benefit packages.

Partners selling your product under their own brand benefit in several ways. They may broaden their product offering, avoid capital outlay on developing new products themselves, reduce time to market for a new product and reduce their risk exposure. When your partners rebrand your product to sell to their customers, they are engaging in a form of SAME CUSTOMERS, DIFFERENT PRODUCT (page 105).

By buying in non-strategic products and labelling them as their own, partners can focus their resources on strategic products. At the same time you can remove a potential competitor and gain an extra sales channel.

For companies with existing products and brands, a WHITE LABEL strategy can deliver additional sales from new buyers. However, due care needs to be taken to ensure that the third party brand will bring new buyers. If the brand attracts the same customers, conflicts will result and revenue will be affected.

Price-sensitive customers who discover that your product is being rebranded and sold at a different price may opt to buy the cheaper version. This will erode profit margins on the more expensive brand. If this happens, consider ways to create barriers or incentives to reduce the leakage.

Variations Companies can create their own additional brands to tap additional market segments. In some cases these brands offer genuinely different products. For example, the cars sold by Toyota's Lexus division stand apart from the other Toyota car models – 'Lexus' is not just a model, but a distinct brand in itself.

However, launching additional brands is expensive and time-consuming. Reusing an existing brand can be far cheaper. Another way of doing this is by licensing a brand.

Related work

WHITE LABEL and WHOLESALER (page 217) patterns are both concerned with someone else selling your product. The key difference is the role of branding: in the WHOLESALER pattern your product is sold under your brand by someone else, while in the WHITE LABEL pattern your product is sold under someone else's brand.

There is a COMPLEMENTOR, NOT COMPETITOR-style relationship (page 309) when a potential competitor chooses to place their label on your product. Rather than compete with you, they are working with you.

Examples

Numerous Chinese and Taiwanese manufacturing companies – such as Acer, Asus, BenQ and Quanta – started life as contract manufacturers with their output badged by better known names such as Dell, HP and Compaq. Some of these companies have developed their own design capabilities. Attempts to develop their own brands have a mixed record. While Acer has succeed, BenQ had to retrench: see *The BenQ story* on page 212.

The ABC Software Company signed a white label deal with a major Scandinavia telecoms company. Until this deal the two companies had similar products that competed in the same market. The Scandanavian company discontinued their own product (reducing their costs) and instead sold a rebadged version of ABC's product. ABC gained a new revenue source and effectively eliminated a competitor – thereby using COMPLEMENTOR, NOT COMPETITOR (page 309) and IN BED WITH THE ENEMY (Weiss, 2007).

Virgin Mobile provides mobile telephony services in a number of different countries, but it doesn't own its own network in any of them. Instead it works with an existing network operator, Sprint in the USA and T-Mobile in the UK. This works well, because the Virgin brand appeals to young people and brings additional traffic and revenue to the actual operator. For Sprint or T-Mobile, aggressively targeting the youth market with advertising and offers may undermine their brand strength with corporations and older people.

The BenQ story

BenQ started life as Acer Peripherals before being spun off in 2001. Initially the company was a contract manufacturer of mobile phones and other equipment. BenQ soon began to design products for its customers as an ODM – *original design and manufacturer*. From there the company moved to produce products under its own brand.

These changes were at least in part driven by the corporate urge to grow. Companies like BenQ need to increase their activities and revenues if they are not to stand still. Contract manufacturers are under pressure from their customers to reduce prices, so one way to maintain profits is to move up the supply chain and design products. Supplying designs to customers increases revenue, but this too soon comes under price pressure. Moving further up the chain means that they need to sell their own products under their own brands. Only by having their own brand can they control the customer relationship.

Marketing own-brand products requires different skills, resources and even culture to contract manufacturing and design. Contract manufacturers aim for low costs and thus keep a tight control on inventory, supply chains, processes and manufacturing. Brand building and marketing require imaginative thinking and customer knowledge.

In 2005 BenQ acquired the Siemens mobile phone handset business in an attempt to grow branded business, gain marketing skills, market knowledge and economies of scale. The Siemens acquisition did not go well and in September 2006 BenQ closed the unit.

Products carrying the BenQ brand brought the company into competition with its own customers. Motorola phones built in BenQ factories would compete in the market with BenQ phones designed and manufactured by BenQ itself. Consequently Motorola and Nokia stopped using BenQ as a manufacturer.

This was the start of problems for the company. In September 2007 BenQ split in two. The BenQ brand continues as a much smaller company: ironically it now resells other manufacturer's products under the BenQ brand. The bulk of the company returned to contract manufacturing under the name Qisda.

INDEPENDENT RETAILER

Figure 44. Best Buy entered the European market in partnership with Carphone Warehouse

---

Fry's, Best Buy, Comet, Electro World – different companies, different countries, but the same idea: many brands of similar products under one roof. From Best Buy, for example, you can buy everything from a vacuum cleaner to a fully featured home cinema centre.

Want a new PC? They have HP, Sony, Acer and others all sitting next to each other. Printer – Lexmark, HP, Canon, Epson or Brother? Inkjet or laser?. The choice is yours. They don't much care which brand you buy, because they make money on all of them.

Context While Internet retailing continues to grow, traditional retail still accounts for the bulk of sales. According to the UK Office of National Statistics, by the end of 2008 the Internet accounted for less than 4% of monthly sales. In categories like electronic equipment, this increased to 26% of sales.

Problem *Where do I place my product so that many people can see it and buy it?*

Forces Your product is intended for a broad consumer market. But the Internet and mail order channels do not reach every consumer. Some consumers will only make the final decision when they can touch and feel the product, and a little attention from a salesperson can help close the sale.

Your own shops may be part of the solution, but BRANDED SHOPS (page 172) are expensive to set up and may not be enough alone, possibly because the revenue from your product will not support your own shops, or because you do not have time and resources to build a chain.

When a product is aimed at a mass market you need to get it in front of as many customers as possible so they can buy it and take it home. But the Internet has limitations: physical products still need to be delivered, not everybody shops on the Internet, and even those who do may still wish to experience a product before they buy.

Solution

Have independent retailers sell your product at locations where many customers will be able to see it and buy it – in malls, on main streets and in specialist shops.

Chains such as Best Buy (USA) and PC World (UK) sell a wide range of computer equipment and software. Home and small business buyers visit these stores for much of their equipment. In some cases other types of store can provide a mass-market outlet; for example, computer games are often sold by the same shops that sell films on DVD and music on CD.

Getting your product into multiple independent retailers is a sales job in its own right. There are many small retailers who might sell your product, but finding and persuading them to do so takes time. There are fewer big retailers (with many stores) but even these have limited shelf space and your competitors also want to be there.

While your final customer may be Joe Public, you first have to sell your product to the person who will sell it to Joe. WHOLESALER (page 217) can help to get your product into individual shops and small chains; for bigger chains, you may need a specialist sales force to sell to the retailers and partners who can help.

Once your product is in the retailer's showroom, you will need to support it with advertising, sales literature and competitor comparisons. The stores and their sales staff are not experts in your product and will have little time to learn about it, so make it easy for them.

Remember to tell the stores who your competitors are, so that they can put you next to them: you don't want your tax return software sitting next to the USB cables. Stores may charge you to place your products in a prime spot in the store, such as at the entrance or by the checkout till.

Even in large retail units stores only have so much space, and seek to maximise the return per square foot. If your product cannot produce the returns of competitors' products, they may stop selling your product. Stores may expect you to share the advertising and marketing costs, or offer customers special deals.

Consequences Your product can be widely available quickly when you sell through established retailers. You will benefit from a broad range of shops in good (and some not so good) locations, experienced sales people and from having your product in the place where customers expect to find such products.

Using existing retailers requires less capital and is faster to start than establishing your own shops. But retailers often exist on narrow margins; they will only stock products they are sure they can sell. They may expect to buy on credit or on a sale-or-return basis. Getting a new product from a new company into a store isn't easy. The biggest retailers, such as WalMart and Tesco, may expect to be paid for the shelf space your product takes up.

You lose a lot of control when you sell through independent retailers. The bigger the retailer, the greater their power to dictate price. They may squeeze your profit margin, or dictate a sales price they think is appropriate for your product. The retailer chooses how and where in the store to present your product, and they may choose to discount the product if it doesn't sell. This can affect your branding and market positioning.

Selling the same product through independent retailers and your own channels at the same time may create damaging competition with yourself. If an independent retailer cannot match an online price they may decide to drop the product rather than carry stock that turns over slowly. Consider selling different products through different channels.

Variations Apple, and before them Compaq, IBM and others, allows independent retailers to brand themselves as 'official Apple distributors'. These retailers borrow elements of BRANDED SHOPS (page 172) in their presentation and product line-up, even though they are independent of the brand. Official distributors may be prohibited from selling competing products.

Related work The WHOLESALER (page 217) pattern can be used to address some of the consequences of this pattern.

Examples

Microsoft, HP, Cisco and others offer their products through chains such as Staples (office supplies) and Fry's Electronics.

Retailers come in all shapes and sizes. Department stores like Sears in the USA and John Lewis in the UK sell brand-name computers and software in their electrical departments. Retailers like Best Buy (USA) and Kesa (Comet and Darty in Europe) sell a variety of goods in small and large shops. Other retailers specialise: for example, Carphone Warehouse limits itself to mobile phones and closely related items.

When PalmOS launched WebOS phones in 2010, they failed to provide enough support for the retail channels. The people expected to sell the phone didn't known enough about the phone or how it worked to impress enough potential customers.

Wholesaler

Figure 45. Wholesalers stock many products from many suppliers

---

Lion Computers started as a single shop in a suburb of Liverpool. It grew as large as four stores, but never moved out of North West England and only lasted a few years.

Still, it stocked all the big name software – games, office applications, operating systems – and if they didn't have it, they could have it for you tomorrow. It wasn't as if the owner had a deal with Microsoft, Adobe and all the other software companies: he only dealt with one distributor.

The distributor dealt with the big boys and bought software packages from them in bulk. Lion's owner could ring the distributor and get software delivered the following day. The distributor handled returns and logistics and provided credit accounts. Once a month the distributor would bill Lion for all the products they had recently taken.

Context You are using, or intend to use the INDEPENDENT RETAILER (page 213) pattern. You wish to avoid the time and expense of dealing with many different retailers.

Problem *How do you get your product into many independent retailers?*

Forces

Getting into a few well-known retailers can be hard enough – you have to know who to call, get an appointment, convince them your product will sell and then actually ship the product. But getting your product into *all* the well-known retailers, department stores, local chains and Mom 'n' Pop operations is time consuming, slow and expensive.

When you are successful, you have to deliver on your commitments. So you need to get involved in contracts, shipping logistics, payment collection and administration.

Solution

Work with a wholesaler who already has relationships with many independent retailers and can handle the administration and logistics. In doing so you outsource management and logistics and pay for it through a sales margin of the wholesaler.

Choose a wholesaler who works with the type of retailer you think most appropriate for your product. The wholesaler will expect to buy your product at a significant discount, then sell it on to a retailer who will ultimately sell it at (or below) the intended retail price (Figure 46).

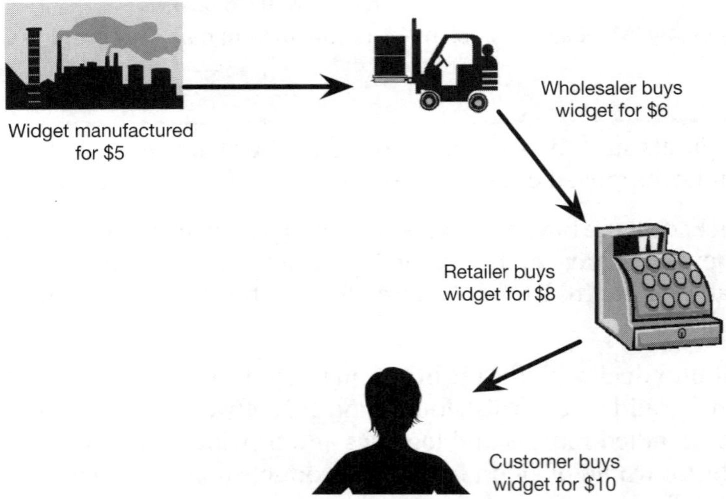

Figure 46. Everyone in the chain needs to make a little money

Consequences

Wholesalers specialise in getting products into independent retailers. They take care of the logistics, administration and the process of selling to downstream vendors. These retailers often rely on one or more wholesalers for many or all of their products. Wholesalers expect their cut of each sale, thus raising your prices or cutting into your profit margin.

By using a wholesaler there is another middleman separating you from your final customers – the ones whose purchases ultimately deliver your revenue. By placing another seller between you and the customer, you also create a further barrier to understanding the ultimate customer.

Variations

'Cash and carry' stores like Makro and Booker in Europe are large hypermarkets that sell to business customers, and in particular to small retailers. The stores obscure the boundary between wholesaler and retailer; they stock a wide variety of goods, from TV sets to frozen chicken portions, including a limited selection of computer equipment and software.

Examples

While more and more software is bought via, and downloaded from, the Internet, some software, like games, is still best distributed on physical CD or DVD. There is still a role for the likes of Sigma Software Distribution, Softline and Mindscape (in Europe) to distribute software to retailers.

Woolworths (UK) was best known for its high-street stores. But the company made most of its profits from a distribution operation called Entertainment UK. This company sold DVDs, CDs, games and other entertainment products to retailers, who competed with Woolworths on the high street. When Woolworths went into liquidation in December 2008, suppliers lost confidence in Entertainment UK. Although the company was a viable business, it could no longer obtain the credit and the supplies it needed. High-street stores that depended on the company for supplies of computer games, DVDs and CD started to experience supply problems.

11

Services

Chapter 1 outlined two broad groups of companies that operate business models centred on developing software: *independent software vendors* (ISVs), which make their money from creating software products that they then sell, and *external service providers* (ESPs), which create custom applications for corporations. New business models, such as *software as a service* (SaaS), blur the boundaries of these, but the two models have always borrowed from one another.

In fact it is all but impossible for companies to employ purely one model; elements of other models always get entwined. For example, successful ISVs need to offer at least basic services such as support and training for their products. Maintaining a clean-cut business model can make it easier to reason about the business, but is an overly simplistic view of how customers relate to products and can be misleading.

For all companies it is a question of finding the right mix of products and services to meet customer needs and allow the company to grow. Each company needs to find its own mix to answer this question, one which fits with the company's history, experience, competitors, investor expectations and current level of technology.

Network effects

One reason why product producers such as Microsoft, Oracle, SAP and Sales-Force.com are massively successful is because, as more individuals and companies use their products, customers experience additional benefit. Take Oracle, for example: the eponymous database is so widely used that there are plenty of engineers with Oracle skills. Choosing an Oracle database ensures that a company can hire from a large pool and will be able to save on training new staff.

When products become as widely used as Microsoft Windows or Office, it becomes expensive to choose another product. This is one reason why, despite its being free, few companies use OpenOffice on Linux.

Economists call this phenomenon *network effects*: the more people and companies choose to use Microsoft Word on Windows, the cheaper it becomes for the next decision-maker to make the same choice. (*Metcalf's Law* is one example of network effects applied to communications.)

Network effects are a fact of life for many ISVs. For a market-leading ISV the network effects can be a powerful ally in making sales. For a challenger, even one with a new product, they represent a significant hurdle.

But network effects are all but absent from the ESP world. Because each product is custom-built, no network effects occur. While ISVs can use network effects to cut out competitors, ESPs cannot. If however an ESP can develop a product, it may harness network effects to support its position and lock out competitors.

Network effects may occur when a product is only part of the total solution. An SAP business suite is never deployed without substantial services support – provided by SAP itself or by third parties. As market leader SAP is not without competitors, but new entrants to the business applications domain would find it hard to challenge SAP, in part because of network effects. Companies wishing to compete in the business application domain might be best advised to work with SAP using patterns such as VALUE ADDED RESELLER (page 203) and COMPLEMENTOR, NOT COMPETITOR (page 309).

Crossover

ESPs may borrow the clothes of ISVs without actually creating products by using PACKAGED SERVICES (page 276), but many go further and create products to supplement their offering. Meanwhile, many ISVs add services to their product line-up. Indeed, it sometimes seems that every ISV really wants to be an ESP, and vice versa, as shown in Figure 47.

Not infrequently ESPs attempt to develop products to supplement, or replace, their services line-up. Often this occurs when an ESP finds it is repeatedly implementing similar solutions for different customers: in response, the ESP embarks on a programme to write a generic product.

This scenario is common enough to warrant a pattern; however, this book does not contain such a pattern. The problem is that, while the strategy is much talked about and frequently attempted, there is no clear and repeatable recipe for success. The discussion that follows outlines some of the forces that make this problem difficult and suggests some approaches.

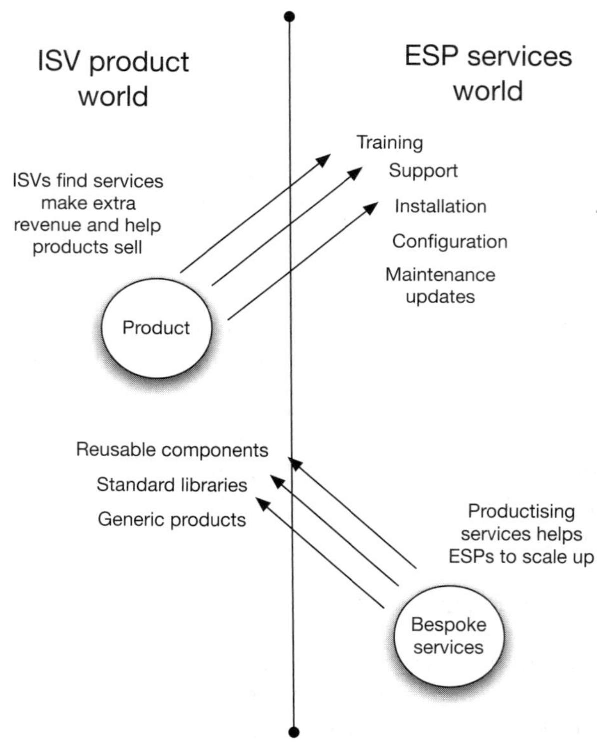

Figure 47. ISVs add services and ESPs add products

For some ISVs this is simply a revenue-chasing exercises. Once a product has been sold to a customer, contacts have been made and a business relationship is in place, so subsequently selling services should be easier. Such follow-on sales are an example of SAME CUSTOMERS, DIFFERENT PRODUCT (page 105). Selling a consultant to support the product can be a quick way of generating revenue – or at least quicker than creating a new product.

At other ISVs selling services is more than just selling more. Selling services is part of a bigger strategy in line with WHOLE PRODUCT (page 131). Rather than sell a product to a customer, the ISV aims to sell an entire solution. The solution includes the product and the expertise to operate and support use of the product.

Selling services is very different from selling products, because selling more services requires more people. Scaling up from selling ten copies of a product to 100 is relatively easy compared with scaling a services business. Selling 100 consultants rather than ten consultants means that 90 people need to be found, recruited, paid and managed. Both economically and culturally, services businesses are very different from product businesses. Expanding from products into services, or vice versa, brings numerous issues.

An ESP is usually motivated to add 'products' by the promise of a *common product* – one product that can be sold to multiple customers. Sometimes this is driven from the business side – the opportunity to reduce costs while simultaneously shortening the delivery cycle – and sometimes from the engineering side – the opportunity to stop 'reinventing the wheel' and to create 'reusable code' rather then writing the same solution for yet another customer. However, moving from ESP to ISV entails a lot more than simply creating another version of a recurring product. Both the business and the engineering sides need to understand the opportunity and challenges, and agree a shared approach.

While there are cases of organisations that have made this transition, there is no as yet identified pattern for making the transition successfully. Such a pattern would most probably be named PRODUCT FROM SERVICES; however, there is no such pattern. *The Missing Pattern: Product from Services* on page 225 describes some of the issues in more depth.

Accenture and Navitaire

Navitaire illustrates one solution to the provision of software products within a services company. Accenture is one of best known professional services companies in the world. Much of this activity is centred on IT. The company develops systems for clients in classic ESP fashion; it will also run IT systems and entire business processes for clients.

In the airline industry there are clear cases where Accenture could provide services or products. Rather than combine the two distinct types of software activity in one company, Accenture has chosen to develop products for the airline industry within a subsidiary, Navitaire. These products include reservation, yield management and operations support systems.

Placing product development in a separate entity allows one company to focus on providing services and the other on providing products. Naturally there will be opportunities for the two to work together with some clients, and probably there is some tension at times.

The Missing Pattern: Product from Services

Many ESPs have developed products for customers and later seen an opportunity to create a generic version of the software to sell to other customers. In the case of an ESP that specialises in a particular domain, this instinct can be very strong. For example, an ESP that specialises in the development of warehouse automation systems will, after developing several such systems, start to consider the development of a common system.

Thus, the problem is: *how does an ESP organise its activities to become an ISV?*

There are a number of forces that make this change difficult:

- *Different revenue models.* ESPs generally receive payment shortly after delivery; in some cases they may receive part payment in advance, or as the system is developed. In either case the payment terms and promise to pay are enshrined in a contract. If necessary the ESP can use this contract to obtain short-term funding.

  In contrast, ISVs develop products speculatively and over a longer period. There the risk appetite and profile is different. Loan funding is rare; instead, companies receive funding from investors who share the risks.
- *Higher costs.* Developing software products can easily be more expensive than developing bespoke software. For a start, ESPs often base their staff on customer sites, while ISVs must house staff in their own offices. When developing for a specific customer, an ESP knows the software will be deployed into a controlled environment, one that they may even specify up front. An ISV, on the other hand, needs to ensure that their software works across a range of operating systems and environments.
- *Testing.* Some ESPs frequently utilise customers as testing staff, either towards the end of development or throughout the process. This option is not generally available to ISVs, who not only must employ their own testing staff, but will

need to test a wider range of environments, and possibly deliver a higher level of quality than an ESP.

- *Intellectual property rights.* ESP customers often assume all rights to the intellectual property (IP), specifically source code, after a product's development. While the ESP retains knowledge in the heads of its engineers, it must usually start each new development from scratch. ISVs own all the IP they create and seek patent opportunities to protect novel ideas.
- *Sales, marketing and customers.* Simply extrapolating requirements, budgets and sales techniques from the current customers may well be a mistake.

  Developing a generic product may well address a different type of customer. Customers who have the money and understanding to commission a bespoke software package might do so because they see unique competitive advantage in it. They may see little benefit in buying the same software as everyone else – indeed, they may not look favourably on a supplier who introduces a generic product. Conversely, potential customers for the generic product will not have the same budget as their richer competitors; they are unlikely too to have the same requirements and expectations.

  In either case inbound marketing must identify the correct market, outbound marketing must address a different customer segment, and sales staff must change accordingly.
- *Change from customer to market; from business analysis to product management.* As discussed in *The ISV / ESP Divide* on page 27, ISVs and ESPs employ different roles to determine what customers need. Both the business analyst (typically employed by ESPs) and product managers (typically employed by ISVs) are concerned with understanding what customers need and how they will utilise the product. One of the most important differences in how these roles operate is how they go about answering these questions.

  Business analysts concern themselves typically with users or customers who are from the same organisation. While there may be multiple users within a single customer organisation, they have needs based on how the one organisation works.

  In contrast, product managers look across a market at multiple users in multiple customer organisations. Their role is to find the commonality between these diverse users and identify the special cases.

  For a company moving from bespoke development to generic product development, there is more to this transition than just retraining business analysts as product mangers: a cultural shift must also occur.
- *Prioritisation.* In an organisation that is developing both bespoke and common software there is conflict over setting priorities and allocating resources. ESP projects tend to have hard deadlines agreed with customers

and payments may well be tied to these deadlines. Conversely, generic products are speculative and will only deliver revenue when finished and sold. Therefore, when allocating resources from a fixed base, client-specific projects have more leverage than generic products. When a client-specific project encounters problems, there is a great temptation to take resources from a generic product development that is not yet delivering revenue.

This is not an exhaustive list of forces that trouble an ESP attempting to become an ISV. The technological differences are relatively easy to spot; the economic differences are usually more complex than most realise, but it is the cultural differences that cause the real problems.

Unlike the other patterns in this book, the solution suggested here has little qualitative evidence to back it up. Thus the suggestions made here are speculative: keep the ESP operating as is and create a separate ISV entity to pursue the opportunity.

The new organisation may take some people, resources and funding from the ESP, but should also seek people and resources experienced in developing products in the ISV model. Additional funding from external sources such as venture capital funds can also help to advise management about how to enter a new market.

If the ESP decides not to set up a separate entity, it should ensure resources – money and people – are ring-fenced from the bespoke activities, perhaps using SEPARATE IMAGINATIVE TEAMS (page 318). The new entity should not seen as a temporary *skunkworks* organisation, it should be created as a permanent unit dedicated to products.

The ESP should seek to supplement existing staff with new hires who have an ISV background. This is particularly important when product managers are considered: business analysts moving to product manager roles should receive addition training in the product manager role.

One of the changes that needs to occur within the ESP planning to become an ISV is to shift from a customer focus to a market focus. Rather than considering one customer, there is a need to consider many potential customers. Initially it may be a mistake to make use of POACHER TURNED GAMEKEEPER (page 91), because the new gamekeeper may bring an excessive focus on one customer.

The question of intellectual property provides another motivation for separating the new product development from the bespoke development. If an ESP customer could show that their IP was included in a new product, the whole development might be endangered. Better still, an ESP may seek to engage an existing customer as a partner: the customer may be prepared to license IP in return for some of the new product revenue. (Assuming of course that the customer does not consider the IP to be the source of competitive advantage.)

Alternatively, the new product group may use CUSTOMER CO-CREATED PRODUCT (page 95) to help guide the development while retaining the IP. Again, care needs to be taken to remember that the partner is not the only customer.

Transforming an ESP into an ISV is a major undertaking and one not without risks. The cultural differences between ESP and ISVs are far greater than is commonly recognised. This is not to imply that one is 'better' than the other, only that each is adapted to its own environment.

Ball Group

Ball Group UK (a pseudonym) sold software to manage investment banks' treasury operations. The company had little capital and found the revenue from selling consultancy services useful.

After a while the company had more consultants than developers and made more revenue from selling services than product. The product was sold cheaply (possibly at a loss) to open the way to consultancy sales.

Like other ISVs, Ball Group sold a product, it sold training for the product, most customers bought a support contract, and while some paid for bug fixes, others bought maintenance contracts. But most of all Ball Group sold consultants to install the product, integrate the product and even operate the product for customers.

One bank had an entire team of Ball Group consultants effectively running the department that used the product. They took over many of the bank's own functions beyond simply working with the product.

The incentive for Ball Group was to cut corners in product development: spending less on quality and documentation made customers more dependent on consultancy services. This was good for the company – lower costs and higher revenues – but it was not so good for customers.

For a while Ball Group flourished and grew, staff numbers increased and new product development began. However problems were lurking. It was difficult to tell where the true core competencies in the company was, or what it was that the customers actually valued. In time the company undercut its own capabilities, and after several rounds of redundancies the company was acquired.

While Ball Group's product added value to the customer's operations, the subsequent services did not; work was merely displaced from pre-sale to post-sale. The need to buy services detracted from value of the product.

Customers were paying twice: once for the product, and again for consultants and fixes. The customers were paying consultancy fees for work which should have been done before the product was delivered. In a shared risk model such as a research project, this might have been acceptable, but customers were not exposed to any of the benefits.

Nor did this model benefit the product. The only work that occurred was to address the immediate problems or to implement customer-requested features that blocked sales. Meanwhile competitors were developing products with a longer-term view.

Tailored Products – 'Specials'

Independent software vendors make their money by building a generic product and selling it to multiple customers. The generic product is designed and built to meet the needs of multiple customers – it is not specific to any one customer. This is what makes ISVs different from bespoke ESPs, which build one product for one customer. (Customer specials are also discussed in Chapter 6.)

But it is not uncommon for ISVs to be asked to tailor a product to the needs of a specific customer. When the ISV accepts such a request – usually for a good fee – the ISV takes on a position closer to that of an ESP: creating a specific product for a specific customer. On the face of it, the ISV has a good deal: a client is paying them to develop functionality they would probably develop anyway, and they get to resell it to others. However in accepting the deal, the ISV places itself in a culturally conflicted position.

For a start, ISVs normally lack the client management skills found at ESPs. ISV culture may initially make the client managers laugh – developers wearing jeans and T-shirts, working unusual hours and playing ping-pong – but the same culture will create tensions when schedules are missed or conflicts arise.

While it might seem that what the client wants for the product and what the ISV wants for the product are aligned, there will almost inevitably be conflicts, both in the functional and non-functional demands. Many conflicts are possible: for example, clients might not share the same quality standards as the ISV, or their desire to get a product sooner may conflict with the ISV's goal of creating a generic product.

There are three questions ISVs need to consider before accepting requests for 'specials'.

Firstly, *will the client allow the ISV to retain all intellectual property associated with the special version?* Unless the ISV can retain the rights to all the work undertaken as part of the customisation project, the question of whether the work is generic or not does not even need to be asked. If the ISV does not retain all the rights they cannot sell the product again, whether they want to or not.

Secondly, *is the request genuinely specific to this client, or is it generic?* If the request is shared by other (potential) customers, and the ISV can retain the intellectual property, then the work might fall under CUSTOMER CO-CREATED PRODUCT (page 95). In this case, the customer requesting the work is a lead customer who will help the ISV create a better product.

Before accepting that the need is genuinely shared by others, the ISV needs to validate whether other customers have similar requirements. If the ISV is lucky, the requested work might already appear on the product roadmap: the customer special request merely brings the scheduled date forward.

A word of warning is required: customers requesting special versions are often prepared to pay good money for them. The salesperson bringing in such a deal – most likely with a suitable reward – will claim, and claim again, that such a customer request is generic. To a salesperson faced with a sale, every customer is generic, every request reasonable and the next sale always the most important one.

It is not enough to rely on a salesman's, or sales team's, view that a customer-specific request is common to all customers: product managers need to independently validate the claim. The characteristics that make salesmen good – focus on individual customers, drive to close a deal – will also lead them to overstate additional benefits in order to make the next sale.

In *Crossing the Chasm* (Moore, 1999), Geoffrey Moore advises start-up companies to avoid special work for specific customers. Agreeing to customisation work means that the product becomes driven by what will sell to individual customers rather than the market as a whole. As a result the company is always chasing the revenue from the next deal rather than producing a product that will sell to many more customers in a wider market. In such circumstances product roadmaps are constantly changing and generic features are rarely delivered.

This is the difference between being sales-driven and being market-driven. Sales-driven companies are always focused on the next sale and the next customer; market-driven companies focus on a bigger target. Paradoxically, though, the bigger target can be harder to hit, because it is less clearly defined and is subject to interpretation.

Cagan (2008) also advises against ISVs accepting customer requests for 'specials'. Cagan warns against specials on the grounds that they are diversionary; they will disrupt the product roadmap and divert resources away from developing the product many customers want in favour of the product one customer wants.

Creating a special version means resources (developers, testers and so on) will need to be taken off other work, which will disrupt delivery of the product roadmap. Even bringing in extra temporary (contract) developers does not solve this problem, because they will require time from the existing developers. Brook's Law implies that the overall pace of development will slow (Brooks, 1986).

Not only will the special disrupt roadmap delivery in the short term; it will have a long-lasting effect on the code base. However the special is integrated into the code base will complicate it, hindering future development.

If the company undertakes multiple special versions of the same product, it can cause a combinatory explosion in the code base, making future maintenance and enhancement far more difficult. Developers find they need to reason about, not one or two execution paths and contexts, but three, four and more. Testing becomes more difficult, because the generic product *and* each special need to be tested. Then there are issues of the interplay between different customisations, which may conflict.

For a start-up, ISV specials represent a particular challenge. Start-ups, more than other companies, need the money on offer, so are more likely to accept a deal that involves a 'special'. But start-ups are locked in a race to bring their world-changing product to market before their competitors and before the market opportunity passes. Taking a diversion to create a special product loses precious time. And by complicating their code base with customer-specific code, they increase their maintenance burden and impair future work. However, it needs to be remembered that developing customer-specific products is a valid business strategy and one that many companies will decide to pursue.

Thus the third question any ISV should ask themselves before accepting a client 'special' request is: *are the company and product structured to undertake customer specials?*

Because of Conway's Law the two parts of this question are intrinsically linked: product and system design are reflections of one another (Conway, 1968). Answering 'yes' to this question does not come about by chance. If a company wants to seek out and undertake specialisation, it needs to position and prepare itself for such work.

ISVs do not find themselves successfully undertaking customisation projects by chance: it needs to be part of their strategy. Unless the company is expecting and seeking out customisation opportunities, it will not be organised and staffed to undertake such projects. To undertake such work, the ISV needs to have the skills and resources available, and managers need to understand the bespoke/generic trade-offs that will need to be made.

Products that are designed for customisation will fair much better than those that have customisations hacked into them: configuration options, plug-ins, APIs, scripting options and so on will all help products accept customisation more easily. The key to success is to have a product that is open to customisation, as described in CUSTOMISABLE PRODUCT (page 115).

To extend this debate further, the move to software as a service (SaaS) further complicates this picture. When individual clients had their own installations of software, it was possible for two customers to have two different special versions of the same product. This complicated development and testing but each version could exist in isolation.

When software products are supplied as a service, multiple customers will be using the same installed version of the software – perhaps just one version. Thus special code must not only be developed and tested, but must coexist at execution time. This further increases the complexity involved with development and testing.

Special requests – product management failure?

Company N regularly had requests for special versions of their product with particular features. This arose because the product management function was poorly understood by senior managers and consequently understaffed. As a result salesmen returned from customer visits with shopping lists of features: "If we can add X, Y and Z then the Norwegians will buy".

This could work well when the features could be implemented generically for all customers. In effect the sales team were acting as product managers. It could also work terribly: no clear understanding of what was needed, constantly changing priorities, no direction for the development team, poor prioritisation and impossible schedules dictated by sales targets.

If customisation requests are arriving regularly and it is not the ISV's stated strategy to seek out such requests, then questions need to be asked about the effectiveness of the product management. It is the product manager's job to understand what 'the market' – the broad section of potential customers – wants from the product and to build a roadmap to deliver such products.

By understanding individual customers and the overall market, product managers try to look into the future and determine what software products need to in order to be useful. As such, product managers should be one or more steps ahead of customers and see special requests coming before they are requested.

If customers are asking regularly for special requests that are shared by multiple customers, it may be a sign that product management is not effective.

Customise or Co-create?

The questions that need to be asked when deciding between CUSTOMISABLE PRODUCT (page 115) and CUSTOMER CO-CREATED PRODUCT (page 95) are shown in Figure 48. Between these two patterns there is a large grey area of less desirable options.

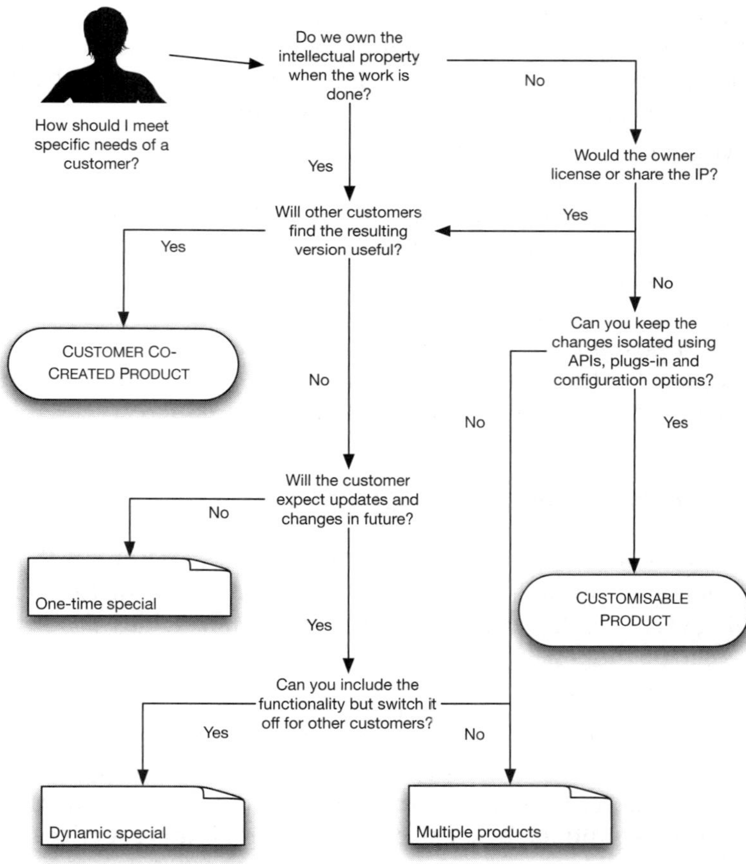

Figure 48. Options for handling a special

Three of these options are shown in the diagram:

- *One-time special.* The special version for the customer is truly a one-time special version. You can branch the source code, produce the special and then return to the point you were at before. But issuing any updates (or fixes) for the release is expensive because it is a separate product. Work has to be duplicated and tests repeated. Meanwhile, the customer has cut itself off from future upgrade deals.

- *Dynamic special.* Maintain a single product (and source base) by allowing the special functionality to be switched on and off. This makes testing more difficult, so it takes longer (each switch needs to be tested on and off) and thus more expensive. After only a few special versions there is a combinatorial explosion, and before long the specials start to require conflicting changes.
- *Multiple products.* Changes required spill out all over the product but cannot be included in the mainstream product, so there are two products. You will need to maintain multiple products: one generic and others specific. This is expensive: resource intensive and test intensive.

  With a suitable architect this approach can be sustainable, provided careful attention is paid to common code and special code. Given enough time, and proper architecture, this approach is likely to look like CUSTOMISABLE PRODUCT (page 115). However, if attention is not paid to the architecture, the result will come to resemble a BIG BALL OF MUD (Foote & Yoder, 1999a).

None of these options completely resolves the forces at work. If the company is not in a position to do a deal based on CUSTOMISABLE PRODUCT (page 115) or CUSTOMER CO-CREATED PRODUCT (page 95), then it may be better to walk away from any deal involving delivery of a special product.

When Services Distract from Product

Unfortunately there is a potential problem for organisations that offer services to supplement a product, and their customers. When companies earn revenue from selling services, they can be deterred from undertaking product improvements. This can be thought of as a dysfunctional version of the pattern LIFETIME SERVICES FOR PRODUCTS (page 252).

For example, the case of Ball Group (page 228) describes a real example of a company that earned most of its revenue from the provision of services after a product was sold. In at least one case the development team were told not to improve the product, because doing so would impact services revenue.

Other less extreme cases exist, for example when customers buy maintenance contracts to receive bug fixes. Were the software maker to produce bug-free software, the maintenance revenue might dry up and opportunities for the company to show how responsive it is disappear – see *Peter's story* on page 236.

Whether such positions are sustainable in the long run is doubtful. Certainly any company that deliberately hinders product development makes itself vulnerable to competitors. However, this assumes that competitors exist and are not pursuing the same strategy themselves.

Table 6 summarises the four positions that are possible. In the long run only selling both product and services at a profit is truly sustainable. In the short run one or other may be sold at a loss, provided the other makes enough profit to cover the cost of both. However, this embeds conflict in the business model, because one element is subsidising the other, and thus creates opportunities for competitors.

Table 6: Source of profits determines incentives when using LIFETIME SERVICES FOR PRODUCTS

	Services sold at a profit	*Services sold at or below cost*
Product sold at profit	1. Good position for seller – be careful not to overcharge the customers, or they may find an alternative supplier. (LIFETIME SERVICES FOR PRODUCTS (page 252) is being used.)	2. Only sustainable in the short run; incentive for suppliers to create a product that does not need service, so this is good for the buyer.
Product sold at or below cost	3. Sustainable if both sides understand the model and incentives are aligned. (LIFETIME SERVICES FOR PRODUCTS is being used.)	4. Not sustainable. If you can't make money for either product or service sales, you should quit the market.

Selling the product at or below cost, and selling services at a profit (quadrant 3) is only sustainable if both sides agree to this model and the implied trade-offs. For example, if Software Co. agrees to delivers an application to Mega Corp at a fixed price, but charges for each bug fix, then it will be in Software Co's interests to deliver a low-quality product and make profits on bug fixes.

If on the other hand Software Co. agrees to a fixed-price sale with a fixed annual service fee, it will be in their interests to deliver a high-quality product to start with, ensuring that ongoing service costs are minimised. Of course Software Co. may still deliver a low-quality product, and in the short term this may save them money, but in a long term this is not in their interests.

One potential variation is to offer bug fixes and updates for free by way of a *total quality guarantee*. A software company may charge a premium price for their high-quality product and make fixes available free of charge – effectively selling at a loss. Provided that the company really can maintain high quality and thus justify a high initial price while minimising rework, then quadrant 2 of Table 6 may prove competitive and sustainable.

The economics of software development mean that a total quality guarantee might not be the fast route to bankruptcy that many might automatically assume – although it might well be. According to Jones (Jones, 2008), bug-fixing is the second most expensive activity undertaken in software development – only documentation is more expensive. Thus a company that can maintain high quality may find that it can charge a premium price, keep costs low, quality high and customers satisfied. Conversely, for a company that cannot maintain high quality, a total quality guarantee and free bug fixes could be a fast route to bankruptcy.

Implemented badly, LIFETIME SERVICES FOR PRODUCTS can be a lose-lose situation. The supplier can ship inadequate product, knowing that they can hide the defects behind their service contracts. Over time these contracts and the product will become more expensive. The customer loses, because they get an inferior product and an increased total cost. Eventually, they will change supplier.

This is not to damn all attempts to support products with services. When implemented well, LIFETIME SERVICES FOR PRODUCTS can be a win-win tactic for both supplier and customer. The supplier wins because they get to increase their revenues and learn more about the whole product lifecycle, which in turn allows them to improve the product.

The customer also wins, because they get a complete solution and better value for money from their supplier and service organisation. Over time they get an improved product, because the supplier is able to use what they have learned in servicing the product to improve the original product, and improvements to the product should bring down the cost of services.

Peter's story

Today Itopia is an IT consulting company based in Switzerland, but it used to have a software development group. This group created Internet server applications based on a software application framework that companies licensed; they usually also signed a maintenance agreement for their applications and the framework. In return for an annual fee the customers received software updates and support. Itopia's developers were reluctant to change known problems with the framework, because such changes increased the chances of breaking released applications.

In 1998 Peter saw Kent Beck and Erich Gamma demonstrate *Test-First Programming* with JUnit, and realised that if their framework and the applications based on it had a set of tests, changes would be far easier. While quality was already taken seriously, adding automated unit testing would make it better still. The safety net of a good test suite also helped with the release of newer framework versions without the high risk of breaking too many existing applications, again increasing the underlying quality.

If a company increases quality, what do we expect to happen? If we believe the research of IBM and Capers Jones (Jones, 2008), better quality (fewer bugs) will lead to shorter development schedules, lower costs and more satisfied customers. One might expect more satisfied customers to buy more products, so revenue goes up while costs come down.

Technically 'test-first' was a success: the product quality started to improve and customers were happier. But because customers were not contacting the company about quality issues, there was less contact with customers. The company had fewer occasions to demonstrate how responsive it was, and in time customers stopped renewing maintenance contracts, so revenues fell.

Perhaps this shouldn't have been such a surprise. Similar phenomena have been seen in companies that adopt *lean production* and then see sales fall. When a company adopts lean production, quality increases, so customers need to buy less, because they know that less of the product they buy will be faulty.

Lean companies supply on a just-in-time basis, so once customers see the supplier delivery schedules improve, they know products will arrive on time. Consequently they can run down or dispense with any buffer stocks they may hold. While this is happening they may not need to buy any products at all from the newly lean company (Cooper & Maskell, 2008). Lean operations reduce sales and cash flow in the short run.

Many software development companies depend on revenue from customers buying bug fixes. Few other industries would tolerate such a business model, so it is debatable whether it has a long-term future. Itopia chose to leave software development and focus on consulting, but what other paths could it have chosen?

The obvious option is not to change: keep customers buying bug fixes. But by not changing the company would open an opportunity for another company using these techniques to produce a better competitor product.

Itopia could have changed its charging model, perhaps by moving to a licensing model in which customers re-license the software every year. For software that can be sold as an online service this works well, but for application frameworks it would be more difficult.

Alternatively the company could diversify away from their application framework product. SAME CUSTOMERS, DIFFERENT PRODUCT (page 105) would suggest that the company look at its customer base to see what other products customers would be interested in buying. It would then use INNOVATIVE PRODUCTS (page 313) to help develop a PRODUCT PORTFOLIO (page 296). Alternatively, it might adopt a VALUE ADDED RESELLER (page 203) stance and sell other company's products to its customer base.

Closing Words

Companies in the technology sector and elsewhere have expanded from products into services. Less often recognised, and perhaps often less successful commercially, is the tendency for service companies to adopt product strategies.

Combining service offerings and products in the same company inevitably leads to conflicts and tensions. To the engineering mind it might be preferable to keep the two separate, but this is seldom possible. Indeed, increasingly the new innovations combine elements of products and services; consider Apple's iPad and AppStore, or Google's Android OS and online services.

Companies that straddle the product/services divide can succeed while bring better products and services to their customers. Certainly companies attempting a WHOLE PRODUCT (page 131) strategy need to pursue both activities.

However, there is more to making software products than most services companies realise, and more to delivering services than most product companies realise. In this middle ground there are business models that look as if they work, and may even deliver several years of profit and growth, but which are not sustainable in the long run.

12 Patterns about Services

For an ISV, achieving the right balance between products and service is an ongoing debate. While services can offer a lucrative addition to work, they can also prove a distraction. Yet without services there are sales that cannot be made and opportunities that cannot be exploited.

ISVs are, by definition, not primarily service providers, but they must include services in their offering to be truly successful. Problems occur when an ISV does not understand why it is providing services, or how they should be provided. ISVs need to borrow techniques from ESPs, but adopting too much of the service model will turn them into ESPs. In some cases this might be a good thing and desirable, but to drift from ISV to ESP without a coherent strategy will create conflicts and problems.

The pattern sequence in Figure 49 starts with the company recognising the need to sell services in tandem with products. At first the company applies INITIAL HELP (page 248) to help new customers use their products. Over time the company continues to support customers by using LIFETIME SERVICES FOR PRODUCTS (page 252).

Later the established company faces a number of opportunities, some of which are complementary and others mutually exclusive. The company may decide to change the nature of its products business, or it might decide that the supply of services is a more lucrative endeavour and adopt COMPLEMENTOR, NOT COMPETITOR (page 309). Whether moving to a service-only model or continuing to supply products, the company may also adopt a PACKAGED SERVICES (page 276) model to

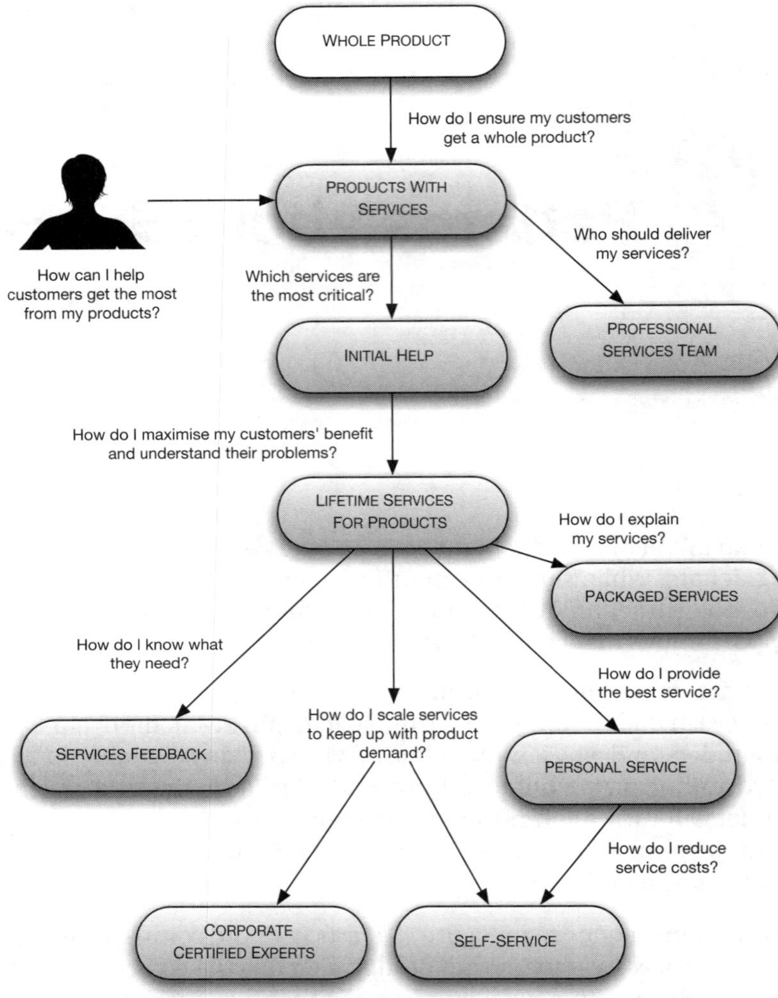

Figure 49. A pattern sequence for services patterns

simplify the sale and delivery of service offerings. When services are offered to supplement a product, their role changes over time. Recognising this change will help organise and structure the services provided.

Whether pursing the services model or not, the company may decide to leverage its existing customer base by using SAME CUSTOMERS, DIFFERENT PRODUCT (page 105). To implement this pattern, ACCOUNT MANAGEMENT (page 187) can be used. However, since active customer management is a time-consuming business, the company may also adopt SALES/TECHNICAL DOUBLE ACT (page 192) to spread the work.

Successful products will increase the demand for associated services. This can present problems when growing the company to meet the new demand. Alternatively the company may decide to apply SELF-SERVICE (page 268) and CORPORATE CERTIFIED EXPERTS (page 272) to reduce the demand on its service offerings. By certifying outside providers, the company can both grow its own ecosystem and offload some of the services work.

The company may apply SEGMENTED CUSTOMERS (page 141) to differentiate between customers. Strategic customers may be offered the highest-quality service (using PERSONAL SERVICE, page 265) while SELF-SERVICE is used for less critical customers. A similar segmentation strategy may be used in services for consumer and business customers.

PRODUCTS WITH SERVICES

Figure 50. Online gaming services are an intrinsic part of modern game consoles

---

Customers expect to have a help desk to call, and they increasingly expect to receive updates and bug fixes long after they buy a product. Yet services can be about much more then just keeping a product working. Traditionally services existed to support a product – they might only be invoked when things went wrong. Services associated with today's products increasingly extend the product itself.

XBox and PlayStation gamers expect to be able to play against competitors in far-away places. That requires a service as well as a product, and it gives the supplier a chance to keep on earning money long after the initial purchase.

Context You produce a technically advanced product and aim to solve customer's problems as completely as possible.

Problem *How do you help your customers get the maximum benefit from your products?*

Forces Technically advanced products often solve many customer problems, but also bring problems of their own: software contains bugs, manuals need to be read, customers require training, installation is hard, software needs updating.

Customers may have bought your product, but they are not using it to the full. Some users may be unaware of valuable features; others may have encountered problems on first use and not tried again.

You want to increase your revenue and reduce your dependence on one-off sales events. But once a customer has your product you have nothing more to sell them. It takes time to bring new products to market and competitors are always trying to displace your gains. Product sales are inherently transaction-based: you deliver a product and the customer pays. Selling upgrades, additional copies and different products can enhance the product sale, but it is still a one-time transaction.

Solution *Supplement your product with services. Start with basic services like technical support and training; later you can expand this with additional services. Good services complement the product and enhance the ownership experience. In the best cases it is hard to tell where the product ends and services begin.*

Services may help your customers use your product (for example, support services and training), services may extend the product's usefulness (for example, Apple's iTunes complements their iPod), or services may supplant the product as the unit of sale, with the product becoming your way of meeting a customer's need (for example, Bharti Airtel buys wireless minutes from Ericsson's services arm, not wireless network equipment).

There is a vast range of services that can be provided to supplement a product; providing the right services can produce a win-win situation: your customers are happier and you improve your revenue.

Table 7 lists some of the services provided to customers. Those at the top of the table usually involve some additional charges, while those lower down the table may be provided free, albeit for a limited period.

Table 7: Some of the types of service provided to customers

Service	Description	Example
Product as service	Rather than sell the product, the producer sells a service that utilises the product. The producer undertakes operation and maintenance of the product to guarantee a level of service.	Aero-engine makers such as Rolls-Royce and General Electric lease and maintain engines on a 'per hour of thrust' basis.

Table 7: Some of the types of service provided to customers (continued)

Service	Description	Example
Remote functionality	The total product consists of two (or more) parts: a product the customer owns works with a service to deliver the overall functionality.	Computer backup agents monitor data changes and send changes to online storage.
Complementary service	A service extends the functionality and usability of the product. Service and product can be used separately or together.	Apple's iTunes complements the iPod, making music easier to purchase and collect.
Installation services	Services that help customers install a product, customise it, configure it and connect it to the environment.	Long common for enterprise software, companies such as Best Buys and Carphone Warehouse offer installation services for consumer electronics.
Training	New customers are provided with courses in how to use a product. May be a legal requirement for some products.	Widely used in the enterprise software market. Driving lessons are normally required to pass a driving test before one can drive a car.
Product update	Customers receive updated version of a product they have purchased.	Antivirus software can be updated automatically multiple times a week.
Support desk	Provides customers with assistance on how to use the product or to resolve technical issues.	Most software companies provide a support desk. Traditionally this has been a telephone helpline, but increasingly online forums are being used.

Do some analysis before rushing to complicate your offering with services. It may be that a better understanding of the problem domain may result in a better design, with consequently less need for services. If your competitors market a complicated product with services, you may gain the advantage on them by offering a simpler product without services.

In the technology sector even pure product companies will find the need to provide basic technical support for their products. This may be offered free of charge for an introductory period, say the first year, after which customers may be expected to pay either a fixed sum – perhaps 10% of list price – or on a pay-per-call basis.

Products are normally sold for a lump sum payment; this typically includes some limited services, such as 60 days of help desk calls. Additional services, or ongoing services, are normally sold on a subscription basis.

There are many variations on this model: for example, mobile phone operators often give away handsets (products) and recoup the cost on subscription charges. Nokia's *Comes with Music* phones offered the reverse model: the more expensive phones came with 'as much as you can eat' music downloads.

Consequences

Resolving customer problems will allow you to increases usage of your product and deliver more value. Increasing the product's value to the customer will increase the chances of further orders.

Sending trainers and consultants to visit customers will allow you to identify and fix problems with product usage. This might be as simple as helping a user with a difficult action, or it might involve simplifying features in a future release.

Services are inherently relationship-based. The relationship continues through the exchange of service and money. Services provide for regular, repeatable earnings. Industry analysts may regard service-based cash flow as of better quality than product-based cash flow, because it is more predictable and long-lasting, with the result that your company is given a higher valuation.

Charges for services provide an alternative revenue stream. However, services can be expensive to provide: support desks must be staffed, even when there are no calls. A low-quality product may result in more calls and thus more expense.

For a company that considers its core competence to be creating technical products, it may be hard to justify services and to position them in the organisation. Services run against the culture of companies that have been built on products. You will need to explain why the company needs to engage in services, and bring in experience from elsewhere to help with the change.

Providing services might mask problems with your product. Sometimes products are complex out of necessity; for example, the problems they address may be complex, so adding a service element is beneficial. On the other hand, products may be unnecessarily complex. This creates a 'make work' situation in which your own experts are needed to handle these complexities. Rather than selling customers additional services, a better solution is to simplify the product.

Variations If you are not able to provide the services yourself, you may choose to collaborate in partnership with an organisation that can provide all or some of the required services. You must ensure a feedback mechanism is in place so that you hear about customer problems and needs.

Related work The other patterns in this chapter, INITIAL HELP (page 248), LIFETIME SERVICES FOR PRODUCTS (page 252), PROFESSIONAL SERVICES TEAM (page 258) and SERVICES FEEDBACK (page 262), provide more discussion and advice on these topics.

As you supply more products and services to a customer, both parties become more dependent on each other: the customer on your products and services and you on their revenue. This provides the opportunity, indeed the need, to engage in ACCOUNT MANAGEMENT (page 187), so that both sides understand each other well. In doing so you will improve your CUSTOMER UNDERSTANDING (page 146) and find more opportunities to help them with products and services, which in turn will create greater revenue for your company.

Companies that are successful in offering services to supplement their products might in time find that the services side of the business is more profitable and has brighter prospects for growth. COMPLEMENTOR, NOT COMPETITOR (page 309) can help to deal with such scenarios.

Examples Most software companies offer a support desk for users. Increasingly this is a SELF-SERVICE (page 268) desk using online forums, FAQs and knowledge bases. Larger software products usually come with some automatic update system, and many ISVs that supply enterprise applications offer some training and other professional services to help customers.

Early customers of MP3 players, and the first versions of the iPod, had to transfer their music collection from CD to the device themselves, or use third-party (and possibly illegal) websites to download tunes. With the iTunes service, Apple simplified the process, guaranteed legality and created a new revenue source for itself.

Apple's iTunes store laid the foundations for the AppStore and, with the introduction of the iPad, the opening of many more retail opportunities for Apple in magazines, books, films and beyond.

INITIAL HELP

Figure 51. New users need first aid to get started with a product

Public domain image created by US National Parks Service

The author worked for an ISV that developed and sold software tools to mobile telephone operators. The product was very powerful and could be customised in a number of ways. Some of these customisations were simple and could be done by users; others required a high degree of product knowledge. The company provided professional services consultants who could tailor the product to customers' requirements and embed the product in the customers' methods of working. Providing consultants reduced the burden on the buyer to do this work and reduced the barriers to use.

Context You are an ISV selling a technically advanced product to other companies and following WHOLE PRODUCT (page 131). Your products need to be installed, integrated and configured.

Problem *How do you help customers get past initial barriers so that they can see the full value of your product?*

Forces Your business strategy is to make money from selling products. But customers find it hard to use your product out of the box.

The product is difficult to install and requires specialist knowledge to get it working, but once installed it provides worthwhile benefits. With an advanced product these difficulties are not the customers' alone: when customers are deterred from buying and using the product, they are the manufacturer's problem too.

Customers might have overcome some difficulties in getting the product up and running, but have still to realise the full potential of the product. Consequently the product looks overpriced, and it is hard to justify the price to new customers. Without training, customisation and integration, the product may be useless.

End users need training before they can use the product, but since the product is proprietary to your company few, if any, independent trainers are available to help.

To use a new product effectively and obtain maximum value, company processes may need to be modified and even organisational structures changed. But it can be hard to find experts who know what needs to be done when a new product is proprietary.

Solution

Provide professional services to help customers get started with the product. This includes training, integration, customisation and support for your product. Your staff may do all the work, or just assist customers in doing it themselves.

For a complicated product it is worth holding the customer's hand for a while. Your consultants can undertake the work that needs to be done, answer user's questions and advise on organisational and process changes needed.

Your support desk needs to be staffed and equipped to do more than just take bug reports. Even if they have training, new users will have questions about how to use the software and what to do when it doesn't work as they expect.

Training services can help users get more from your product. New users can be helped through the initial learning process; more experienced users can benefit from learning about new and advanced features. Work with your customers to understand their training needs and how you can best help.

When products are complex and frequently require configuration and customisation, it is worth forming a dedicated PROFESSIONAL SERVICES TEAM (page 258), rather than borrowing staff from internal functions. This is especially true when the product is a CUSTOMISABLE PRODUCT (page 115) with many means of configuration and customisation.

Customers should pay for the help they receive. You may choose to include the cost of these services as part of the purchase price to the customer, or bill them as extras. Either way, be sure you know how much the work is costing and how much revenue it is generating. Even when these services are essential, money needs to be apportioned between service work and product development so that it is clear where the costs are incurred.

The objective of these services is for the customer to be using your product in a sustained and beneficial manner. When customers no longer need routine help the engagement – this pattern – is complete. Services and help may continue as lifetime services, as described in LIFETIME SERVICES FOR PRODUCTS (page 252). Customers may not notice a difference between these two patterns, but the underlying motivation is different.

Consequences Your consultants can get customers over the initial hurdles of using your product. When a product is installed, integrated and customised to a specific environment, there will be a greater acceptance of the product. Customers are less likely to use a competitor's product and more likely to buy from you again.

By having your people work with the customer, and by tailoring your product to the customer's needs, you will create a closer relationship with the customer; this is good for both sides.

Providing consultants is not cheap; in addition, travel and accommodation costs are often incurred when working with customers. These costs must be covered somehow. If the costs are included in the product price, then the overall price will be higher. Alternatively, these costs may be billed separately, in which case the customer must be persuaded to pay them in addition to the product costs.

Customers may be put off by the costs of customisation and training. Products such as SAP are reputed to cost a lot in terms of time and money to install, customise and train users.

Variation This strategy can be the basis for a business that does not develop products itself, provided that they have an in-depth understanding of the product. For example, Open Source products can suffer from the same issues as commercial ones, but the developers may not want or be able to provide the necessary services to get new customers started.

Related work Selling services provides for a second revenue stream, but you should be clear where your competitive advantage lies. If your added value lies with the consultants rather than the product, it might be time to consider LIFETIME SERVICES FOR PRODUCTS (page 252) or COMPLEMENTOR, NOT COMPETITOR (page 309). Some companies become overly dependent on selling services rather than products without realising it.

Corporate Certified Experts (page 272) provides another route for solving this problem; it may be used in combination with or as an alternative to this pattern.

Secrets of Software Success (Hoch et al, 1999) also discusses these topics.

Examples

Smith Communications (a pseudonym) had one product, an advanced e-mail system. The company made its money from selling the product, but it needed to be integrated with a customer's other systems, such as database and accounts systems. So the company set up a professional services group that worked with customers directly to integrate the product.

Professional services were sold near cost; sales staff would even throw in several days of consultancy to sweeten a sale – consequently, the professional services group never made a profit. When the company hit financial trouble and layoffs were required, the professional services group was the first to be cut.

However, the product still needed to be installed and configured, so some of the staff found themselves hired back on *ad hoc* contracts.

LIFETIME SERVICES FOR PRODUCTS

Figure 52. Rolls-Royce aero engines are as likely to be leased as sold

Image from Rolls-Royce media resources

Rolls-Royce doesn't just design and build aero engines, it monitors them in flight and maintains them for the airlines that fly the planes.

Jack Welch (2001) tells how during the 1990s General Electric (GE) entered the service business in a big way. What had been thought of as 'after-sales service' became a major contributor to profits. At the start of the 1990s the company was already a leading maker of aircraft engines; by 2000 over 60% of engine revenue came from servicing such engines – both GE engines and those of competitors such as Rolls-Royce.

Context You are successful in your market and are looking for growth opportunities.

Your product has a long lifespan; the sale is only the beginning. Over its lifetime the product requires ongoing service and maintenance. These requirements go beyond INITIAL HELP (page 248).

Problem *How do you ensure that your customers get the best experience from your product and you grow your company at the same time?*

Forces You know a lot about the lifetime management of your products, but you consider yourself a designer and manufacturer. Indeed, you may be one of the leading designers or manufacturers, but that is where your responsibility ends; customers are expected to arrange and pay for ongoing service themselves.

In a competitive market you need to undercut your competitors to make a sale, but a low price may not be profitable. You have been concerned traditionally with the sale price of your product, but customers are, perhaps increasingly, concerned with the total cost of ownership over the lifetime of the product.

Customers understand that complex products need to be maintained, but they don't necessarily want to do this themselves. In fact, they may view such activities as distractions from their core business.

You are one of the leading companies in the market, but this means that growth opportunities are limited. Being number one in the market is great, but shareholders still expect growth.

Solution

Provide services to your customer over the lifetime of the product so that your objectives are mutually compatible. Your customers will get more from the product; you will get more work and more revenue. Use your product and industry knowledge to improve the customers' entire ownership experience and allow you to produce better products.

Sell the customer a complete solution that addresses the product, the ownership of the product and the reason they are buying the product. Taking a wider perspective on the consumer experience will provide new opportunities for innovation, revenue growth and improved customer satisfaction.

Customers continue to consume your product long after the sale is closed. As the developer and manufacturer of a complex product, you have specialist knowledge of the product. This knowledge can be used throughout the product's lifecycle to enhance ownership.

Having people on site with a customer provides good opportunities to understand what the customer wants from the product, how they use it and what features they need and value – SERVICES FEEDBACK (page 262). This can be of benefit to both supplier and customer.

Obviously you know your own products best, yet competing products will not be too dissimilar and these will also need to be serviced. You may choose to offer service work with these products too; this will increase the size of your market, provide a fuller service to customers and help you to understand the competition better.

Remember to balance your product development operations against your service operations. Product development generates little revenue by itself and costs are incurred long before revenue is generated.

In service operations the cash will arrive shortly after the service is performed. However, services continue to be delivered, so cash continues to arrive in the business. Managers must seek to smooth the flow of work in progress to ensure a steady flow of work and high utilisation of resources.

Your service operations should add value for the customer; it is no use shipping a low-quality product in the hope of charging for service to fix problems. Customers may feel stung if they receive a poor product and a hefty service bill. (*When Services Distract from Product* on page 234 discusses this issue too.) It is important to understand the incentives created on both sides by your sales model.

Gaining an ongoing revenue stream may allow you to reduce your sales price to gain a sale. It also means that your company's future income is in place and is less dependent on the next sale. Once you have a firm understanding of the work involved in supporting your product over its lifecycle, you can consider charging a combined price for product and service, or leasing the product with service included.

Competitors may still win the business if they can show that the total cost of ownership of your product is higher than the total cost of ownership of theirs. However, such figures are difficult to calculate and some customers may be prepared to pay a higher price overall if they can reduce their initial capital outlay.

Consequences The sale and INITIAL HELP (page 248) are only the start of a commercial relationship between buyer and seller. The initial revenues can be just a small part of the overall revenue stream. For such a product the ongoing service revenue, over a number of years, may be far greater than the initial sale price.

Considering the product's lifetime allows your objectives and the customer's to be aligned for mutual benefit. Buying your product solves one problem for the customer, but creates others. They now own a complex product that needs support and maintenance. As the seller you know this first and best; you can solve the customer's problem, make your product more attractive and generate a revenue stream for yourself.

In the software business scaling up a services business is different to scaling up a product business. Delivering more services means selling more consultants and service technicians, thus you need to hire more people. Delivering more software products means cutting more CDs or providing for more software downloads. To put it another way: the marginal costs of scaling services are far higher than the marginal costs of scaling software products.

Apportioning costs and benefits becomes very difficult – ultimately they start to blur. In the short term it may be more profitable to hold back on new features and quality improvements to reduce costs and boost fees. However, in the longer term this risks the product becoming dated and uncompetitive.

Opportunities are created by having design, production and maintenance within one organisation. This allows for SERVICES FEEDBACK (page 262) and better CUSTOMER UNDERSTANDING (page 146). For example, GE has designed software into its aero engines to provide additional information for maintenance services; increased development costs will be offset by reduced maintenance costs.

Variations

This pattern can be extended to competitors' products and Open Source products. Competitors' products are likely to have much in common with your own, so much of your knowledge is transferable. Of course you will not be able to improve the original product, but you can provide a one-stop shop to customers who use both your products and your competitors'.

If you choose to service competitor products in addition to your own products, you must respect your competitors' intellectual property rights. Incorporating competitors' innovations into your own products will violate intellectual property law. Using a PROFESSIONAL SERVICES TEAM (page 258) can help to keep confidential information away from those who should not see it, but reduce the benefit of sharing information.

Although described in business-to-business terms, this pattern is also be used in business-to-consumer markets: Apple's iTunes and AppStore provide lifetime services to iPod and iPhone buyers; McAfee, Symantec and others provide updates for antivirus software.

This pattern is itself a variation on the classic 'razor sales technique' – sell the razor cheaply and make the money on the blades. Other examples include games console manufacturers such as Sony and Nintendo, which make their money on the games, and printer manufactures like Hewlett Packard and Lexmark, which make money on ink cartridges. However, in the case of this pattern it is a knowledge-based service that is being sold rather than consumables.

Related work IT'S A RELATIONSHIP, NOT A SALE (Rising, 2002) advises us to look beyond the current transaction and consider the long-term relationship, during which there may be multiple sales.

INITIAL HELP (page 248) discusses the need to provide services to get a product installed and working correctly. LIFETIME SERVICES FOR PRODUCTS goes beyond this model and shows how ongoing services can be sold in addition to the initial product.

Examples The author has seen this pattern applied in both its functional and dysfunctional versions. The *Ball Group* example on page 228 illustrates a dysfunctional example of the pattern.

Microsoft, Adobe, SAP and others continue to support their software and issue updates long after a customer has bought the product. Sometimes these are free, sometimes customers need to pay a subscription for the services.

Services Trump Product?

When originally drafted these patterns included one called *Services Trump Product*. This pattern described the ultimate step for a product company after LIFETIME SERVICES FOR PRODUCTS (page 252) and COMPLEMENTOR, NOT COMPETITOR (page 309) – that of leaving the product business altogether and staking everything on services.

The pattern drew on the Lou Gerstner strategy for IBM (Gerstner, 2003). Under Gerstner's leadership IBM moved away from products and increased its service offerings through IBM Global Services. The strategy, continued by Gerstner's successors, has seen IBM become one of the biggest IT service providers in the world, with the Global Services division contributing more than half of total revenue.

However, the evidence that a strategy of switching from products to services is successful seems somewhat ambiguous. While IBM is indeed one of the biggest service providers, it retains a large products business, accounting for the remainder of its revenue. IBM Software ranks as one of the world's largest software providers, and IBM continues to dominate the mainframe business.

Other companies have also come unstuck with a services strategy. In retail, both the chemist chain Boots in the UK and Home Depot in the USA have backtracked from attempts to switch from product sales to services sales. IBM itself has had difficulties with the strategy and needed to buy the consulting arm of accountants PricewaterhouseCoopers for $3.5bn in 2002 to reach its current position.

The logic of combining services and products continues to attract corporations. Dell's 2009 purchase of Perot Systems for $.39bn followed Hewlett Packard's 2008 purchase of EDS for £13.9bn. While such deals allow product companies to go well beyond LIFETIME SERVICES FOR PRODUCTS and COMPLEMENTOR, NOT COMPETITOR in their service offering, none of these companies intends to leave the product business.

It is unusual to find a services company buying a product company on this scale. It seems that while services can complement products, abandoning products in favour of services is unproven.

PROFESSIONAL SERVICES TEAM

Figure 53. Delivering professional service requires dedication

Author Fabio Alessandro Locati from WikiMedia (Creative Commons Attribution-Share Alike 3.0 Unported)

A London-based ISV was pursuing a WHOLE PRODUCT (page 131) strategy. A complete solution could command a far higher price than the generic products the company had sold before. But that meant customer features and functions had to be added for each sale – even if it was just putting the customer's logo and colour scheme on each page.

The company added a script system to the product as per CUSTOMISABLE PRODUCT (page 115), and created a PROFESSIONAL SERVICES TEAM. The team included consultants to undertake the customisations, pre- and post-sales technical account managers and the support desk.

Context You are following PRODUCTS WITH SERVICES (page 242) and supplying services to supplement your product offering.

Problem *Who in your company should provide the services?*

Forces Companies – especially small ones – that use their development engineers to provide services to customers find that their product development is disrupted. When engineers are taken away to work on customer-specific projects, it becomes impossible to stick to schedules and deliver product roadmaps.

Development engineers may not be the best people to provide consultancy services: temperament and personal objectives often differ between backroom and customer-facing staff. Such staff may have deliberately chosen a backroom position to avoid customer contact; they may not be happy living out of a suitcase and staying in hotels.

Some of your product development engineers may be willing to undertake customer assignments, but product development skills do not always transfer to customer-specific work. Delivery cycles are often shorter, work is more specific and less general, compromises are sometimes required that are different to those valued in product development. Also, you don't want development engineers making changes to the core product just for one customer (as discussed in CUSTOMISABLE PRODUCT, page 115.)

Solution

Create a dedicated team of professional service staff to undertake customer engagements. Staff the group with people who have the right skills and aptitude for customer-facing work – and make sure they are willing to travel.

In a small company where everyone is happy to muck in, services may be provided by development staff. As the company grows, having staff move repeatedly between development and customer engagements will prove disruptive to both endeavours.

When creating a professional services team in an existing organisation, move some existing staff into the team. As well as the customisation consultants, you may include trainers, pre-sales and posts-sales consultants, and maybe the support desk on the team. This will allow the team to look after the entire technical relationship with the customer.

In addition you will need to hire consultants with experience of such teams. Finding people with the particular mix of skills required may be difficult. They need to be technically savvy, happy to work closely with customers and build relationships, understand the customers' business and your product.

Having some movement between product development and professional services teams can benefit both teams and employees. Rotating staff between teams is not disruptive as long as it does not happen too frequently, or as a knee-jerk reaction.

The team will need to work closely both with the engineering (product development) and sales teams. Initially the relationship might be closer with the engineering team, but over time it should become closer to sales.

In some organisations the team reports to the engineering function. However the customer-focused nature of the team means that priorities differ between the teams and tension can arise. Alternatively the team may be a stand-alone unit on an equal footing with engineering, or it may report to the sales function.

Ensure that there is a clear understanding of how the team delivers revenue to the business: either by charging for all work or by ring-fencing revenue from sales. If the team cannot demonstrate revenue and profit in its own right, then it is in danger of becoming a drain on resources.

Consequences Having separate dedicated teams for product development and service delivery will reduce disruption. You can set staffing levels strategically to meet your expected work within your budget. This will end the conflicts that occur when product development work and customer-specific projects compete for the same resources.

Separating product development from customer-specific work removes a source of conflict, reduces variability, allows both teams to focus on what they are good at and improves roadmap delivery and customer experience.

Staff can work on the kind of projects and in the kind of environment they are happiest. This will improve the quality of their work and your staff retention rate.

Development work and customer projects each need to be managed in the most appropriate way, using the most appropriate skills.

Setting up a services team represents a financial undertaking that many small companies are unable to make. In addition, there is sometimes a belief that such teams reduce the flexibility of an organisation to respond to 'special' circumstances. Too much flexibility is a bad thing when translated into variability in operations, and undermines schedules.

There can be friction between the product development engineers and services engineers. The former may see the latter as less competent, while the latter see the former as disconnected from customer needs and realities.

Variations Third parties can supplement the team, either as short-term contractors or as alternative service providers. CORPORATE CERTIFIED EXPERTS (page 272) can be used to ensure the competence of these providers.

Related work The team is likely to supply the technical staff for the SALES/TECHNICAL DOUBLE ACT (page 192) and PERSONAL SERVICE (page 265).

Decoupling customer-specific work from the core product contributes to CUSTOMISABLE PRODUCT (page 115) by exploiting Conway's Law (Coplien & Harrison, 2004) – one team on each side of the architectural boundary.

Examples Most enterprise software vendors eventually create a PROFESSIONAL SERVICES TEAM (also called a *professional services organisation*) to deliver integration, customisation and ongoing support to customers.

The Open Source development JBoss recruited professional services consultants from its pool of contributors. This allowed the company and contributors to profit from an Open Source product. However, some of the consultant contributors tired of the travel demands it made, and left to found the Apache Geronimo application.

In addition JBoss provided traditional support services for this Open Source product. While the product itself was free, the support services, provided under a typical maintenance contract, provided recurring revenue and allowed the company to expand (Watson et al, 2005).

SERVICES FEEDBACK

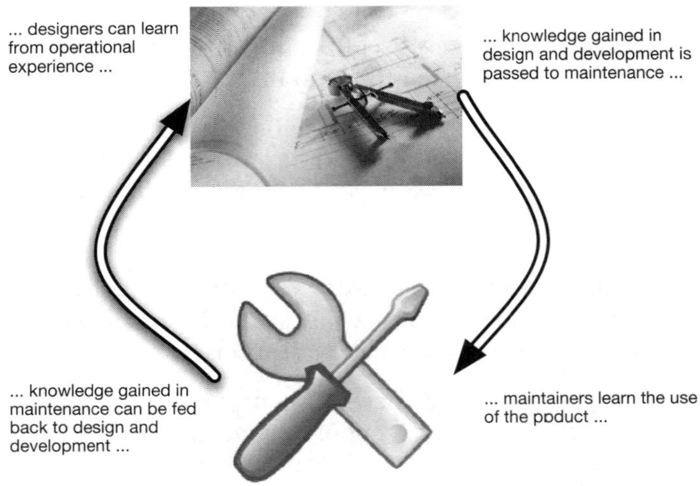

Figure 54. Create a virtuous learning circle between development and maintenance teams

Tools illustration by David Vignoni from WikiMedia (Creative Commons Attribution-Share Alike 3.0 Unported)

One of the author's colleagues sat in on a customer training session. After observing what was being taught and how users responded, he was able to recommend several modifications to the product to make it easier to use and thus reduce the training needed.

Context You are building products and delivering services to support the products; you may be using PRODUCTS WITH SERVICES (page 242), INITIAL HELP (page 248) or LIFETIME SERVICES FOR PRODUCTS (page 252).

Problem *How can you harness the services team to create better products?*

Forces You want to improve the product but, without customer feedback, you will just be guessing. *What do customers find difficult? What features do they consider to be missing? What features will they need next year?*

Your consultants are experts, not just in your product, but in customers' businesses and integration issues. Consultants who are regularly seeing customers and dealing with their problems are a valuable source of information when it comes to deciding what to develop next.

Solution

Build mechanisms, events and artefacts into your product development cycle to collect feedback from your services team. Encourage the service team to provide feedback on customer experience with products – give them a place and time to provide feedback and make sure someone is there to listen.

Your services team has direct contact with your customers, so are well placed to help CUSTOMER UNDERSTANDING (page 146). When your people work closely with customers at their sites and are in regular contact, they have good opportunities to understand what the customer wants from the product, how they use it and what features they need and value.

Knowledge gained in design and production may be applicable later in the product's life, particularly in maintenance. Similarly, knowledge gained later in the product's life may be fed back to design and production phases. This allows you to create the virtuous circle of learning shown in Figure 54.

Have your consultants provide regular feedback to product managers and the development team in person. Have them speak at team meetings, company-wide events and BROWN BAG (Manns & Rising, 2003) sessions.

Have your product managers review customer projects: they should look for the common themes from customer requests, the customisations that are being done and the services that are being delivered. These clues should inform the product roadmap.

Training sessions for customers can be another valuable source of feedback. Developers and product managers should sit in on some sessions and observe how new users react. *What the questions are being asked? What ideas do new users have?*

Watch out for training that is covering up problems with the product: it can be a substitute for making a product that is easy to use. Companies that rely on training its users rather than making simpler products are vulnerable to competitors with genuinely simpler offerings. Periodically, look at your training programmes – both their content and delivery – and consider what material could be omitted were the product to be changed or simplified.

Look at the queries being raised with your help desk. These can be a useful source of ideas and problems, but can also be misleading. Most users don't call the help desk: it tends to be those new to the product, who don't really understand it, and those who have used it for a long time – the most advanced – so the queries raised don't on the whole represent the issues most users have.

It is not just your customers you need to consider. Look at what your own service team is spending its time doing. When you are following LIFETIME SERVICES FOR PRODUCTS (page 252), changes to the product can improve – or reduce – the service your own team delivers.

Try and put your services team out of business by being one step ahead of them. Foster friendly competition, so that the development team stays one step ahead of the real competition. There will always be more services that customers want, so the services team's jobs are safe.

Consequences Offering support and other services can help you understand your customer in more depth and extend your knowledge of the domain. Providing a support desk will make you more aware of customers' difficulties. Even simple queries ("How do I...") can provide information on how the product is used and perceived. More complicated problems ("It crashes when I...") may demand an immediate fix and highlight issues concerning future products.

When your people engage with customers in service roles, they can learn what customers find difficult, what features the product lacks and what future opportunities exist for your product(s). So make sure you provide customer-facing staff with a channel to feed back such information to the product managers.

Related work Feedback can help implement patterns such as CUSTOMER UNDERSTANDING (page 146), WHOLE PRODUCT (page 131) and SIMPLE PRODUCT VARIATIONS (page 121).

Examples Many software companies insist that software developers spend some time working on the technical support desk, so that they become familiar with customers, their questions and their approach to products.

Personal Service

Figure 55. Butlers attend to your every need

In the USA drivers are sometimes able to choose between self-service gas pumps and full-service pumps, where they pay extra to have their gas pumped. Frequently both options are available at the same station, although its usually cheaper to pump your own.

Some people will consider service when making their purchasing decisions; they still value personal service and are prepared to pay more for better service.

Context Your company sells similar products to your competitors and you would like to differentiate your offering.

Problem *How can you differentiate your company when its basic product is the equivalent to your competitors?*

Forces You want to realise extra revenue from the segment you have identified. To do this, you need to differentiate your product, but economies of scale mean you must stick close to the basic product.

Using a self-service model keeps prices down, but there is a quantifiable difference in the quality of delivery. Some customers would prefer not to use self service and can afford pay more.

Using more staff would allow you to differentiate the product, but such staff are expensive to employ and you would be forced to raise prices to cover the cost. Raising prices will reduce sales.

More staff in uniforms may look better, but if these staff are not given authority the customer's experience will suffer – staff will spend much of their time referring to managers with greater authority. Similarly, staffing a call centre with plenty of knowledgeable staff will not improve service if its staff are not authorised to take action.

Solution

Provide customers with better service when buying or using your product. Make the service personal, have named contacts and let the same staff deal with the same customers each time. Customers who value your approach to quality service will choose your product over your competitors' and be prepared to pay a bit more.

Staff should be trained such that they can provide a high level of service, and be encouraged to resolve problems. Allow staff to make decisions, and even spend money so that the customers' experience is immediately improved.

It is particularly important that staff are able to rectify problems when they occur and make compensatory arrangements when they can't. People accept that things sometimes go wrong and will remember a good recovery – unexpected events are your chance to shine in the customer's memory.

Some of your customers will value higher-quality service, but others will only be interested in price regardless of service. Segmenting your customer base will help you to understand what different customers value. Pursuing a better level of service, with its associated extra costs and price increases, may lose some of your customers who are seeking low costs.

You might need to employ more staff than absolutely necessary so that each customer can be given personal service in a timely fashion. Your product will be differentiated from the competition, allowing you to increase prices by more than is needed to cover increased staff costs. Even if you lose some customers, your profits should improve.

Consequences

Providing a better level of service when competitors provide the minimum can increase differentiation of your product. Staff who are knowledgeable about the product, helpful and have authority to act and make decisions will further increase your differentiation from competitors employing 'McWorkers' – standard staff.

The personal attention given by the staff makes customers feel valued and privileged. This helps to justify the extra price your company charges for what is essentially the same basic product.

Some customers will accept higher prices for better services. Customers who experience good service are more likely to return and purchase your product again. There will always be some people who avail themselves of your services and then buy elsewhere on price; focus on those you sell to rather than the few who play your system.

Staffing levels based on peak load ensure that customers can be served in a timely fashion. Consequently, at other times staff may appear idle and unproductive; this is a natural result of staffing for peak load rather than for optimal throughput.

Employees are able to understand a customer's needs and demands better. This places them in a good position to cross-sell additional products, and thus recoups some of their additional expense.

Variations Rather than associating customers with individual staff members, you might create staff teams to service groups of customers.

Related work ACCOUNT MANAGEMENT (page 187) and SALES/TECHNICAL DOUBLE ACT (page 192) act as a form of PERSONAL SERVICE used for specific ends.

Examples The British bank First Direct (a division of HSBC) is a telephone and Internet-only bank, yet the bank shuns automated answer systems; onshore staff members always answers customer calls, no matter how small the query.

American supermarkets often employ grocery packers to help customers at the checkout. One British supermarket copied this idea, but instead of employing extra staff, expected the checkout operator to pack and scan, making for longer queues. Since customers were already accustomed to packing their own groceries, the longer queues made for unhappy customers.

Best Buy entered the UK market at a time when other high-street electrical retailers like DSG were in retreat. A key part of Best Buy's strategy was to employ staff who understood and could explain increasingly complex home electrical goods. This contrasted with stores like Dixons, where staff seldom knew very much about any of the products on display.

SELF-SERVICE

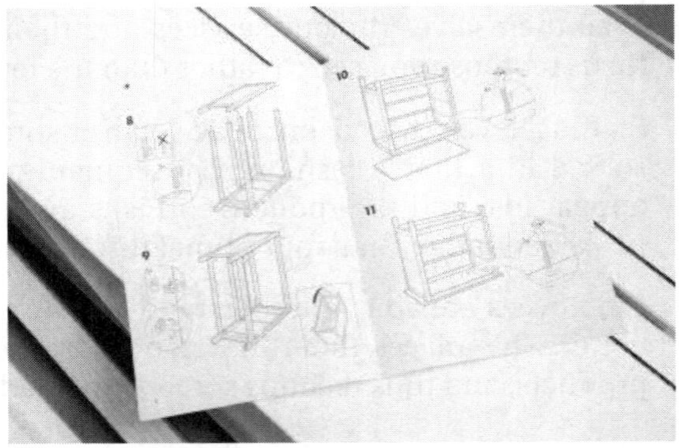

Figure 56. Self-service assembly is integral to Ikea's business model

---

Banks, petrol stations and supermarkets all encourage customers to serve themselves. Ikea has extended this to bulky furniture purchases, which customers pick themselves from the warehouse selves.

The odd thing is that customers often prefer the self-service approach, perhaps because they feel more in control, or perhaps because they feel more involved. Some people may recognise that they are helping to keep costs down and appreciate lower prices; others are happy to use their own time and efforts if it means less time waiting.

Self-service can provide opportunities that would not be viable in a 'served' approach – customers can check their open support tickets as often as they like, they can choose options for the hell of it, or proactively seek out other services.

Context To obtain your product or core service there are some preliminary steps you need to go through with your customers. You may be seeking to reduce costs in delivering services, or to improve customer experience.

Problem *How can you provide customer service without costs running away as you grow?*

Forces The preliminary steps are not particularly taxing or complicated, but do take time and require staff. These steps don't add much additional value to the core product, but they do add cost. With growth comes more customers and more costs.

Customers are cost-conscious but still care about service. If you make them queue for too long they will (eventually) choose another supplier, even if that supplier is more expensive. It is hard to keep costs down while keeping queues short and providing good service quality.

Customers don't usually enjoy queues; they like staff who pay attention, look after them and provide personal service. But customers also like to be in control of the process themselves; they don't like being dependent on others. There is more to good service than short queues and good staff

Solution

Build a service process that can be operated by customers and allow customers to serve themselves. People like to feel empowered, so give them the tools to take control of the process themselves, help them save time and access extra benefits.

Be prepared to start with small ideas. Over time, with creative thinking, more and more processes can be given to customers. Try process modifications, try self-service options and see what happens; not all changes will work, but you can learn from your experiments.

Start from a customer perspective. Consider what customers do when they buy your product or use your service. Look for places where they might be able to help themselves: *when do they come into contract with your staff? When do they wait or queue? What needs to be done for them?* All of these could be opportunities.

Next, examine your processes for fulfilling customers' requests. Processes may need to be simplified or split into discrete steps, offices may need to be redesigned – for example with more front-office space for customers and less back-office space for staff – or new simple-to-use technology introduced for customers to use.

Easy to use ATM-like machines can help with some processes. At other times it is information that is important to provide customers with up-to-date information sources – via the web, SMS or Twitter – and background sources, in FAQs, documents and knowledge bases. Discussion forums and open question and answer sessions can help customers to help one another.

Run pilot schemes before converting your whole operation to self-service. This will help you to understand what can be achieved, what problems you will encounter and to gauge customer reaction. If the pilot scheme is successful, gradually expand it to include all your customers.

There are limits to how much process can be turned over to customers. For example, security and safety concerns mean that asking airline passengers to screen their own baggage would not be wise. Legal restrictions may also present barriers.

Not all customers will want to use self-service all the time. Some customers may resist any change, while others may not like the new system. For example, self-service checkouts at supermarkets are welcomed by many shoppers, but are difficult for a parent with a young child.

Keeping a personal service option and giving customers a choice can overcome this problem. However, offering two alternatives may be expensive and, if you are looking for aggressive costs savings, it might be economic to accept the loss of such customers.

Alternatively, retain both self-service and personal service options, and charge more for personal service, as US gas stations do, or include personal service as part of a premium package, as airlines do with check-in options.

Consequences When customers perform tasks previously undertaken by employees, fewer workers are needed, companies may reduce their work force and their wage bill, thereby reducing direct costs. Lower costs may be passed on to customers, so improved services and lower prices may both be possible.

Despite shifting some of the work from employees to customers, your customers may consider the result to be better quality. They now have a sense of control over the process; they are no longer dependent on another person.

For a growing company the need to hire more workers can limit the speed of growth – it takes time to hire people. Thus, companies employing a SELF-SERVICE model may be able to expand faster than rivals.

With most of the simpler tasks undertaken by the customer, your staff will find their role changed. While some of their time will be spent helping customers with the new process and machines, more time will be spent with customers whose needs are more complex.

Additional costs may be incurred while you switch to the new processes, for example refitting office/shop space, investment in machines, self-service tools and training staff in their new role.

Losses from theft – 'shrinkage' – and customers taking too much advantage of self-service will also push up costs. Experience shows that the savings usually outweigh the costs, but remember to conduct your own studies on your own systems and customers.

The hands-off, scripted nature of self-service deprives the organisation of opportunities to get to know its customers and understand their needs. This makes it more difficult for companies to see new opportunities and cross-sell products. For example, an old style behind-the-counter storekeeper can always recommend a complementary product to a customer, but a supermarket checkout operator and has little opportunity to do so.

Variations

You may choose to only allow trusted customers to use self-service. For example, initially airlines only allowed frequent flyers to perform self-service check-in. This can help to enhance the sense of privilege for these customers.

Related work

PERSONAL SERVICE (page 265) is the opposite of this pattern.

This approach has also been called 'outsource to customer'.

Examples

Examples of SELF-SERVICE are abundant: petrol (gas) stations have long expected customer to fill their own car; supermarkets increasingly are expecting customers to scan their own goods, and airlines increasingly expect customers to check themselves in for flights.

The Internet has created many more opportunities; for example, customers can now read product specifications online instead of asking a sales clerk. Even more advanced transactions are candidates for self-service. For example, Amazon uses self-service over the Internet not only for purchases, but also for returns. Customers can print out their own return forms, complete with bar codes.

One London-based enterprise software company introduced an online support portal for customers to log and track issues. Many customers found that this made the process quicker – no more waiting in a phone queue – and provided more visibility of their issues once logged. The software company itself was able to service more customers with the same support staff, and to spend more time on the most difficult issues.

CORPORATE CERTIFIED EXPERTS

Figure 57. Chefs wear uniforms for practical reasons and as a sign of their qualifications

---

During the late 1980s and early 1990s, Novell Netware was the most successful PC-based networking system, but it was difficult to install, configure and administer. So Novel created the Certified Novell Engineer (CNE) programme. If you needed a Novell network, you hired a CNE to look after it. Individuals found that they were worth more if they were certified, and several service organisations added CNE services to their offerings.

Context You are marketing a technically complex product that requires a few expert users to operate it correctly.

Problem *How can you and your customers know who is proficient to use your products?*

Forces The product may expose several different interfaces, but at least one requires in-depth knowledge; for example, a vending machine may appear simple to casual users, but very different to the service technicians who repair such machines.

Your PROFESSIONAL SERVICES TEAM (page 258) can undertake advanced work such as installation and configuration for customers, but this makes customers dependent on your service organisation.

You need to be able to distinguish between expert and non-expert users of your product. Users outside of your service organisation may be capable of performing the necessary work, but how do you, or your customers, know who has the advanced skills and experience necessary and who doesn't?

Some organisations may not want to be dependent on your service organisation, and if your product is very successful the service team may not be able to serve all potential customers, resulting in lost sales.

Individuals want to be associated with your brand and offer services to your customers, but you don't want just anyone associating themselves with your brand. If it is too easy for people to claim knowledge of your product, they may damage the reputation of your company's offerings.

Solution

Segment your user base by creating a certification programme for expert users. Target documentation, training and features at different types of user; your customers will know who is capable of undertaking work on your product.

Create a test for those seeking certification. You will need to produce materials for those studying for the test and ensure that those certified are up to date with changes. For example, certification might be tied to a product version, or re-certification may be required every year.

It may be helpful to create multiple certification programmes for different products or different aspects of the product; for example, Novell certifies Netware Administrators, Netware Engineers and SUSE Linux Professionals. Multiple levels of certification such as 'professional' and 'expert' can be used too. You may also want to create certification for trainers who can train others in your products.

Make sure you cost the programme and understand its funding in detail. Creating a certification program can be expensive: materials must be created, tests set and administered and the programme kept up to date. Ideally, the programme would be self-funding (people pay for certification), but if you have a small customer base it can be difficult to make certification return a profit.

Rather than create and maintain the programme and materials yourself, you might engage a partner who has experience of running such programmes. They can brand the programme as your own and let you set the quality thresholds.

Big companies with well-known brands will find it easier to create certification programmes because they have the resources and brand exposure to create the qualification, and they can afford to wait while the programme becomes established. For a small company, however, such a programme may represent a drain on finances that it can ill afford.

Consequences By distinguishing between users you can target different interfaces and materials (for example documentation and training) at different types of users and levels of experience.

Your service organisation is no longer the only one to contain people who can undertake complex work. Customers can now choose from your service organisation, a certified third party organisation or an individual, or they can train their own people to a known standard and do the work in-house.

Even when your service organisation is fully utilised, sales can be made to customers who could buy the necessary services elsewhere. However, letting others replace your own service organisation may weaken your relationship with your customers, both by increasing the distance between them and you and by involving third parties.

Third party organisations may decide to add your product(s) to their service portfolios. This may result in reduced revenues for your service organisation, but increase sales of your product. If this is not your aim it might be better to build the reputation and image of your own people and seek ways to stop unauthorised people from working with your products.

Individuals may find that certification makes them more employable and allows them to command higher wages.

The existence of individuals and organisations who can support your product will enhance your market credibility and make your product a less risky purchasing decision, thereby increasing sales.

Network effect suggests that the more people who are certified to support your product, the more acceptable it will be to customers and the more difficult it will be for competitors to establish a foothold. By certifying experts in your product as such, these individuals have expended time, energy and money on your product rather than on the competition.

Variations

If you are seeking truly to certify experts, then the training and testing process should be rigorous and ensure that only experts are certified. If however you are seeking to allow individuals to associate themselves with your brand and to feel part of your team, you might offer a less rigorous certification process. Allowing individuals to collect your 'badge' will buy loyalty and squeeze your competitors.

Red Hat certifies partners to provide support and services for the Open Source JBoss product. Hewlett Packard and IBM are among the companies that partner to provide services for, and products built with, JBoss. These partnerships have allowed JBoss to grow faster than would otherwise be possible.

Related work

A certification programme can help when finding and designating a VALUE ADDED RESELLER (page 203).

Examples

Novell's Netware certification programme helped Netware to become the leading network operating system in the late 1980s and early 1990s. After purchasing SUSE, Novell expanded the scheme to provide Linux certification.

Microsoft and other enterprise software providers offer similar schemes for their advanced products and technologies.

PACKAGED SERVICES

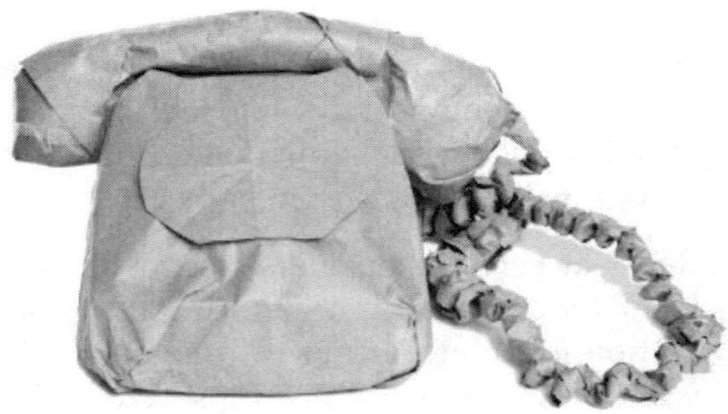

Figure 58. Packaging services can require inventive thinking

Compare two descriptions taken from the Internet websites of two software service providers on 27 November 2007:

'Blue Skyline offers a mixture of consultancy and mentoring to assist the team at the same time as enabling the delivery of the system.' `www.blueskyline.com`

'We help companies in the chemicals industry drive their performance to new heights by capitalising on important business and technology opportunities.' `www.accenture.com`

Which gives the best description of what the consultants actually do? The best description addresses the needs and concerns of the customer. The services offered by these two very different companies may appear very similar in delivery, but they target different needs.

Context You are an external service provider (ESP) delivering technology business services to corporate customers, or an ISV following PRODUCTS WITH SERVICES (page 242).

Problem *How do you explain to customers what your services are?*

Forces Services are infinitely flexible, but that makes it difficult to explain to customers what those services are. The more variable the service is, the harder it is to explain. Using value statements and generalisations in the descriptions can make it difficult to explain what you do in a few words.

Customers expect consistency in service delivery. They may come to know and trust an individual consultant. But if they only buy that consultant's time you lose the flexibility sell their expertise anywhere else. If each consultancy assignment depends on a named individual consultant, it is difficult to grow a business. To be effective, consultancy businesses need to be able to swap individuals on assignments.

Many customer problems look alike on the surface; managing a data centre for company X can be a lot like managing a data centre for company Y. But there are also unique problems; applications developed for company X might be very different to the ones developed for company Y.

Customers often engage consultants to reduce costs, but sometimes they are looking for strategic services to create a competitive advantage. Sometimes cost reduction is strategic.

Solution

Think of your services like products; explain what you do as a well-defined product with a defined cost and a defined outcome. Define who your customer is and speak to that customer's needs. Your potential customers are an audience. Describe your services in terms they will relate to. If you customers want to know what you do, tell them what you do; if they want to know what the result is, tell them the result; if they want to know the kind of problems you solve, then tell them. Keep it short.

Demonstrate that you understand the customer's needs that your services are addressing. Add product-like attributes to your services. Market your services as products for defined problems, with defined actions and defined outcomes. Explain the benefits your services will generate and how others have already benefitted.

Know your customer by using CUSTOMER UNDERSTANDING (page 146) and SEGMENTED CUSTOMERS (page 141). Identify their problems and identify the ones that occur again and again. Devise common service solutions that can address these problems. Separate the unique problems and deal with them as unique solutions.

Maybe take a leaf out of the ISV handbook: appoint senior consultants as product managers and make them responsible for identifying customers, understanding them and managing the service products.

Initially you need to work on marketing. Market your services as products:

- Identify the common problems, common causes and common 'pain points'.
- Speak at conferences, blog, Twitter, make a noise about your services. Produce case studies and datasheets for your services. Show how your services solved the problems.
- Identify organisations that you expect to have the same issues, and engage with them.

Next you need to work on your delivery to create common solutions to common problems:

- Break the services down into repeatable steps, and where possible offer a defined price for a defined benefit or outcome. Commonality will allow economies of scale to be extracted.
- Consultants need to be trained to find, and rewarded for finding, commonalities across services and service engagements.
- Consultants need to be motivated to share personal findings with each other.
- Avoid selling individuals and instead sell results.

You will need to decide the financial model behind your service products. A defined problem that results in a defined outcome suggests a fixed-price service rather than one that charges for services on a time and materials basis.

All consultants are part sales people; the dividing line between consulting and selling is far vague than with products, so help your consultants to understand at least the basics of sales.

Consequences Treating your services like products makes it easier to describe what you actually do and what the end result is. The more you make your services look like products, the more consistency customers can expect and will come to expect.

Customers buy a specific product rather than a specific individual, so it is easier to swap consultants during the assignment. This does not mean that customers will welcome the replacement of an experienced consultant with a new hire. It may pay to send new members of staff out with experienced consultants at no charge to customers until they learn the basics.

Commonality benefits customers, because services are delivered more quickly, at a lower cost and with fewer complications. However, offering different customers the same packaged service treats all customers the same – all solutions come from the same 'cookie cutter'. The specific needs of an individual customer may be lost. Where needs are different, they must be treated differently.

When a customer seeks to minimise cost, they may be happy with a cookie cutter approach, because it delivers maximum cost reduction. But they will then not recognise any competitive advantage if you deliver them the same services as their competitors.

Over time commoditisation of the services may occur. When this happens you may either lead the transition to commoditisation, or change your strategy.

Offering a customer a fixed price on a service contract can be difficult and leave little room for unexpected problems. Indeed many organisations find that charging for unexpected problems is profitable. See the discussion in *When Services Distract from Product* on page 234.

Examples

In July 2006 the Financial Times said this about IBM: 'These days, IBMers talk about 'productising' services, turning them into clearly defined offerings that can be marketed and delivered in much the same way that new mainframe computers are. [IBM's] small and medium-sized business unit, for example, now distributes a catalogue outlining its main services.' (Waters, 2006).

13

Patterns about Organising Product Companies

The patterns in this chapter fall into two groups: patterns to be used early in the company's existence, and patterns to be used for later growth. Between these are patterns that can be used at any time; these are found in other chapters.

As noted in Chapter 3, the actual formation of a company is relatively easy: anyone can do it. The difficult bit is staying alive – generating revenue and making a profit. If a company cannot do this, it will quickly fail. To make a profit, the focus of a new company needs to be on the product or services the company has been created to produce and deliver. Once a company is beyond its early life, its chances of survival increase as its age increases. Unlike humans, companies do not have a natural lifespan of three score years and ten; as Arie de Geus has discussed, few companies live this long, although a few do (De Geus, 1997).

A new company needs revenue: to earn it, it can either supply services or it can sell a product. Thus the pattern sequence in Figure 59 has two entry points, one for companies starting with services and one for companies jumping straight to products. Some companies will continue to deliver services, while others will move to product development and leave initial services behind. It is the product companies that are the focus of this chapter; indeed, these companies are the focus of much of this book.

Traditionally software products have been delivered physically, on a tape, a CD or at least a package download. Increasingly software is delivered as a service, for example the sales force and CRM system offered by SalesForce.com. In the

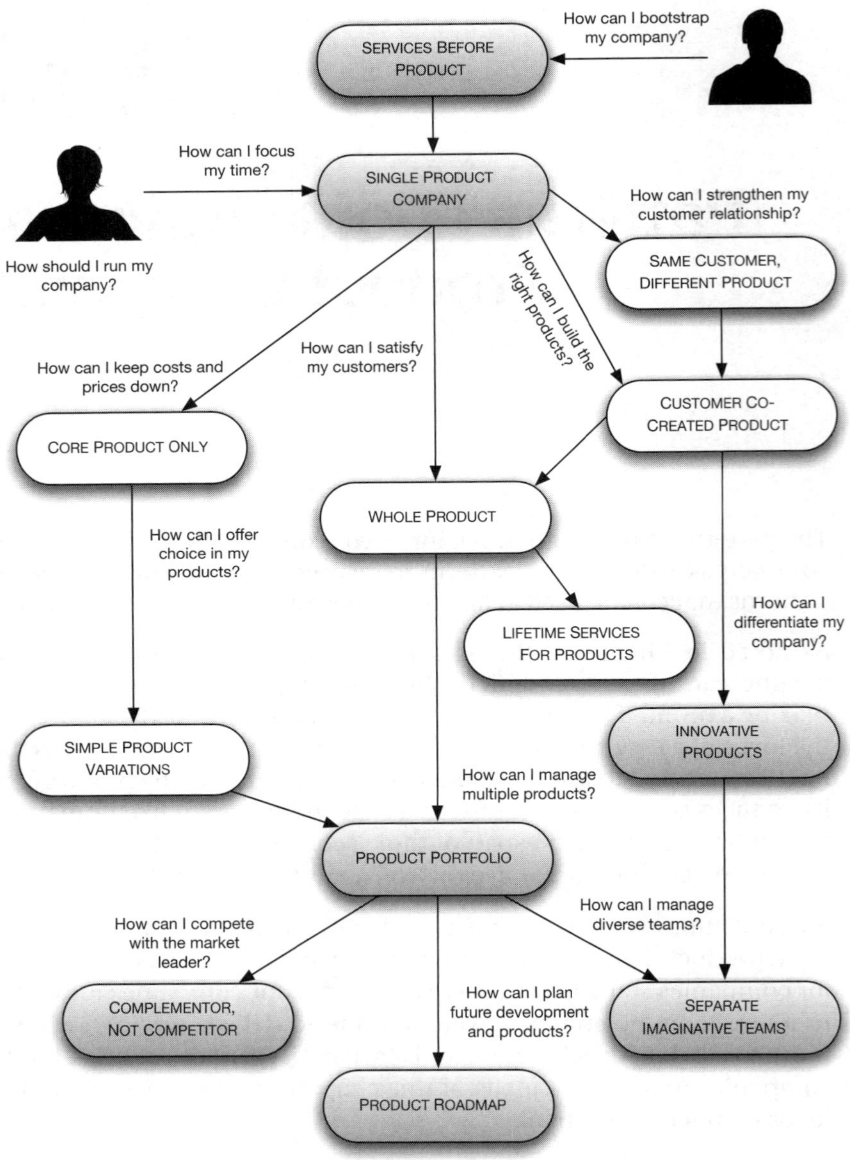

Figure 59. Pattern sequence for organising a growing company

context of this book such services have most of the characteristics of a product, even if they are delivered as services.

Some companies will succeed with one product through sheer chance. Indeed, the opportunities made possible by advancing technology and software mean that a few companies have some success through pure luck. However, companies that succeed with their first product through luck cannot rely on luck for the second: relying on luck is not a well-regarded business strategy, even if it is a common one.

New product companies face two challenges. First, to make their product successful enough to survive. Second, to position themselves to repeat the success.

The key to this double challenge is to create a culture that respects customers and technology, to put in place the people and roles for successful delivery, and to develop the practices and processes that allow the company to grow, create and support more products, and serve more customers.

Capabilities

Many of the patterns in this book assume explicitly or implicitly that a company has, or will gain, particular capabilities. The exact capabilities a software company needs to develop will vary depending on the nature of the product, the market, the regulatory environment, its expansion intentions and many other factors. Still, there are some capabilities that are relatively common and deserve a few words of description.

As described in Chapter 3, all software companies need a sales capability and a software development capability. The sales capability will vary depending on the distribution channels used: it might be a lone super-salesman or a mass of individuals working all hours in a call centre. If multiple channels are to be used, then multiple sales teams may be needed, with each specialising in a different channel.

Nor is it enough to have a development group. The group needs to be able to deliver software reliably and in a timely and cost-effectively manner. These days the group – sometimes called ‘development’, sometimes called ‘engineering’ – is likely to be following one of the Agile methods (Kelly, 2008; Highsmith, 2010). Following the traditional ‘waterfall’ approaches is unlikely to provide products in a competitive timeframe in today’s market.

As a company grows it becomes necessary to create other capabilities in the organisation. Creation of some, such as a legal department, can be postponed for a long time, perhaps indefinitely, by using external contractors and advisors when necessary. Others, technical operations, are increasingly needed at an early stage.

A mistake made frequently is to see technical operations as merely an extension of development. While some of the technical knowledge overlaps, the nature and skills of technical operations are quite different to development. Technical operations contains many routine, possibly boring, activities, and occasional firefights when things go wrong. The objective of operations is to be routine and minimise the unexpected. In development, by contrast, there is little routine; development by its nature is about developing something different.

That said, a trend has recently emerged for bringing development and operations together in so called *DevOps* teams. Some companies have taken separation of operation and development too far. Both groups posses the ability to make the other work harder or easier. Bringing them together makes sense as long as their differences are respected.

The other capability that becomes necessary in all but the smallest software company has already been mentioned in earlier chapters: marketing. Marketing divides into two groups: outbound and inbound – telling people *about* the product and learning what people want *from* the product.

Outbound marketing further divides into product marketing – concerned with specific products – and corporate marketing – concerned with marketing the corporation. In a SINGLE PRODUCT COMPANY (page 292) these two functions are so closely related as to be possibly the same thing.

Software companies frequently leave the creation of both product marketing and product management capabilities too late. When they do move to create marketing groups, they make them subgroups of another group. Product marketing is often made an extension of sales – where it is likely to work on short time horizons and be unable to effectively influence strategy. Similarly, product management is all too often made part of development.

While it is useful for developers to understand customers and users, to meet them, to observe them and talk to them, the task of deciding what the software should do and setting the development priorities is too important to be left to developers. The roles of business analyst and product manager exist to deal with these questions.

One capability that proves particularly difficult for software companies to get right is that of *human resources*[1] (HR). Hardly surprising then that the Financial

[1] This author has a particular dislike of the term *human resources*, since it reduces people to the level of computers, cars and paperclips: resources. The older term *personnel* seems to be far more humane.

Times reported that 73% of HR professionals did not consider themselves to be the best people to recruit IT staff (Thomas, 2007). Perhaps this situation arises because those who work in HR departments are oriented towards the human aspects of business, while those who work in technology groups are oriented towards the technology aspects.

Done well, HR can improve recruitment, reduce staff turnover and enhance individual development and learning. Done badly it adds bureaucracy, costs and slows recruitment and change. To date no patterns of human resource management have been written, and it is difficult to know what forces create the difference between effective and bureaucratic HR. These differences may largely be down to the individuals who staff these roles.

Why not outsource development?

It is, in theory at least, possible to outsource software development and have another company undertake the 'dirty work' of coding. Doing so would in effect turn the first company into a super-distributor that controls sales, marketing and branding of the products, but sells products created by another company. This route it not common for a number of reasons that are largely to do with intellectual property (IP).

During the development process much IP – knowledge – is created. While contract agreements may state that this IP belongs to the super-distributor, the reality is that most of it exists inside the heads of engineers. It is impossible to remove this knowledge and difficult to prevent the knowledge being used in future products.

In outsourcing development capability the super-distributor is in effect creating a potential rival. The organisation undertaking the development will acquire much knowledge of how to develop the product in question and what is required of it. However the bulk of the profit will rest with the super-distributor. As illustrated by the BenQ example in Chapter 10 (page 212), the development company may not settle for this arrangement.

Secondly, new product development is a risky business. It is unlikely that the development company would wish to take on all or even a substantial amount of this risk. The super-distributor would be left paying the bills and taking the risk, but with limited direct control over the process.

One more reason why software companies usually seek to control development and control the IP themselves is that it can lead to patents. Patents are valuable entities in their own right and opportunities for patents, and existing patents, are often considered by potential investors.

Structure

The question of how to structure a software development company is beyond the scope of this chapter. While some suggestions are embedded in the patterns in this book no complete solution is offered: each organisation must decide for itself. That said, there are two points that are worth making about organisational structure because they occur regularly.

Firstly, product management only appears in software product companies. In ESPs and corporates, the equivalent role is business analyst. Unfortunately companies neglect to create a product management function for various reasons:

- An attitude of 'the developers know' is too often prevalent when deciding what the product should do.
- Developers are kept responding to sales requests, so enhancements are customer- rather than market-driven.
- Enhancements are driven by what competitors' products do. A 'follower' strategy is perfectly legitimate – and cheap – as long as there is acceptance that it will not allow the company to get ahead of the competition.

Consequently, product management is created late in the day, if at all, and often finds itself part of development. When this happens the result is too often overly technical, complex and feature-orientated products.

Product management and product marketing are very different activities with different priorities. For this reason it is best to keep these two groups separate. It is not uncommon to see one person filling both roles. This might be acceptable on a temporary basis, but to do both jobs well requires dedicated people in each role.

It is also best to keep these groups independent, even at the price of the CEO having more reporting channels. Product management is sometimes placed under development (also called 'engineering'), while product marketing is sometimes placed under sales. For more discussion on this topic, see Cagan (2008).

Secondly, many companies organise themselves along functional lines: product management, development, testing and so on. The problem with this type of organisation is that these groups need to be coordinated to produce any product. According to Conway's Law (Conway, 1968; Coplien & Harrison, 2004), such an organisation tends to create a similarly segmented product.

The alternative approach focuses on the product and creates a team of many skills around it, as for example team X, which contains a product manager, several developers, testers and others necessary to deliver the product X. The same pattern is applied to team Y and product Y and so on for all products.

In an effort to reconcile these two approaches, some companies adopt *matrix management*. This approach is seldom popular with staff and there is some evidence that it results in lower productivity in the software development environment (Jones, 2008).

Patterns exist from other authors concerning team structure (Weir, 1997; Bricout et al, 2004; Hvatum, 2009). Coplien and Harrison have compiled an entire book of such patterns; several of their patterns relate closely to this discussion, including TEAM PER TASK, UNITY OF PURPOSE and LOCK 'EM UP TOGETHER.

SERVICES BEFORE PRODUCT

Figure 60. Service in a restaurant is experienced before the product is tasted

Start-up companies need cash flow and may well take odd jobs developing software, fixing existing packages or integrating components to make ends meet while they develop a product.

The author once worked for a British company that pioneered hand-held PCs. The founders had left a previous company and undertaken consultancy projects, writing *ad hoc* software while raising enough capital to develop an 8088-based pocket PC.

Context You are starting out in a new business, perhaps on your own or perhaps with partners. Your first priority is to generate some revenue.

Problem *How do you leverage your existing expertise to get closer to your goal of creating a product?*

Forces You have an idea for a product; you have some expertise and a little money, but not enough of either.

You need money to develop products, but outside investors expect to see product prototypes, business plans, market research and a lot more. All this requires time and money to create. Worse still, there may not be anybody willing to risk money in your field.

To understand the market and develop business plans, you need to get into the market, but you can't get into the market without something to sell. Analysing the market, reading reports and talking to potential customers is useful, but only by being in the market can you see what and where money is being spent.

Founding a company requires good timing. Founders need to be ready to quit their jobs and join the new company, business plans should be laid out, funding should be in place and the sales pipeline should be ready to go. But getting all factors to coincide can be difficult and delay the endeavours. Delays may lose customers (who find other suppliers) or founders may be offered attractive positions elsewhere.

Solution

Fund your new company by providing professional consultancy services in the same field as your envisioned product initially. Increase your expertise and knowledge of the field and improve your cash position. Use the knowledge and cash from consultancy sales to develop products ideas.

Selling expertise through consultancy services requires less preparation than developing and manufacturing a product. Cash can be produced relatively quickly, allowing the company's founders to eat while developing products and business plans.

You still need to find the consultancy work, which doesn't grow on trees; this will take time and money. Start by setting out your stall with a website and letting your contacts know you are looking for work. Make some noise by way of public relations, journal articles, speaking engagements and through your network of contacts. Remember to be clear and concise about what you can do and what you are looking for.

Success at winning and undertaking consultancy work can crowd out product ambitions. Consultancy work brings in money and keeps people busy, but leaves little time for the original objective. This may be a sign that you have created a perfectly good service business and you would be well advised to pursue this avenue.

If you still wish to create a product, ring fence some time or people and some money. Use these resources to develop your product ideas. In many countries this research and development can qualify for tax breaks.

Once a business grows big enough to recruit people beyond its initial founders, revisit your original ideas and check which type of company you want to be. Provided you are successful at offering services, then why not continue doing so? Just because you originally envisaged producing products does not mean you have to produce products. If there is good money to be made in services, then there is no reason to stop supplying them.

When recruiting additional people it helps to be clear about the role you are recruiting them for. Consultants and product developers are often different. People hired to work as consultants may not want to work on product development when the time comes to switch. Similarly, product developers might not like the idea of spending time with customers and in hotels until the cash is available for product development.

Consequences You have entered the market by selling yourself. As a short-term move this gets you exposure to the market and generates cash, and allows you to enhance your technical knowledge and understanding of the market.

Being in the market allows you to identify potential customers, their needs and where existing products fail. You will be able to meet potential competitors and complementors, refine your product ideas, your marketing and strategy, and expand your contacts. Even if you have not been able to start developing a product you will be able to make a better case for it, and your experience in the market will increase your credibility when you start seeking outside funding.

This move buys time to get organised – the company's founders don't all have to join on day one. As you develop the sales pipeline, you can bring more people on board. However, while you are organising and improving your knowledge, the market is moving forward and you have provided time for potential rivals to enter the market. Wait too long and the market opportunity might have passed.

There are risks in changing your business model. Changing from a services-based to a product-based company is not simply a case of flipping a switch: culture, people and financing are all different.

Consultancy work can provide a steady and lucrative cash flow. This can be addictive. Using your staff for product development will cut cash flow until the product is ready. Product launch can be expensive and risky; the promise of cash today may be more appealing than cash tomorrow.

Related work When formulating a business strategy it is important to know whether you are selling services as a prelude to developing a product, supplying services as an alternative to developing a product, or selling services in addition to a product.

Once in the market other opportunities may appear. Rather than develop your own product you may follow COMPLEMENTOR, NOT COMPETITOR (page 309).

Examples

John was CEO of a small software company in central England. The company made money by developing software for other businesses. Profits were then used to help develop the company's own products, identify markets and investigate technology.

Prior to meeting a new client the author was told "There are really two businesses inside this one. The first develops software components, which they sell to equipment manufacturer, the second creates portals for end customers". Both businesses were successful, but the second business generated a lot of work in progress and left little time for the first business to develop.

SINGLE PRODUCT COMPANY

Figure 61. 1925 Model-T Ford

After several iterations Henry Ford finally found commercial success with the Model-T Ford. The Ford Motor Company focused initially on just producing this one car and, famously, in only one colour: black.

Early Ford operations were totally integrated and focused on producing one car in one colour. This helped Ford to enter and dominate the early motor business, but also provided opportunities for competitors. However this strength was also Ford's weakness. By offering customers choice in their products, General Motors was able to compete with Ford.

Context You have identified a need in the market and have decided to start a company to address it. You believe the need is best satisfied by a product rather than a service, so you will not use SERVICES BEFORE PRODUCT (page 288).

Problem *When you start a product company, what do you do first?*

Forces When you start a company the world is your oyster. There are countless opportunities for new products and vast untapped markets.

Companies are normally brought into being to do something specific: to address a need in the market, an opportunity with a specific customer, or to exploit a new technology. But there are many ways you can go about addressing the *something*; it is hard to know where to start, and even harder to know whether you are addressing it in the right way.

There are many things a new company has to do: legal status, accounts systems, recruitment, customer accounts and so on, but the company founders only have so much time, energy and money to devote to all these issues. All companies have limited resources, and new companies are more limited than most.

Solution *Decide on one product and focus all your attention on developing the product, delivering the product and marketing the product.* Bring this product to market as quickly as possible.

Ask the question "*What is stopping us from delivering this product tomorrow?*" Direct your time, energy and money to resolving the issues identified by this question.

Identify your target market and target customers as early as possible. Engage with them before the product is finished; they may be happy to offer advice, to beta-test the product, or act as a lead customer – see CUSTOMER CO-CREATED PRODUCT (page 95).

Ensure your target customers can pay for the product one way or another. You may sell the product in a single transaction, charge a monthly fee, or offer your product free and sell advertising around it. However you decide to monetarise your product, make sure the revenue will cover your costs and give enough profit to justify the investment.

When the chosen market is large and the problems to be solved are many, then define your own niche to improve your focus. Deliberately put some opportunities out of bounds. By defining the part of the market you will address, you will improve your own focus and reduce the amount of time you need to deliver a product. Having a clear idea of who your target market is and what you have to offer should make it clearer to communicate your marketing message.

Focus on the core problem the product is solving, limit extra activity and work on both the product and the company as a whole. Leave extra functionality out of the product and limit the growth of the company organisation. Defer non-essential activities like setting up a human resources department, or do them differently, perhaps by renting services or outsourcing work.

While developing your product, avoid the distraction of offering services and the temptation to develop additional products. Focus on your market, focus on the product you are developing, focus on your potential customers.

When your product is available, this advice no longer holds. You may need to supplement your offering with services or additional products, as described in WHOLE PRODUCT (page 131), and from there to PRODUCT PORTFOLIO (page 296).

There is no guarantee that your first product will be the right one. While researching the market, building the product or even after product launch you might identify a more interesting prospect and decide to change focus. Consider using EXPEDITIONARY MARKETING (page 153) to help to refine your product ideas.

Once established, most companies relax their focus on the single product. They may add additional products and services around the original product, as in WHOLE PRODUCT, or they may diversify with new products – see SAME CUSTOMERS, DIFFERENT PRODUCT (page 105) and PRODUCT PORTFOLIO (page 296).

Consequences Knowing what single product you are producing, and what single problem you are solving, will make it easier to focus your resources and limit distractions.

By keeping features and functionality to a minimum you can reduce development costs and shorten the development cycle. However, this means the features you do implement need to be the right ones to make your product attractive.

Focusing on the product will detract from building the company organisation and infrastructure. In the short term the company needs the product – and the resulting revenue – more than it needs the infrastructure of human resource departments, public relations and so on. But delaying such capabilities too long can have negative consequences. Companies may work sub-optimally if new business units and functions are not created when they are needed. For example, a dedicated technical support desk may be a distraction at the start, but when there are many customers it is more disturbing to have engineers answer queries directly.

Similarly, once the product is established and revenues are flowing, companies need to consider supplementary and additional products. Delaying new products may leave opportunities for competitors to enter the market. Use WHOLE PRODUCT (page 131) and PRODUCT PORTFOLIO (page 296), and product services such as PRODUCTS WITH SERVICES (page 242), INITIAL HELP (page 248) and LIFETIME SERVICES FOR PRODUCTS (page 252).

Marketing is easier when your (new) company name is associated with one product, for example Hoover in Europe or Q-Tips in the USA, although they also make it more difficult to control your trademark.

Companies that do not expand their product portfolio are often acquired by larger companies, where they form part of a portfolio.

Variations

Companies that do not follow this strategy from the beginning can still adopt it later. To create focus, shed additional products, withdraw from non-core markets and decline customer business outside the core area. Review employee incentives to ensure everyone is focused on the same thing. It is no use focusing on quality if engineers are still given bonuses solely for achieving delivery dates.

Focus need not be product-related, although for software companies it usually is. Companies may focus instead on a particular customer and its needs, or on specialist activities.

In some markets customers may expect to buy a set of similar products. For example, a customer buying a lipstick may expect to buy matching nail varnish; if they cannot, they may buy nothing.

Related work

SINGLE PRODUCT COMPANY (page 303) is a company-level version of HOMOGENOUS CUSTOMERS (page 136), usually used when the company itself is just starting. HOMOGENOUS CUSTOMERS is directed at the individual product level.

CORE PRODUCT ONLY (page 110) and SIMPLE PRODUCT VARIATIONS (page 121) describe how to manage costs by focusing on a single product and how to increase revenue with additional sales or variations.

Examples

Most start-up companies pass through a single product period in their early days. Originally Apple only sold the Apple II computer, while Intuit started with Quicken alone.

PRODUCT PORTFOLIO

Figure 62. Nokia makes many different models of cell phone

Collage created from Nokia media resource image

Few large companies sell just one product. For example, by 2008 Nokia was selling a range of cell phones to suit all tastes and budgets: you could choose between a small 6300, a large N95 with a hard disk or a Blackberry-like E61. Different phones appealed to different customer segments – a 6300 for the casual user, the N95 for the power user and the E61 for those who needed e-mail on the go.

Context You have successfully used SINGLE PRODUCT COMPANY (page 292) and WHOLE PRODUCT (page 131). It is time to grow the company and you are following SAME CUSTOMERS, DIFFERENT PRODUCT (page 105).

Problem *How do you decide which products to continue selling, which to introduce and which to discontinue?*

Forces Company strategy is no longer synonymous with one product. Your new strategy needs to encompass multiple products. But your resources are still limited and your potential products all demand resources. Some trade-offs and compromises are necessary, but nobody wants to lose resources.

New products need time to demonstrate significant sales, but demand development resources. Old products might be profitable, but they are near the end of their life and vulnerable to competition. Even if you do not wish to grow the company, you still need to consider new products, as customer needs and tastes change over time.

Products age in the market: competitors enter and new technologies change production options. Introducing new products, changing existing products and retiring old products all takes time, money and effort. You need to decide how to allocate your resources between these activities, and how to reduce risks.

Being a single-product company has brought you success, but you now need to grow the company. Maintaining focus on one product brought the success but, by definition, you cannot focus on too many things at the same time: each additional product detracts from the focus on the others.

What is in the best interests of the portfolio may not be in the best interests of a specific product, and vice versa. Tension arises between products serving one market and products serving another market. Further tension will arise because products are build by different teams: decisions about individual products affect the portfolio and vice-versa.

By following WHOLE PRODUCT (page 131) you have developed a cluster of products around the original one. But as this cluster grows, and as more and different products are added, it is difficult to see the common elements. Each additional product – or service – requires management attention; the same managers have more work to do.

Solution

Manage the collective product portfolio as well as managing the individual products. Look at how the products compare, who they target and at what stage they are in their lifecycle. Delegate management of individual products to specific teams and managers. Each *product line* can then focus on its product(s), while company management should then focus on the overall portfolio of products.

This is easier said than done. There are many criteria and conflicts to manage. The portfolio needs to balance the need for an orderly introduction of new products and retirement of old products, and balance the customers' needs for a range of products to choose from or switch between.

There are many criteria that may be used in creating a product portfolio, so it pays to define your criteria before evaluating the portfolio. Criteria need to be based on company goals and objectives, risk aversion, approach to innovation, cost of producing new products, customer needs and many other factors.

With the right criteria in place the portfolio will reflect company strategy. If you are driven by near term-profits, then all your resources should be put into the most profitable products. Conversely, if you are looking for growth you may tolerate loss-making products that may bring in new customers and growth in the medium term.

For some companies the customers' need for a selection of products will dominate: for example, Nokia's mobile phone range. Or companies may offer customers a range of products designed for the different stages of their lives. For example, Ford Europe offers the small Fiesta model for young drivers short of cash, the Focus for couples with young children and the Galaxy for large families. In the world of software, Microsoft markets many different versions of the Windows operating system, for example for desktop use and for mobile use.

A range of products also allows a company to balance positions in the product lifecycle. Established, aging but profitable products can be balanced against new, unproven introductions. Stability and continued support may be important in some sectors, while innovation and fresh products are important elsewhere.

Your product portfolio needs a unifying theme, or *core competency.* The theme may stem from your capability with some technology, from servicing a particular type of customer, or from solving a specific type of problem.

When constructing the portfolio, consider how customers' needs differ, why they might change, what they will need (or want) next, and provide a product to match these factors. By covering a variety of positions, you have multiple products to offer your customers as their needs develop and change.

Both the criteria used to evaluate products and the methods used to manage the portfolio are large topics and outside the scope of this pattern. Two approaches to constructing a portfolio are detailed in *Vertical and horizontal portfolios* on page 300 and *BCG product Growth Share Matrix* on page 307. Many other approaches are possible.

Consequences Setting portfolio criteria and positioning products against each other will highlight product priorities and inform resource allocation. The portfolio view will help to balance product introduction and retirement by exposing product lifecycles. This in turn will help reduce risk.

Studying the portfolio as a whole will help to identify gaps and opportunities for new products. You will also see product overlap, where one product is stealing sales from another, and see which products are in decline. Declining products may be revived by further investment, or 'milked' for further sales and cash without investment.

Introducing new products can offset slowing sales of an aging product. Alternatively, you may be able to rejuvenate the aging product by introducing it into a different market segment.

By offering a selection of products you can retain your hard-won customers as they look for new and different products. When you have a relationship with your customers they will want to do business with you again; when you sell them more products, you will strengthen the relationship – as demonstrated by the SAME CUSTOMERS, DIFFERENT PRODUCT pattern (page 105).

Company strategy is now concerned with the range of products you offer and how those products relate to one another. Each product group can continue to focus on their product, while you focus on the portfolio.

Tensions between different products, and between individual products and the roadmap or company strategy, are easier to recognise, even if they cannot be resolved.

Rather then focusing on a *whole product,* you are looking at the *whole company.* Delegation becomes possible and individuals can be allowed to focus on individual products.

A balanced portfolio will allow you to invest in new products and take risks with the products you develop and introduce, without jeopardising the security of the company. The portfolio will also allow for the organised retirement of older products, so that customers can be migrated to new products and support wound down.

Without a unifying theme your portfolio, and company, will start to resemble a conglomerate. Although conglomerates have advantages, they often trade at a discount when listed on stock markets.

Portfolio management can lead to sub-optimal decisions for individual products. Some products may be held back for fear of damaging others or cannibalising sales. Competitors may be able to exploit such gaps by introducing their own products. For example, IBM initially held back the PC so as not to damage sales of minicomputers, but competitors raced to enhance the capabilities of the PC.

Variations

Venture capital companies pursue investment strategies based on portfolios of companies. Richard Branson's Virgin Group follows a portfolio approach with different companies within the group, using the same brand to sell many different products. Customers associate with the Virgin brand – keep fit at Virgin Active sports centres, talk on a Virgin phone, fly on holiday with Virgin Atlantic. Virgin Group can be seen as a disguised private equity portfolio, with all companies leveraging the same brand and approach to marketing and service.

Related work

Use PRODUCT ROADMAP (page 302) for each product, then synchronise the roadmaps. SIMPLE PRODUCT VARIATIONS (page 121) should lead to a portfolio of products. These may include CORE PRODUCT ONLY (page 110) and SIMPLER PRODUCT (page 100).

SIMPLE PRODUCT VARIATIONS may be help in containing costs of the overall portfolio.

Examples

Product portfolios abound; most large companies offer a range of products. The BCG matrix is a widely cited and critiqued example of a portfolio management technique (see *BCG product Growth Share Matrix* on page 307).

Vertical and horizontal portfolios

Portfolios may be *vertical* or *horizontal*, or a mix for both. In a horizontal portfolio the products fulfil a similar need. For example, Dell's laptop portfolio is arranged horizontally. The laptops are broadly comparable but are alternatives aimed at different users: Inspiron models are aimed at home users and Latitude models at business users. An individual buyer will choose the laptop that best meets their needs, but is unlikely to buy more than one.

Vertical portfolios are made up of products that link together. Buyers are likely to buy several products from the portfolio to work together. For example, IBM offers the Z Series mainframe, which runs the Z/OS operating system, on which can be run the DB2 database and on top of that Office Vision office automation software, as shown in Figure 63. In a vertical portfolio one product leads to the next.

A WHOLE PRODUCT (page 131) strategy creates a horizontal portfolio of products that serve a specific need. The layers of the stack are unimportant to the final customer, who just wants a solution to some problem. Each generic product will have its own mini-portfolio of related products and services. Some of these may be products in their own right if developed correctly.

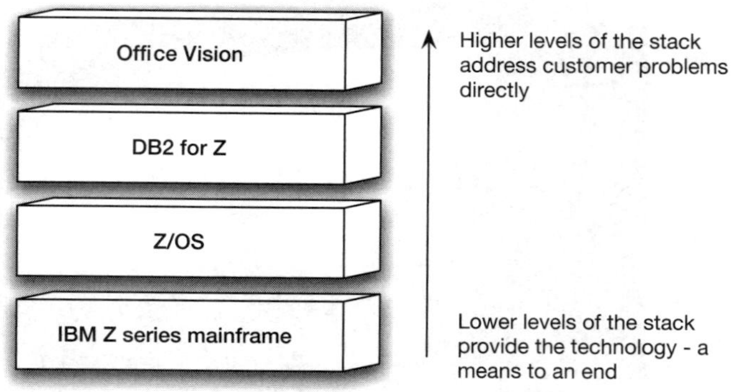

Figure 63. IBM offers a vertical portfolio of mainframe products

Product Roadmap

Figure 64. Items on a roadmap may appear closer than they are

From Flickr user Rarewren (Creative Commons Licence 2.0)

'It's tough to make predictions, especially about the future.'

Yogi Berra, American baseball player and philosopher

'One of the biggest roles of science fiction is to prepare people to accept the future without pain and to encourage a flexibility of mind.'

Arthur C. Clarke, science fiction writer

You can't predict the future for your product, but you need to base your activities around a map everyone can agree on – or at least all see and discuss.

Context You have an existing product in the market. Now you have to tell customers and staff how the product will develop.

Problem *How do you plan for a product's future, and communicate this to customers, employees and partners when the world changes so much?*

Forces Without new products, and new versions of existing products, your company will not advance. Without a vision of what will be in future products, it is difficult to plan for the future and impossible for your engineers to start building.

It is always difficult to foresee the future, but lots of people want to know what your products will do in future: your customers want to know what your product will do in future; your organisation needs to plan for the future – what resources will it need? When will it have a new product? But you cannot answer their questions with absolute certainty.

Lots of disparate groups have an interest in knowing and suggesting what a product should do in future, but how do you incorporate their ideas? And how do you explain the result? The product will need to meet future customer needs; it needs to take advantage of new technology, needs to fit with the company strategy, and will help shape future strategy.

A plan can be formulated from these ideas and opinions, but plans take time to develop and even longer to implement. During that time things change, and some things take longer than expected.

Different groups might feel the need to create different visions of the future. The product management group might create a roadmap that addresses customer needs, while research and development create one that looks at future technology development. But multiple roadmaps will fragment your future vision; they might even conflict and confuse customers.

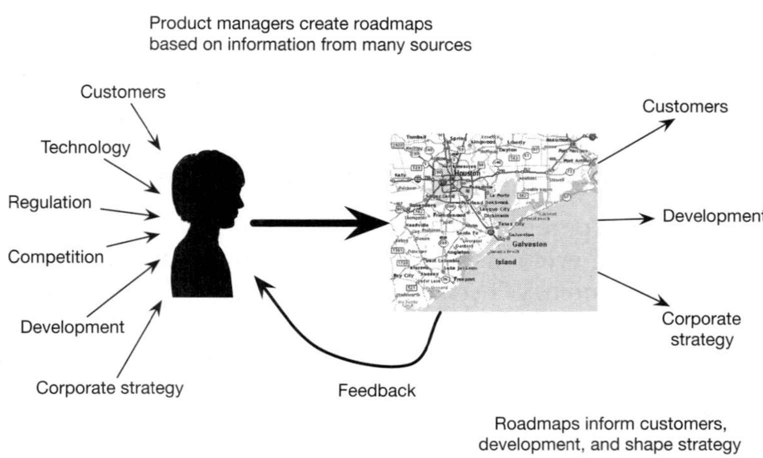

Figure 65. Roadmaps consolidate information, project and inform

Public domain map image (US Federal Government)

Solution

Create a product roadmap to show a vision for the future. The roadmap does not contain a lot of detail; it is more about vision than execution, it shows where you are going rather than a detailed route.

The future is uncertain, but there is still a lot you do know about it, things that are predetermined by the system – dates of trade shows, technology updates, population growth and decline. These can all be marked and help your understanding of the future.

Legislation changes, important financial reporting dates, anticipated competitor actions and dates important to your customers are all key events that can be marked on the roadmap too.

Before building the roadmap, decide who the stakeholders are and find out what they want from the product in the future. Customers are the most obvious (and important) stakeholders, but the actual users of the product are important too – often but not always the same people. People in your company will also have needs and suggestions that will be useful.

Divide the roadmap into 'time buckets', perhaps by quarters or perhaps into the next three months, the next year, the next five years – whatever works for you. Put different objectives in different buckets and keep timescales vague.

When there are lots of enhancements, features and changes to make, group them into themes. Each theme should address a specific aspect of customers' problems.

Show the roadmaps to the stakeholders and listen to their feedback. Present the roadmap to the whole company and listen again. Use their feedback to change the roadmap. Roadmaps are living documents and subject to change. Expect to update your roadmap at least quarterly, and certainly not just for the annual report.

Incorporating different groups and listening to feedback will help to bring everyone in the company to agreement on a single roadmap. Technology development and customers' needs can – and should – be shown on a single map that is simple to understand. Careful attention needs to be given to timelines so that technology introductions and changes can be made.

Avoid making commitments based on the roadmap; you will need to commit to some things, for some dates, but the majority of the roadmap needs to be flexible – work might take longer than expected, or needs may change. The closer something is on the roadmap, the more definite it is. Items that are further away (for example five years out) may be removed long before the date shown.

It may not be wise to show customers your full roadmap. Such a roadmap may contain information you don't want them to have, such as features for their competitors. You may wish to show customers versions of the roadmap that emphasise the things they are interested in and hide other elements. Avoid such problems by never letting a salesperson conduct a roadmap presentations alone.

Consequences The roadmap provides the future vision for people to work towards. It is always a best-efforts map because things always change.

A roadmap describes one version of the future and provides a base for further discussion. Some psychologists call this a *transient object* – an object that exists to help you learn. You cannot foretell the future exactly, but the roadmap allows you to talk about it and plan for it.

The roadmap, the picture, accompanying documentation and verbal description are the result of many inputs. Some people will see their suggestions immediately, others will need to be shown. Some suggestions will be absent from the roadmap because they don't fit with the product strategy. The roadmap will allow you to explain what was left out and why. If every idea was included, the roadmap would be impossibly large and complicated. What you leave out is more important than what you include; there are always some requests that are best turned down.

Creating a single roadmap which reconciles different departments, such as marketing and research and development, will create a unified vision across the company.

Developers can start to develop the products and features on the roadmap. Although items on the roadmap will change, there will be enough certainty at the start of the map to start work. Regular updates between roadmap owners and developers will be needed to accommodate changes on both sides.

Sales people can use the roadmap to sell products by promising features. This can help to improve sales but can be problematic when sales people sell features that are later delayed or removed, when dates changes or are deliberately misrepresented.

A roadmap will raise expectations and perhaps inevitably form the basis of commitments; when a roadmap changes, some commitments will be broken. Sometimes this is difficult to avoid, but when commitments are being broken on a regular basis it is a sign that something is wrong. Look for the underlying reason: perhaps the roadmap is being interpreted too literally, or is too optimistic; perhaps sales people are over stepping their authority; perhaps the planning and roadmap creation process needs to be improved; perhaps the development team needs more resources; perhaps you were too optimistic.

Roadmaps can be used to sow fear, uncertainty and doubt about competitors' products, and to retain customers with promises of new features. This should not be the primary use of a roadmap.

Roadmaps show priorities, so adding a new theme or feature means deciding its priority relative to other items. Conversations about the roadmap quickly turn into conversations about relative priorities – and shows there is *no free lunch*.

Related work Creating the roadmap is a learning exercise; as it is created, you will be forced to think about the future. Once created, the roadmap is also a tool to help stakeholders learn about the future and consider options. A roadmap may be considered a scenario for the future.

Scenario planning (Schwartz, 1991) is a well-developed field and you might borrow some techniques from it. For example, try creating several roadmaps and select the most realistic. Once a roadmap is selected, the organisation begins to build the product described. It is worth continuing to monitor the roadmap/scenario: which of the events envisioned came to pass? What changed? Periodic updates to the roadmap are essential; the planning, creating, monitoring and changes is an ongoing process.

If you are also following PRODUCT PORTFOLIO (page 296) remember to synchronise your various roadmaps where necessary. It may also be useful to produce a high-level portfolio roadmap.

Examples The author has worked with several ISVs that have successfully used product roadmaps.

BCG product Growth Share Matrix

The horizontal and vertical view of the product portfolio describe how a portfolio is presented to customers. Another way of looking at a portfolio is the *Growth Share Matrix* from the Boston Consulting Group (BCG), as shown in Figure 66. This approach aims to maximise the return for the whole company.

The matrix divides products into one of four categories based on whether the company has a high or low market share and whether the market as a whole is experiencing high or low growth.

Companies that follow the matrix are advised to maximise their returns from *cash cows* while minimising investments because the market is not growing. Companies are advised to discontinue *dogs* – products with low sales and little potential growth – and invest in *stars* that will produce profits in future. There is no standard advice for *question marks*, those products that have potential but are currently underperforming. These products require specific attention.

Such advice can be simplistic, particularly for small technology companies. More detailed analysis may consider the profitability of products and their role in providing for a WHOLE PRODUCT (page 131). An unprofitable *dog* product may in fact be providing vital support for another product.

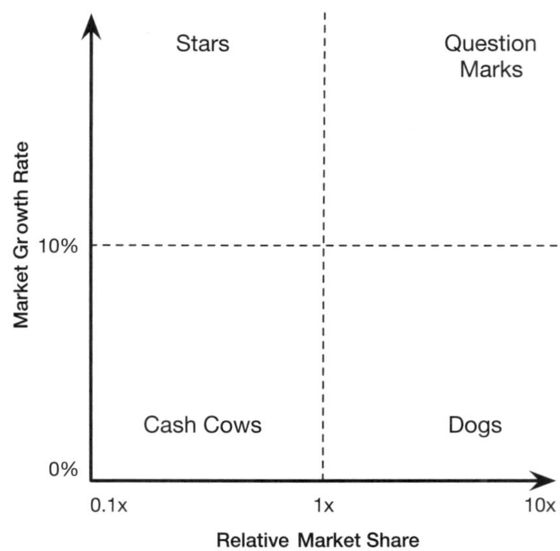

Figure 66. Simplified Boston Consulting Group Growth Share Matrix

One problem with the growth matrix can be defining the market. *Crossing the Chasm* (Moore, 1999) advises companies to define the market as narrowly as possible in order to focus action and present the company as the market leader. Following this advice renders half the matrix pointless, because we have defined our market as a market we dominate. Thus there are no *dogs* or *question marks*. Conversely, an expanding company may redefine its market more broadly in a search for growth: at a stroke a *star* product can be turned into a *dog*.

The question of market share and market definition can have a profound effect on company action. During the 1980s General Electric famously pursued a strategy of being 'number one or number two' in every market it operated in. The company abandoned those markets where it could not achieve first or second place (Welch, 2001). However one way to achieve leadership was to define the market narrowly. In doing so the company could miss profitable opportunities in a wider market.

Complementor, Not Competitor

Figure 67. Strawberries do not compete with cream

'Three years, a lot of activity, and a few billion dollars later, we still weren't [application software] leaders…

However, one thing we were doing exceptionally well was irritating the heck out of the leading application providers – companies like SAP, PeopleSoft and JD Edwards. These companies were in a great position to generate a lot of business for us…

What we said to them was "We are going to leave this market to you; we are going to be your partners rather than your competitor".'

(Gerstner, 2003)

Context Within your product portfolio you sell two or more products that are complementary and usually sold together; it might not even make sense to buy them individually. Your competitors offer one or other of the products, and customers often mix-and-match. One of your products can hold its own against the competition, but the other cannot.

Problem *How do you arrange your product and services portfolio so that you maximise your profits and don't lose money on products?*

Forces

Your have two complementary products: let's call them 'Strawberries' and 'Cream'. Strawberries sells well and makes money, but Cream sells less well; it loses money, and even some of your Strawberry customers prefer to buy their Cream from another vendor.

You have traditionally sold customers a total solution of both Strawberries and Cream. But, while your Strawberries are very good, there is better Cream on offer elsewhere. Customers who buy Strawberries elsewhere are unlikely to buy your Cream too.

Developing both Strawberries and Cream has allowed for innovation in the past, but now it is competitors who sell only Strawberries or only Cream who are generating the innovations. Having both does not offer a lot more opportunities for innovation.

Traditionally your own Strawberries and Cream, and the innovation possible, has given you a strategic advantage. But the market, business strategy and core competencies have changed over time, and you no longer get the advantage you once did.

Selling both products together makes for a bigger sale with more revenue, but when costs are broken down, most of the profit comes from the Strawberries.

Both Strawberries and Cream are expensive to develop; while Strawberries makes money, Cream is losing money.

Solution

Concentrate your activities on the most profitable part of the solution; discontinue the less profitable parts and replace the missing parts with ones from other vendors. Rather than competing with everyone, seek to complement those who can help you sell more of your most profitable products.

Customers will want to buy Strawberries and Cream; now that you no longer compete with the Cream manufacturers, they can be a source of customers. You will need to form partnerships to align your goals and methods. Your staff will need to know partners' products and ensure partners' Cream works well with your Strawberries.

You need to prove to your new partners that you are committed to this strategy. Move fast and decisively to show that you are now a friend and not an enemy. Cream makers could still recommend one of the other Strawberry suppliers, so work together to produce the best Strawberries for their Cream.

Consequences You no longer supply a total solution with your own products; instead, you sell your most profitable product and complement it with third-party products to offer a total solution.

Opportunities for innovation between Strawberries and Cream are more difficult to find and exploit; however, you can be more focused on innovation for Strawberries.

Discontinuing a loss-making product should immediately help your balance sheet. By partnering with others you can increase sales revenue for your profitable products – a classic win-win situation.

Sales of Strawberries alone may be smaller, but they will be more profitable; in addition, you are hoping to sell more Strawberries by working together with the Cream makers. You may be able to make revenue from consultancy services too.

You have saved the cost of developing an expensive product. Product development costs are lower; the cash released may be used elsewhere, say in new products or services.

However, you will need to ensure that your Strawberries are compatible with the Cream from various vendors. Ensuring compatibility can in itself be a timely and costly endeavour.

Customers are no longer locked into your products; they now choose your products because you have the best solution to their needs, not because they have no choice.

New partners may seek to lock you into their product; if you become dependent on one Cream maker, you will be in a weak position if they ask for special consideration and price cuts. So work with several Cream makers to give you the choice to walk away from a deal if a partner asks too much.

Variations Products may be service products. You might stop offering your physical product while offering your services in support of your traditional competitors' products. Conversely, you may discontinue your own services offerings and encourage third-party suppliers to offer services to support your products.

Related work Contrast with LIFETIME SERVICES FOR PRODUCTS (page 252), where the sale of one product – possibly at a loss – allows you to make money from a second.

IN BED WITH THE ENEMY (Weiss, 2007) also describes how companies can work with former and even current competitors.

A WHOLE PRODUCT (page 131) strategy can lead companies to produce supporting products that in time end up losing money in their own right. As long as customers see a total solution to their problems, it is not important whether all components come from one supplier or many.

Examples Games console manufactures usually lose money on each console sold while making large profits on the games for the consoles. After selling over 6 million Dreamcast consoles and losing $500 million, Sega left the market in 2001 and chose to focus on producing software for Sony, Microsoft and Nintendo consoles.

Competitor, not Complementor

There is a mirror image to COMPLEMENTOR, NOT COMPETITOR. Sometimes a company that could be a complementor in a market decides to enter the market as a competitor. For example, at around the time Sega decided to leave the games console market, Microsoft entered the market with their first Xbox console.

The company spent millions of dollars researching and developing the new console to enter the same highly competitive market Sega was leaving. Microsoft could have chosen to play the role of complementor and develop games for Sony and Nintendo consoles, but instead chose to become a player in the market themselves.

Microsoft reasoned that, despite the cost of entering the games console market, it was important to their overall strategy. Eventually the move would deliver enough profit to justify entry. To enter the market the company leveraged their existing core competency of software development, but had to develop new competencies in hardware development and console marketing.

INNOVATIVE PRODUCTS

Figure 68. Innovative products

Innovation lies at the heart of all successful start-up companies, and rare is the software or technology company that does not depend on innovation for growth. Yet innovation remains easier to talk about than to accomplish.

While many companies talk about innovation, few are prepared to bet the company and make it central to strategy and ongoing advantage.

Context Your company wishes to create innovative products, perhaps so that you can break into new markets; perhaps so you can serve your existing customers better and expand your customer base, perhaps so you can command higher margins on your product – or perhaps so you can do all of these things.

Innovation allows products to be differentiated from competitors' and command a higher price, or it may provide for a much cheaper version of an existing product. The innovation itself might be in the product itself, or in the process used to manufacture or deliver the product or service.

Problem *How can a company create a stream of innovative products?*

Forces

A company might want to produce new innovative products or services, but it is not easy to come up with new ideas on demand. Innovative ideas come from people, they cannot be repeatedly produced by a formalised process; indeed, a formal process might drive innovation out.

From time to time opportunities for new products arise spontaneously, apparently out of the blue. But successful companies do not rely on chance happenings. To remain competitive, companies need to create such opportunities.

Generating an innovative idea is necessary, but is not enough: companies need to turn ideas into marketable products. Research suggests that '*most companies are sufficiently good at generating ideas; the 'bottleneck' in the innovation process actually occurs a lot further down the pipeline.*' (Birkinshaw et al, 2010).

New product ideas may be attractive to individuals, but not all of them are attractive business propositions. The company needs some means of deciding which ideas to pursue and which to discard.

Existing products cannot guarantee competitive advantage, but new products take time to create. Companies need cash flow to survive while creating new products, so existing products and markets need to be sold and serviced effectively. Thus the company will need to *do two things at once*: create new products and support the existing one(s).

Solution

Seek to understand customers and their needs, then to apply your technology skills to create innovative solutions. Create a corporate culture that values and encourages innovation, and take practical steps day-to-day to seed, identify and experiment with innovation.

Encourage employees to generate new ideas for products, apply company technology and competencies to new domains. Do not reject ideas out of hand, give people time to develop ideas: even if one idea goes nowhere, it may encourage employees to try again.

Don't penalise people for ideas that don't work. For every success there will be many failures; each of these is itself a learning opportunity. If employees feel ashamed of their failures learning will be inhibited and they will be less likely to try again. Immediately after the 'failure' might not be the best time to learn – people want to nurse their wounds – so let the dust settle a little before inspecting what happened.

SAME CUSTOMERS, DIFFERENT PRODUCT (page 105) suggests you work from your existing customer base. You have these relationships already, so find out what else your customer needs. How can you serve their needs better? What products would complement those you have already sold them?

Get to know your customers in depth to truly understand their needs and aspirations: use CUSTOMER UNDERSTANDING (page 146) and EFFECTIVE LISTENING (Rising, 2002). By understanding the customer, understanding the problems they face, and how they use existing products, it becomes possible to see opportunities where existing products fail.

Remember that all customers are not equal, so use SEGMENTED CUSTOMERS (page 141) to divide your existing and potential customers. Seek to understand the different segments and the opportunities they offer.

Establish a company structure that encourages people to think and work beyond their existing products and segments. The structure may not be right on the first try; it may take several attempts before a suitable structure is found. Groups that were previously separate will often need to work together, so build multi-disciplinary teams and encourage cross-functional staff.

Where new products can be imagined but details are unclear, use EXPEDITIONARY MARKETING (page 153) to map the market space and find what customers are prepared to pay for.

When the corporate environment is stifling new product ideas and development, try SEPARATE IMAGINATIVE TEAMS (page 318) to give the innovators space.

Sometime the company can envisage a product, but some aspects of development, distribution or marketing fall outside of the core competencies. Use CUSTOMER CO-CREATED PRODUCT (page 95) to involve customers in creating a product they need.

Alternatively, build on what your company does, your *core competencies,* and seek to apply these skills to new markets and products. You will need to look beyond your current markets and customers. Finding partner organisations can help here, even if it means getting IN BED WITH THE ENEMY (Weiss, 2007).

You will need a mechanism for reviewing projects, deciding which to continue and which to discontinue. Beware that mechanical approaches to market evaluation – such as return on investment

(ROI) calculations (for example IRR (internal rate of return) and NPV (net present value)) – and traditional business plans may undervalue the opportunity, because it is difficult to value new ideas. The more radical the idea or product, the more difficult it will be to value it.

To achieve focus on new products the company may need to leave some market segments, either because new products are available or to improve company focus. This may be done directly – through sale, closure or write-off – or indirectly through outsourcing and licensing.

Consequences Although you cannot guarantee innovation on demand, providing a supportive culture and opportunities to pursue ideas will increase the chances of ideas being shared and acted on.

A proactive approach to understanding customers and their needs will provide the basis for spotting opportunities. Developing capabilities and technology know-how will provide the tools to address those opportunities.

The review process provides a way for closing down unpromising ideas, but may also kill off the those with the greatest opportunity because they are also the riskiest and have more unknowns. Such a process needs to avoid sending mixed signals to staff about the value placed on innovation. Staff who feel aggrieved when their favourite project is killed may even leave the company and take the idea with them.

Splitting resources between existing products and new product development is never going to be easy. By recognising the process and placing a value on it, managing the balance should be easier.

Not all new products and markets may be viable; some efforts to establish new market space will fail. It can be hard to predict sales of radically different products ahead of time; demand may be slow to build and multiple iterations of the product cycle may be needed in order to understand the market and refine the product before a profitable configuration is found.

Entering the market with a minimal CORE PRODUCT ONLY (page 110) will keep costs low and time short; EXPEDITIONARY MARKETING (page 153) and SIMPLE PRODUCT VARIATIONS (page 121) can be deployed to experiment in the market and find out what customers want.

Innovative products may open new revenue streams, but the new products may reduce revenue from existing products. Failure to launch new products – either consciously or subconsciously – provides opportunities for competitors to launch such products.

Variations

Being innovative is not for all companies. One alternative is to adopt a *fast follower* approach: let others develop the innovative product, and when they have success, copy them quickly. To be a successful fast follower you will need to:

- Watch the market and customers to spot new innovations when they occur
- React quickly when a new product is spotted
- Deliver rapidly before the gap becomes too wide.

Follower companies may be able to copy individual innovations, but they will be forced to play catch-up and compete on price while an innovative company moves on to newer, more innovative products and services that can command a premium.

Related work

Fearless (Manns & Rising, 2003) describes how to introduce new ideas to an organisation.

Examples

3M embraces the idea that continual innovation provides competitive advantage: divisions are required to generate 30% of revenue from products introduced in the last four years. The company's '15% rule' means that all researchers must spend 15% of their time working on their own projects (Nonaka & Takeuchi, 1995).

Google extended 3M's 15% rule to '20% projects' where staff are expected to spend a day a week on their own innovative ideas. In practice this means some staff (such as product managers) find opportunities with customers and the market, then find engineers to work on these projects. When the project reaches some viability threshold it is reviewed and possibly formalised.

Although both Google and 3M are famed for these rules, reports from employees indicate that they are not applied at all locations or to all workers. Intensive work schedules mean that staff sometimes need to find the time for such personal projects from their own time.

SEPARATE IMAGINATIVE TEAMS

Figure 69. The SR-71 'Blackbird' was the result of a Lockheed 'skunkworks' programme

Public domain image created by US Air Force personnel

Sun Microsystems set up a 'black project' in 1990 to develop what later became the Java programming language and environment. The small team was located away from Sun's own offices, was secret, had lots of money and was free of Sun's usual development strategy and bureaucracy (Naughton, 1996).

Context The company is competing in an established market and has developed an infrastructure to support its existing products. Existing products sell well and make a profit, but the product line is ageing. The company now wishes to follow an INNOVATIVE PRODUCTS (page 313) strategy.

Problem *How does a company create a truly innovative product when corporate culture resists innovation?*

Forces Large companies may stifle innovation. Development of new products (if any) tends to be incremental in nature. Company bureaucracy tends to restrict innovative products; people can become scared of failure.

Research and development may be able to create new and innovative products, but the company organisation, culture and bureaucracy serves the existing products efficiently, stifling innovation.

Incremental development of existing products is cheap and can show a clear return because it builds on existing sales data, but fails to produce real innovation. Competitors are able to undercut the established market through innovation.

Companies do not lack innovative people; most large companies will have researches and designers, but such people find their ideas rejected at an early stage, or are perceived as rocking the boat. Some may choose to leave the company to pursue their ideas if they cannot innovate within the company.

Solution *Form a team of innovative employees and separate them from the organisation that constrains them.* Separate them physically in a new location and provide them with the resources they need.

The team needs to be staffed by people who are both innovative and entrepreneurial. The team will be outside the company, so it is no use staffing the team with people who prefer a large corporation.

Leadership and management of the team must be particularly entrepreneurial, as they will need to create a start-up environment and make many of the decisions traditionally made by start-up founders. Such people may be difficult to find in a large organisation that, by its nature, contains managers and staff who are at home in a large company.

Teams need to be motivated and directed without overly confining and controlling them.

The new team needs a 'clean slate' – to be free of company bureaucracy, politics, existing assumptions and legacy systems.

Resources must be made available to the team. In some variations the team is given everything they need; at other times such teams must operate on a shoestring, or even obtain outside funding.

Consequences There will be start-up costs associated with creating such a *skunkworks* project, such as leasing new office space.

Such teams may find it difficult to leverage company assets, knowledge and resources, because they have been set up separately outside of the main processes and hierarchy. Attempting to leverage these resources may expose the team to the politics and bureaucracy it was trying to escape.

Existing employees may see the separate team as a threat to their jobs or a slight on their skills. Companies sometimes choose to keep the team secret, but this can add to resentment when the team is made public.

Once the project is complete the team and product needs to be folded back into the original organisation. Simply disbanding the team may be efficient, but may miss opportunities and entail its own risks. Team members may have become accustomed to their independence and dislike returning to the big company. The ideas and values that surrounded the independent team and support creativity may be lost in the change.

Even if the skunkworks group creates a great product, the company has not actually improved its ability to create new innovative products. The very one-off nature of the project makes it difficult to repeat, and the company's original problem remains unsolved.

Motorola's successful Razr phone was the result of a skunkworks development team; however Motorola was unable to repeat the success: it was unable to build on the skunkworks development, and the company's share of phone sales has resumed its long-term decline.

Variations

Sometimes the skunkworks project is not completely approved of by management and seeks to hide itself away. Tracy Kidder's story of the Eclipse project at Data General describes a team with limited resources seeking to create a new computer in competition with a more well-established effort in the same company (Kidder, 1981).

The ultimate separation of innovative teams occurs when corporations engage in *corporate venturing*. In these cases companies set up their own internal venture capital groups and seek proposals from within the company. Entrepreneurs inside the company must produce business plans and finance requests to the corporate funders and possibly other outside financiers. Groups that receive funding may be required to resign from the parent company in order to create true start-up incentives.

Related work

This pattern is broadly similar to SKUNKWORKS (Coplien & Harrison, 2004), but differs in two aspects. Coplien and Harrison say '*the very existence of a Skunkworks team should be a secret*' – this is not suggested here. Secondly, this pattern places more emphasis on the difficulties of re-integrating products and teams into the corporate structure.

Examples

One of the most famous example of a company separating an imaginative team was Xerox' creation of the Palo Alto Research Centre (PARC) in California. While Xerox' management and mainstream engineers were based in New York or Texas, the PARC team were located far away, with the remit to invent technologies to sustain Xerox beyond photocopiers. Although PARC developed much new technology, Xerox itself was unable to capitalise on the developments and failed to fold any of the products back into the company or generate innovation elsewhere. Many of the PARC researches went on to found successful companies, such as Adobe and 3Com, based on what they learnt at PARC, or helped other companies to capitalise on the innovations, such as Microsoft and Apple.

Mazda's Miata/MX-2 sports car was developed by as 'guerrilla' project. The team was placed in a different building to the main engineering organisation and given a remit to develop a distinctive car outside of the usual multi-project strategy (Cusumano & Nobeoka, 1998).

A

About Patterns

The patterns presented in this book form part of a growing *pattern language* about business, and software businesses in particular. As additional patterns are added, more are identified. Patterns within this language are assembled together in *sequences*. It is natural to find that the application of one pattern creates the opportunity to apply another pattern. There is no mandated, or even *right*, sequence through the language; each organisation needs to find the sequence(s) that works for them.

Patterns, by their nature, capture existing knowledge rather than create new knowledge. By documenting this knowledge in pattern form it can be made more accessible to a wider audience, thus making it more accessible to the managers, engineers and others who are tasked with implementing business strategies.

In some cases this knowledge may not have been captured before. Although known to some individuals and groups, it may previously have only existed tacitly inside the heads of individuals, or embedded in practices, processes and market mechanisms. Presenting this knowledge in pattern form allows it to be communicated and combined with other knowledge. Once captured, these heuristics can be examined, enhanced, refined or even deprecated.

Whether applying patterns or documenting new ones, patterns are by their nature generative. We apply one pattern and find an opportunity for a second. Similarly, when we document one pattern, we often find another. Most of the patterns presented here have been identified by the author from his own experience and investigation. During the pattern review process, reviewers have identified additional patterns, many of which have been developed and included here.

What Is a Pattern?

The short answer to the question "*What is a pattern?*" is usually given as '*A solution to a problem in a context*'. However a pattern is more than this. A pattern is a story about how to solve a recurring problem. The story has structure and form; although the structure and form may differ from pattern to pattern, the important thing is that its author follows a structure and form.

The possession of a (variable) structure and form means that patterns are in many ways similar to poetry. Both patterns and poems tell a story; both seek to convey feeling and knowledge. Both follow a predetermined format and both are named, simplifying reference and communication.

Like the best poems, the best patterns are short. Brevity is important: a short pattern is more likely to be read and remembered. A long pattern is often better expressed as several shorter patterns that fit together. Details may be omitted, both to keep the pattern short and to allow the reader to impose their own experience. Unlike a poem, however, a pattern is a working thing. It is written to convey knowledge about how to resolve a problem. Conveying this knowledge is the reason the pattern exists.

There is a further way in which a pattern may be like a poem. In the same way that there is no prohibition on writing another love poem, or a poem of sorrow, there is no prohibition on writing a pattern on the same subject as an existing one. The second pattern might contain knowledge missing from the first, it might be more current, or it might simply be more readable. Of course, if a pattern already exists that says everything you would like to say in an accessible form, then there is little point to writing it again. But like any art form, retelling a story often adds something.

Patterns and patterns

There is no restriction on the word *pattern*; it has an everyday common usage. There are plenty of books, journal articles and conference presentations that discuss 'patterns' but are not concerned with the type of patterns discussed here.

It is sometimes useful to characterise the casual use of the term *pattern* as 'pattern' with a lower-case 'p', and the more formal use as 'Pattern' with a capital 'P'. The latter are pieces of literature that document and explain recurring solutions. Casual patterns (lower-case 'p') might be little more than coincidence, convenience or idiom. Careful examination may lead from a casual 'pattern' to a documented 'Pattern', but there is no guarantee. (One might also use the term *Alexandrian patterns* to signify roots in Alexander's work (Alexander, 1977), or *Design Patterns* to signify shared roots with software patterns. Both terms may also lead to additional implications.)

Recurring events or behaviour that lead to (casual) patterns has interested other authors and researchers, leading to work such as *Profit Pattern* (Slywotzky et al, 1999), *Patterns in Strategy Formation* (Mintzberg, 1978), *Pattern Based Strategy* (Gartner, 2009) and *Spotting Patterns on the Fly* (Coutu, 2002). Apart from the word 'pattern', the common connections are recognition of recurrence, an attempt to understand what brings about the recurrence and efforts to benefit from the recurrence.

Alexander's ideas on patterns have influenced many writers in many domains, but this does not mean that every writer who uses the word 'pattern' is using it in the same context. The word 'pattern' is used to communicate different ideas for different authors. Some authors will be influenced by Alexander and some not. The underlying basis behind all this writing may be similar, but it is interpreted and used differently. Indeed, Alexander himself has not stood still. His own thinking about patterns has advanced with work such as *The Nature of Order* (Alexander, 2002). This is only to be expected, but similarly, the software pattern community's thinking about patterns has also developed and moved on. Along the way the two have begun to diverge.

The Patterns in this book take as their basis Alexander's work in the 1970s as developed by the software patterns community in books such as *Design Patterns, Fearless Change*, the *Pattern Oriented Software Architecture* series (Buschmann et al, 1996; Schmidt et al, 2000) and at PLoP conferences – specifically EuroPLoP and VikingPLoP. Consequently there may be some divergence from Alexander's more recent ideas.

It is important to understand what we mean by a *pattern* when building on Alexander's work. Here, and in related works, a pattern has a precise meaning:

> *A pattern is a piece of structured writing that describes a solution to some recurring problem within a common context.*

Context is a particularly important condition. Sometimes context is broad and widely shared, while at other times it is narrow and highly specific.

When discussing patterns in the Alexandrian sense we need distinguish three types of pattern:

- *Undocumented pattern*: a pattern that has not yet been identified and documented.

- *Informal pattern*: a pattern that has been identified, may be documented, but has not been written in structured form. This book contains many informal patterns scattered throughout the text.
- *Formal pattern*: a pattern that has been identified, written in a structured form and probably peer reviewed and revised. Most of the patterns in this book are formal patterns.

An underlying pattern of events and things may exist, but it is a formalisation of these sequence into a piece of structured literature that is the 'Pattern'. For the remainder of this appendix the word 'pattern' is restricted to this definition.

Elements of a pattern

Patterns typically come in sections. Each section carries a specific element of the pattern. Although pattern form varies, there are standard elements that occur in most patterns. Several elements are considered essential in a good pattern:

- *Problem statement*: every pattern is expected to resolve some problem. If we are to resolve a problem, we must first define what the problem is.
- *Forces*: these are the things that define the problem and make it difficult to solve. Pattern writers are advised not to bother with trivial problems and those with obvious solutions. Rather, patterns seek to resolve difficult problems that involve multiple and often contradictory forces.
- *Solution statement*: a description of how to solve the problem described in the problem statement and the forces. Writers are encouraged to give practical advice and describe how to build a solution. General advice, or philosophical solutions, are discouraged.
- *Name*: all patterns need to be named to allow them to be referenced and discussed. As we shall see later in *How to Write a Pattern* (page 338), the naming of patterns helps to improve knowledge sharing. Unfortunately there is no mechanism for ensuring that patterns have unique names: names like 'Strategy' and 'Template' tend to be used by multiple patterns.

No pattern is complete without these four elements as a minimum. However there are several more elements that are commonly considered desirable in a pattern:

- *Context*: not all patterns are applicable in all contexts. The context helps to set the scope of the pattern by defining its applicability.
- *Picture*: including a picture allows the author and reader to share a visual stimulus as well as textual description. Whether the picture shows the problem, the solution, an example or simply seeks to stir the reader's emotions, it can help the reader, literally, to visualise the pattern.

- *Consequences*: when a pattern is applied there will be consequences; some will be good (benefits), some will be undesired (liabilities). Consequences usually follow the solution description and often describe explicitly how each force is resolved after the solution.
- *Known uses*: the pattern community places great store by documenting known solutions. Patterns are not the place for original thinking: the objective of a pattern is to capture existing knowledge (more on this below). As such it should be possible to demonstrate that the pattern has been used before. Three examples are normally preferred, showing beyond doubt that the pattern tackles a recurring problem and solution.

There are several more elements that some pattern writers choose to include and others do not, depending on their style and structure. It is common to find the following elements in addition to those described already:

- *Opening vignette*: a paragraph or two, sometimes in italics, which attempts to give a feeling – often by way of an example – of the pattern that follows.
- *Implementation*: solution sections are sometimes split between a general description of the solution and a more detailed description of how to implement the solution.
- *Example*: patterns may contain an example of specific known uses that are described in more detail than other known uses. In software patterns this may involve program code.
- *Example resolved*: where a more detailed example is included, authors may choose to present it initially with the problem description and then later with solution applied.
- *Intention and Motivation*: when included, these sections attempt to give some justification for why one might want to use the pattern. Personally I find that they duplicate the problem statement.
- *Alias* or *Also Known As*: a list of names and reference by which the pattern may also be known.
- *Benefits* and *Liabilities*: some authors prefer to present the *Consequences* section as two sections, one dealing with the positive consequences – the benefits – and another dealing with the problems – the liabilities.

Finally, authors are free to add additional sections as they see fit or to use alternative names for these elements.

Where do patterns come from?

'Patterns do not come only from the work of architects and planners.'

(Alexander, 1979, p. 199)

Most of the patterns documented in this book draw on personal experience and observation together with publicly available sources. Other patterns are the result of *pattern mining* – that is, they draw on existing literature but are written in pattern form. This provides for a more complete pattern language and helps to make this literature more accessible.

For example, the pattern EXPEDITIONARY MARKETING (page 153) discusses techniques for creating and marketing innovative products derived from *Corporate Imagination and Expeditionary Marketing* (Hamel & Prahalad, 1991). The author has added his own insights and experiences to these descriptions. Wherever external sources have been used, a conscious decision has been made to use public sources, so that readers can enquire further themselves.

Hopefully it is now clear that patterns are themselves *emergent*. Problems that occur once and which are genuinely unique are not the basis of patterns. But problems that occur again and again, and to which similar solutions are found, are. The details and nature of the solution will depend on the things that make the problem difficult (the forces) and the available technology.

When the same solution is used by many people in different places, a pattern is established. At first it is not documented; the knowledge exists, but it is tacit. Some people will learn the pattern first-hand from others who use the solution – tacit knowledge transfer (Nonaka & Takeuchi, 1995). Others will reinvent the solution, and still more people will struggle to find a solution to the problem. Only when the pattern is documented and the knowledge it encapsulates is made explicit can it be circulated widely.

Naturally, once the pattern is documented and passes into common knowledge, it becomes part of the design vocabulary; it is no longer and emergent phenomenon. Now it can play a role as a building block in the emergence of new patterns.

The originator of pattern thinking, Christopher Alexander, believes that patterns are timeless – that the same worthwhile solutions will appear again and again. This may be true for some patterns, but others will change or fall into disuse as technology allows for different – better – solutions, and the forces that brought the problem and solution into being change.

Perhaps it is better to think of patterns as *stable intermediary forms* (Henney, 2004). These are solutions that exist for a period of time: some will have short lifetimes – perhaps so brief that nobody notices them – while others will have lifetimes that last centuries and which may appear timeless to humans.

Patterns capture knowledge about technology. They allow technology usage to be described and shared. Thus they play a role in advancing the state of the art. But as that technology changes, it will change the patterns. In some cases the pattern will rendered useless by such changes, but new patterns will emerge. The implicit context of all patterns is the technology environment in which they exist. As technology changes, patterns will change and evolve.

Pattern forms

Pattern form refers to the presentation and layout of patterns: the sections that are included or omitted, and the text flow of the pattern.

The earliest patterns, by Christopher Alexander and his colleagues, comprised a pattern name, a picture – Alexander claims it should be possible to draw a pattern – and a text description. The description contained all the elements described in *Elements of a pattern* on page 326. The problem statement was presented in bold text to make it easier to find; the problem description and forces would then follow in plain text.

The solution would be introduced by the word *therefore*. A brief problem statement would then be presented in bold again, before a more detailed description in plain text. Someone in a hurry could thus read a pattern as: 'problem statement (therefore…) solution'.

Many authors since Alexander have also adopted this form, or forms very similar. Good examples can be found in *Fearless Change* (Manns & Rising, 2005) and *Organizational Patterns of Agile Software Development* (Coplien & Harrison, 2004). It is in this form that patterns come closest to poetry. Such patterns can be easy to read, but they can also be among the most difficult to write.

Most software developers first encounter patterns when they read *Design Patterns* (Gamma et al, 1995) – often called the *Gang of Four* book because it has four authors. This book uses a very different pattern form that is far more structured. Here each element is given its own section with a large bold heading. Nor do the authors skimp on sections; elements in these patterns are: Intent, Also Known As, Motivation, Applicability, Structure, Participants, Collaborations, Consequences, Implementation, Sample Code, Known Uses and Related Patterns.

At first sight this list may look overwhelming, and it may seem to bear little resemblance to the list presented in *Elements of a pattern* (page 326). However elements like 'motivation' map quite clearly to 'problem', and collaborations can be mapped to related patterns; other sections, like structure and implementation, seem to overlap.

To draw an architectural comparison, Alexandrian form is like an office building in which the supporting service infrastructure is inside the structure. Examining the services requires careful examination inside the pattern. The alternative forms that signpost their structure can be thought of as being like the Pompidou centre in Paris or the Lloyds building in London, in which the supporting infrastructure is on the outside. Indeed, the infrastructure is the first thing one sees.

In this book I have used a hybrid form. Each element is clearly signposted and clearly different from the others. Ideally I would like to think the reader can ignore the signposts and read the body of the text straight through in Alexander-like form. The form has proved popular with readers and has been adopted by other writers, for example Weiss, 2009.

The reason for using this form is twofold. By signposting the sections, it is hoped to make the analysis clearer and help those new to patterns understand the different elements. Secondly, the form deliberately aims to be readable without the signposting getting in the way.

Pattern length is another element of pattern form. A pattern may be long: my own ENCAPSULATED CONTEXT ran to 20 pages when it was finally published (Manolescu et al, 2006). This pattern covers a lot of material, it has a long worked example, and discussion of variations and modification. Alternatively, the same material may be presented as a set of patterns that work together in sequences or as alternatives.

Sometimes a pattern needs to be long because there is a lot of information to communicate. Equally some patterns are naturally short. The pattern author has a choice: one can continue adding more and more to a single pattern, or one can choose to split the pattern. Splitting the pattern is usually the right thing to do. However this not only generates more work – for authors at least – but means both patterns now need to stand alone as well as work together.

More than contingency theory

At first sight it may appear that a pattern is little more than an elaborate contingency theory. The context, problem statement and forces form a set of conditions that, when met, allow a solution to be used. However there is more to a pattern than this.

Firstly, patterns are a type of literature; the comparison to a poem has already been made. Patterns should be readable and even enjoyable to read. Were they just contingent, one could imagine writing them in program-like pseudocode. The author needs to make the pattern interesting to read.

I sometimes like to compare a pattern to a novel. In the beginning (context) the scene is set, perhaps a house in the country. Then something happens, a body is discovered! – this is the problem. The detective investigates and finds many difficult questions to resolve. These are the forces; the most difficult are those that are contradictory.

The problems and unanswered questions create a tension that intrigues and mystifies. The reader is left asking: *with all these forces to resolve, how can we solve the problem? Who is the murderer? And how did they do it?*

Next comes the moment of explanation: the solution – the detective names the murderer. *But how?* asks the gathered audience. "Elementary..." says the detective, and explains how he resolved the case and found the killer – this is the solution. At the end of the story all the questions are answered and the tension resolved – the consequences.

As in the story, that which is unsaid can be as powerful as that which is explicit. There is a balance between describing the situation and allowing the reader's own imagination to fill in the pieces. Using the readers' imagination to help tell the story involves the reader and helps them to see how the pattern can work in their environment.

The second reason why patterns are more than an elaborate contingency theory is the *quality without a name* (Alexander, 1979). Alexander suggested that all patterns should improve the quality of life. This is discussed in more detail below; suffice to say, this objective gives patterns their moral basis.

As we will show, each pattern is part of a larger pattern language. Within the pattern language there are sequences that describe common applications of many patterns. Those using the patterns are free to find their own sequences, but at heart patterns are intended to be used together.

Taken together, these reasons mean that there is more to a pattern, and pattern languages, than contingency theory alone. This also implies that mechanical automatons cannot apply a pattern language to create a whole system without human intervention. A recurring theme in software engineering pattern literature is the automatic discovery and application of patterns. An understanding of pattern languages and sequences show why this is not possible.

Contingency theory

Contingency theory is a branch of behavioural theory that claims that there is no single best way to organise a corporation, lead a company or make decisions. The optimal course of action is therefore *contingent* (dependent) on the internal and external situation the company experiences. Several such approaches were developed concurrently in the late 1960s.

Pattern Languages

'No pattern is an island' *(Schmidt et al, 2000).*

Individual patterns need to be coherent and make sense; each pattern is a short story in its own right and each pattern can be read alone. Individual patterns describe and document some aspect of a system: a set of forces, a problem, solution and consequences.

However patterns do not exist in isolation, and when it comes to their use, patterns are found with, and applied with, other patterns. Patterns are used to build systems, and when brought together a set of patterns interlock and operate together to produce a system bigger than its parts. When this happens patterns create *a whole*, and the system they build possesses the *quality without a name*, or *wholeness* (Alexander, 2002).

The set of patterns provide the vocabulary to describe the *whole* and how it is built; because we can describe the parts, we can communicate this to others. Thus, collections of patterns that share a context are considered *a pattern language*.

A pattern language might describe how to create a home or a town (Alexander, 1977), how to build a computer system (Gamma et al, 1995), how to organise a team (Coplien & Harrison, 2004) or how to introduce change into an organisation (Manns & Rising, 2005). In each case the set of patterns provides us with the linguistic tools to create a shared vision and shared understanding of the problem and the solution we are building. The pattern names act as labels, and the patterns themselves as building blocks.

For example, suppose we are building our dream home. If we employ an architect familiar with Alexander's vocabulary we may ask them to incorporate a WINDOW PLACE into our new home. But if our architect is not a reader of Alexander we would need to ask:

> *"Everybody loves windows seats, bay windows, and big windows with low sills ...*
>
> *Therefore: In every room where you spend some any length of time during the day, make at least one window into a 'window place'."*
>
> *(Alexander, 1977)*

It is because patterns allow us to talk in terms of building blocks and ideas rather than intricate details that we can generate a sense of the whole. Thus pattern languages are more than simply collections, or sets, of patterns. They have a shared *raison d'etre*. These patterns share part of their context and complement one another.

Patterns may exist in more than one pattern language. The only stipulation is that in each language they help build towards the whole. Similarly, pattern languages may exist within pattern languages. Sometimes it is convenient to think of patterns for creating a smaller part of the whole.

We may create our own pattern languages from existing patterns and from new patterns we discover. For example, *A Pattern Language* (Alexander, 1977) sets out 256 patterns for creating communities and homes. Should we decide to build our own home, we may draw on this language. We may decide to use patterns like LIGHT ON TWO SIDES OF EVERY ROOM and ALCOVES. We may also decide to incorporate features found in our previous homes; we may consider these features new patterns. When our house is finished, we have a new pattern language unique to our house. This language contains some existing patterns and some new patterns, some we have borrowed and some we have created afresh.

Alexander (1977) advises pattern writers to strive for patterns that complement and complete one another. Patterns need to be aware of the other patterns around them and fit together. Each individual pattern needs to include all the necessary information, facts and instructions to bring it to life.

Pattern Sequences

When patterns are applied together they are said to form a *pattern sequence.* There may be many ways of combining the patterns in a pattern language, and each pattern may appear in multiple sequences. Pattern sequences show the order in which patterns are combined to make a whole.

It is not always obvious from a pattern description which patterns should be applied together. Even if the pattern writer could specify this information, they may choose not too, either for the benefit of brevity, or to leave the reader with options. Pattern sequences are used to describe which patterns are applied in tandem, and to describe the effect on the whole when several patterns are combined.

Naturally there are many ways in which patterns may be applied. Some patterns are larger than others: they describe a large thing to build. The building of this thing requires the use of smaller patterns. These in turn may require more patterns. For example, in *A Pattern Language* Alexander starts with patterns for distributing towns and cities in a region. He moves on to describe the organisation of the town and from there to the individual buildings.

It is not essential to apply every pattern in a language or a sequence. We choose which patterns to apply and which not to. Few if any patterns are without negative consequences along with their positive ones. In some cases we may decide that despite its positive attributes, we will not apply a pattern. There is nothing automatic in the application of patterns; the decision to use, or not to use, a pattern is purely a human one. Each pattern application will be unique, with variations and changes specific to this instance. Consequently the application of a single pattern language may result in different systems being created.

Again we see why patterns are more than contingency theory, and why the automatic application of patterns is unlikely ever to become common.

When applying a pattern language we will be faced with choices. Not only must we choose whether to apply a pattern or not, but on occasions we will have to choose between different patterns. For example, faced with limited space in a house, we may be forced to choose between WORKSPACE ENCLOSURE and DRESSING ROOMS (Alexander, 1977). Pattern writers cannot foresee every context, problem or force that may lead to modifications when applying a pattern: human judgement is needed to select and adjust individual patterns and sequences.

On other occasions we may find that the application of one pattern forces us to use another. The negative consequences of applying one pattern will create forces; resolving these forces may require the use of another pattern.

So it is that patterns from a common language are applied in sequence. Such a sequence forms a path through a pattern language; the result is a single whole (Coplien & Harrison, 2004). A sequence may be a well-known one or it may be one devised for a specific scenario. Individual patterns may play a role in multiple sequences; indeed the outcome of applying one pattern in two different sequences may be different. Even when patterns come from the same language, not all possible sequences will be useful or even make sense. Patterns taken from different languages might work together or they might not.

The sequences contained in this book, indeed in any pattern book containing sequences, are merely suggestions and record what the author has observed to work. All but the smallest problems are likely to differ in some element from previous problems. We should not expect to be able to apply a previous pattern sequence exactly. Readers are encouraged to make up their own sequences.

When writing patterns it is natural to find one pattern leading to another. In writing this collection of business patterns, the discovery and documentation of one pattern has more often than not led to the discovery of another pattern. Thus as patterns are described, sequences are mapped out.

The application and creation of patterns is an exercise in stepwise refinement. The details of a large pattern are often implemented with a set of smaller patterns. These in turn may require the use of several smaller patterns, and so on.

In part the patterns one discovers depend on the granularity of patterns; one lengthy pattern may cover many scenarios. Alternatively, one short pattern may require several more patterns to cover the same scenarios. It is the writer's decision to decide which course best explains the problems and solutions to the reader.

Improvising with Patterns

Together pattern languages and pattern sequences provide us with maps and routes through the maps. You may choose to follow an existing route across well-charted terrain, or you may choose to follow a different route on the same terrain. You may even choose to change the map by adding your own patterns. You are also free to change and reinterpret the patterns on the map. If a pattern doesn't work for you, then remove it. If you find that a pattern requires modification, then change it.

In all likelihood your projects and endeavours will not follow the maps and routes given here. At best the maps and routes are like the score for a jazz band. The performers are more likely than not to improvise around a score. Sharing a pattern vocabulary helps individuals prepare their minds and create a shared sense of the whole, a shared understanding of the objective.

The people, resources and environment you find as your journey progresses will lead you to your own improvisations. It is not always possible to follow another's map: things change, obstacles arise and opportunities appear. Only through such improvisation and the changes, additions and removals you make from the map can you create your own unique whole.

In a business context *unique* is important. Unique can be what makes your company, your product or your service different – and superior – to the competition. *Unique* can also be what makes your operations complex and expensive. Recognising when uniqueness is valuable and should be retained, and when it is merely expensive and should be eliminated, can mean the difference between a successful business and a failure.

Anti-patterns

Patterns describe a recurring solution to a problem. It is critical that the solution improves the situation in which we find the problem. But not all solutions, even recurring ones, improve matters; some so-called solutions may make things worse. It is therefore natural to ask: *is there such a thing as an anti-pattern?*

The short answer is yes, there is. There is even a book called *Anti-patterns* (Brown et al, 1998), We can expect an anti-pattern to describe a problem and how the problem came about (the forces). While an interesting piece of analysis, this isn't of itself very useful. To make an anti-pattern useful, the author needs to describe how to resolve the situation. To be useful an anti-pattern needs a solution. A good solution should detail the consequences of applying the problem and give some examples.

In other words, to be useful an anti-pattern has to look a lot like a pattern. Both require a problem description, a solution, a description of the solution and some examples. It then becomes difficult to distinguish what is a *pattern* and what is an *anti-pattern.*

Apart from raising a few smiles, the term 'anti-pattern' isn't actually a lot of use. The things we commonly believe to be anti-patterns are in fact regular patterns.

Of course there are problems that occur again and again, and there are poor solutions that are used again and again. These things might look like patterns, but good analysis reveals them to be suboptimal. The subject of good, bad and ugly patterns is discussed in Appendix B.

How to Read a Pattern

The most obvious way to read a pattern is to start at the top and read to the end. That is fine if you have the time to do it, and it is fine as long as you are interested in the pattern. However there are other ways to read a pattern that can save you time and help you decide quickly whether the pattern is for you.

However you read a pattern, start by looking at the name. Pattern names are carefully chosen to describe the pattern, and you can often decide from the name alone whether the pattern interests you or not. As patterns become better known, their names are used as shorthand for the whole pattern and they become a shared language.

If you are in a hurry, read the problem statement next. This should tell you the problem that the pattern is attempting to solve. It may be that you say "*I've never had that problem*" and decide to skip the pattern, or perhaps you say "*Yes! This is a problem I face all the time*" and continue reading.

Next, read the solution, or rather just the first couple of sentences. In this book the first few sentences of the pattern are in italics and aim to give you an overview of the solution quickly.

Having read the name, problem and solution, you should now have a good idea of what the pattern is about. You are now well prepared to know whether the pattern is really useful to you (in which case you will want to read the whole thing), whether it is of slight interest to you (in which case you may decide to read it later, or the next time you come across this problem), or whether the pattern can be passed over altogether.

If you do decide to read the pattern now, then return to the top of the pattern, read the context and reread the problem statement. You may now decide to read the pattern from start to finish. As you read the pattern, try and think about what you have done when you faced the same (or similar) problem.

Most patterns will list a number of forces that make the problem difficult. In some cases all of these forces will apply; in other cases only some of them will apply. This is quite normal; just because your circumstances lacked one or more forces does not mean that the pattern is irrelevant to you. In your case there may be additional forces that are not listed. Not only is it impossible to list all possible forces – simply because we don't know all the circumstances – but even if we could, it would make for a very long pattern, and very long patterns are less likely to be read than short ones.

The solution section of the pattern should describe how to resolve the problem. We can think of this as *What should I build to fix this?* – showing patterns' roots in architecture. You should find some concrete actions to take and a description of what to do. In some patterns this advice is more difficult to give, so more general advice is given. In these cases the onus is on you to decide how you turn the general advice into specific actions.

Following the solution section is the consequences section. This will describe what becomes of the problem and the forces when you have built the solution. Normally the consequences section will describe how each force is resolved and how things look after the solution is applied. The consequences section will also describe other effects of the solution. Some of these will be beneficial and some detrimental.

Few if any patterns have only positive results. It is important to look at the consequences before applying the pattern and decide whether, in your specific case, the consequences are acceptable. If not then you will need to find a different solution.

The consequences also play another role: by describing the conditions that pertain after applying the pattern, they also describe the forces that are now at work. Thus they become forces that lead to another problem and another pattern.

The remaining sections of the pattern: known uses, related work and other names, will provide additional background and reading. These sections both add to the depth of the pattern and tell you where to go next if you want to know more.

When reading a pattern language it is usually more interesting to read each pattern as they are mentioned rather than to read from the first to the last. Rather than turn to the next pattern in the book, look at the patterns mentioned in the one you have just read.

How to Write a Pattern

The first thing to say about pattern writing is that anyone can do it. There is no restriction on pattern writing, or indeed on the term *pattern*. This openness can lead to confusion: what one person refers to as a pattern is not necessarily the same thing as someone else.

I would encourage everyone to try their hand at pattern writing. Put aside any doubt about whether what you are writing is a pattern, or whether it conforms to pattern form, style or theory. Get your ideas down on paper or in electronic form first and leave the theory until later.

Much of the advice above for reading a pattern can be applied to writing a pattern. The emphasis on name, problem and solution is the same. Reading other people's patterns, looking at different forms and styles, can help inform your own pattern writing. Decide what you like about other people's patterns and steal the elements you like.

The most important thing to remember when writing a pattern is that it exists to communicate your knowledge and experience to someone else. Therefore a pattern must be readable and understandable by another person. The pattern community has processes and structures to help review and improve patterns; most of the patterns in this book have been through these processes. However you do not need these process to get feedback on your patterns. You can simply show your patterns to co-workers, relatives and others and get their comments and suggestions for improvement.

Writing a pattern

There is no right or wrong way to write a pattern. As with any creative endeavour, it is impossible to give a recipe for inspiration, insight and creativity. However it is possible to give some guidelines and ideas on how to go about writing a pattern.

The key to writing a good pattern is to know exactly what it is you are trying to explain. So start by getting your idea for a pattern straight in your own mind. I usually start with a sort of mind map to collect my initial thoughts about a pattern.

Usually the process of writing the pattern will help to sharpen the original idea. But the writing process will also lead you to analyse and deconstruct what you are saying; this will in turn create new insights for you and for your reader. Don't be worried if, half way through writing, your pattern seems to have collapsed in on itself. This is usually a sign that you are reaching a better understanding, and a stronger pattern will emerge. Not infrequently it is the collapse of one pattern that leads to the recognition of several more patterns.

Although a name is the first thing we read about a pattern, it is often best to leave naming the pattern to later. It may help to have a working title, but you should be open to changing the name if you can think of a better one.

Normally patterns are given names using nouns, that is, *things*. The name usually describes the thing you build in the solution section to solve the problem outlined. A frequent mistake is to name a pattern with verbs, that is, words that describe what you do to.

It can also be attractive to name the pattern after the problem rather than the solution. However experience shows that solution-based names tend to last longer and are easier to explain.

Next comes the problem statement. The problem statement should pull the reader in, it should motivate them to read more. As the pattern develops you will most likely revise the problem statement again and again and again: the search for a short, crisp, clear description of the problem can seem never-ending.

Although the forces section normally comes next in a pattern, it is best to leave writing the forces until later. Forces are generally considered the hardest part of the pattern to write. As with the problem statement, revisions to the forces are continual.

Deciding what information goes in the problem, the forces and the context section is difficult. Often information moves between these sections. For example, what at first appears as context can become a force later on, and even eventually the problem statement in a pattern all on its own. Context sets the scope of the pattern and can be used to broaden or narrow the content of the pattern. As a general rule, a narrower scope is better.

I often start writing a pattern with the known uses, or with the opening description – the first part set off as a vignette. The opening section often contains a short example, or it may be used to set the scene for the pattern, or even give a brief overview. Whatever its contents, it should prepare the reader for what is to come. Writing the opening section, or known examples, helps to get the pattern and its scope clear in my mind. It also helps seed the analysis process.

In the same way that information moves between the problem and forces sections of the pattern, information moves between the solution and consequences sections. The solution section should describe both what to build and how to build it, while the consequences section describes the state of the world after the thing is built and used.

In some ways the solution section is the easiest part to write, especially if you have built more than one such solution yourself. In doing so one needs to strike a balance between the specific – *exactly what do you do?* – and the general. Too specific, and the pattern will not be of much use to other people; too general, and it will not be clear what to do.

It should be possible to pick off individual forces and find a matching consequence. I regularly print the forces section and the consequences section on separate pieces of paper, put them next to each other and compare each force with its corresponding consequence. This can yield interesting insights, and ensures that each force is resolved – or at the least, explicitly not resolved.

Kevlin Henney has suggested that it can better to leave writing the forces until after the consequences section has been written. This is because the state of the world is clearer after the solution has been solved than before. Given a list of consequences, one can ask: *how did that come about?* and work back to the forces.

Remember that forces are the things that make solving the problem hard. Without a set of contradicting forces, there would not be much of a problem to solve. This insight leads to what is known as the *but-form of forces*. The thing that makes a problem hard is not a single force, or even multiple forces, but when those forces are opposing one another. In other words: *this* but *that*. For example:

- The company has a lot of work to do *but* cannot hire more workers.
- Customers would like more features *but* cannot afford new versions.

By thinking about what makes a force difficult, and contrasting it with an opposing force, the tension in the pattern can be increased. The need for a solution is created.

As suggested earlier, a pattern is like a mystery story. The reader should be pulled in by the problem, the forces describe the complication – then the solution presents a miraculous answer. Ideally reading the solution should create an *'Aha! – that's how they do it!'* feeling in the reader.

The review process

Anyone can review and comment on your patterns. The more people who review a pattern, the better. The pattern community, through the Hillside and Hillside Europe groups, have created a process that helps pattern authors by providing feedback. Should you wish to take your pattern writing to the next level, Hillside and the PLoP series of conferences are the places to go.

The review process is centred around a series of independent conferences:

- PLoP. Traditionally held in Illinois in September each year. In recent years the conference has moved and collocated with the much larger Splash (formerly OOPSLA) conference.
- EuroPLoP. The European version of PLoP: this is held in Bavaria each July.
- VikingPLoP. A smaller version of EuroPLoP that moves between Norway, Denmark, Sweden and Finland. Although usually held in September each year, VikingPLoP has not been held since 2007.
- SugarloafPLoP. Held in Brazil in August, this is the only PLoP conference not conducted in English, but instead in Spanish and Portuguese.
- ChilliPLoP. This deviates from the other PLoPs by focusing on specific 'hot topics' and adopts a different format. It is held each March in Arizona.
- Koala PLoP and Mensore PLoP have been held in Australia and Japan respectively. At the time of writing neither conference is occurring on a regular basis, although they may return in future.

'PLoP' stands for *Pattern Languages of Programming*, and shows the community's roots in the software development arena. For more details of any of these conference, see the conference website and the Hillside website, `www.hillside.net`.

All conferences are open to all comers, from industry and academia alike. Each conference is independently organised, has its own website with dates and its own 'call for papers' announcements. Papers are submitted to each conference in advance, as for other conferences, and papers are reviewed. However, papers are not assessed for academic rigour, original knowledge or any of the other normal conference criteria: instead they are assessed for quality and potential.

Provided that a paper is considered suitable, the author(s) is then assigned a *shepherd* (Harrison, 2006). The shepherd then reads the paper and spend the next few months working with the author(s), usually via e-mail, to help them improve the paper. At the end of this time the paper is reviewed again by the conference organisers, and if it is good enough, is accepted to the conference.

At the conferences papers are reviewed further. A PLoP conference consists of a number of workshops: each workshop consists of several reviewers, most of whom are also pattern authors themselves. The workshops review each paper interactively and provide the author with feedback in terms of comments and suggestions for improving the paper.

After the conference authors are expected to update their papers with as much, or as little, of the feedback as they like. The revised papers are gathered together for the conference proceedings. Many of the patterns then go on to be published in books like this one, or in collections of patterns like the *Pattern Language of Program Design* 'PLoP D' series, or in journals such as *Transactions in Pattern Languages*, 'TPLoP'.

Closing Words

This appendix has provided an overview of patterns, how they are collected together in pattern languages, how they ordered in pattern sequences, and has offered some insight into the pattern writing process.

In the next appendix we will explore patterns in more depth, consider some of the philosophy behind patterns, and discuss the role of patterns in capturing knowledge and creating action.

B

Patterns Philosophy

Business patterns are not intrinsically different from architecture or software patterns – what is true for one pattern domain is true for the others. Each domain seeks to address different, if overlapping, subjects. Patterns in all three domains share a common framework. By understanding this framework, we are better able to judge what is a pattern, what is not a pattern, what constitutes a good pattern and what we may expect of a *pattern language*.

This appendix is written for those wanting to know more about patterns and the theory behind them. In particular it is designed for readers not familiar with the framework within which architectural and software design patterns already exist: as such it continues where the last appendix left off. In particular, the search for *wholeness* (also known as *the quality without a name*) is considered, and how this search influences business patterns.

Patterns and their Implicit Context

> *'There is a central quality which is the root criterion of life and spirit in a man, a town, a building, or a wilderness. The quality is objective, precise, but it cannot be named...*
>
> *'In order to define this quality... we must begin by understanding that every place is given its character by certain patterns of events that keep happening there.'*
>
> *(Alexander, 1979, p. ix)*

In writing patterns, authors attempt to codify and document the events that create the quality Alexander speaks of. The result is a pattern or set of related patterns known as a *pattern language*. However, these are not the patterns themselves, but a human interpretation of the events and the results. As such the patterns reflect the context in which they are written: the time, political climate, technical maturity, economic environment and, significantly, the authors' own views and understanding of the world around them.

In other words, each pattern exists within an implicit context that is not stated and may not even become apparent until later. Pattern writing is not science; although patterns may be grounded in research, theory and examples (specifically the 'three known uses' to demonstrate that the pattern is not a 'one off'), they also contain conjecture and advocacy.

For example, in an age when global warming threatens the planet, when pollution in cities endangers health and public opinion dislikes concreting over swathes of countryside, what are we to make of RING ROADS and NINE PERCENT PARKING (Alexander, 1977)? Indeed *New Scientist* reports that:

> *'Alexander's philosophy has turned many cities, especially in the US, into social and ecological disaster areas, teeming with social[ly] deprived neighbourhoods whose inhabitants are forced to rely on the polluting, petrol-guzzling car to maintain the illusion of freedom.'*
>
> *(Pearce, 2006)*

Patterns, like other domain knowledge, are created in a context and in a period of time that brings with it its own set of assumptions, norms and standards. Patterns both document their implicit context and exist within that context. By documenting and naming events, we may actually change those that are described.

One of the primary reasons for writing patterns is to communicate our understanding. Naturally, it is easier to communicate one's own understanding to another who shares a similar context; the greater the difference in context and environment, the more difficult it is to communicate the idea. This is not just a matter of understanding: it is a matter of applicability.

The pattern NINE PERCENT PARKING would have made little sense to any individual living much before the middle of the twentieth century. This is not because the idea was badly communicated, nor does it reflect on the validity of the pattern. Before about 1950 there was simply no environment in which this pattern would exist.

Some patterns may well be timeless; others may last for decades or just days. While we may identify patterns that are gone and no longer used, it is harder to determine exactly when a pattern ceases to be applicable.

The Quality Without a Name: Wholeness

For Alexander, patterns are not an end in themselves, they are only a means to an end; his objective is to generate the *quality without a name*:

> *'To reach the quality without a name we must then build a living pattern language as a gate.'*
>
> *(Alexander, 1979, p. xi)*

More recently Alexander has chosen to name the *quality without a name*: its name is *wholeness* (Alexander, 2002). As this term is relatively new, much of existing literature still refers to the *quality without a name*, or QWAN for short. In this book the two terms are considered interchangeable.

Alexander is not alone in emphasising the importance of *the quality without a name*. The comments of Dick Gabriel apply equally to software and business patterns:

> *'I believe we cannot come to grips with Alexander in the software community unless we come to grips with this concept [wholeness].'*
>
> *(Gabriel, 1996, p. 34)*

Therefore, if business patterns are to stand alongside architectural patterns and software patterns, we must consider the role of *wholeness*, or the *quality without a name*. A full discussion can be found in Alexander (1979). For the moment we may abridge Gabriel:

> *'The quality is an objective quality that things like buildings and places can possess that makes them good places or beautiful places. Buildings and towns with this quality are habitable and alive...*
>
> *'Alexander proposes some words to describe the quality without a name, but even though he feels they point the reader in a direction that helps comprehension, these words ultimately confuse. The words are alive, whole, comfortable, free, exact, egoless, and external.'*
>
> *(Gabriel, 1996, p. 34–36)*

Interestingly Alexander initially rejected the term *whole* as a description of the *quality without a name*, but later adopted *wholeness*.

Later Gabriel questions whether the writers of software patterns share the same goal:

> *'When I look at software patterns and pattern languages, I don't see the quality without a name in them, either. Recall that Alexander said that both the patterns themselves and the pattern languages have the quality.'*
>
> *(Gabriel, 1996, p. 69)*

However, even if software patterns lack QWAN, they can still be useful and play a positive role. Gabriel outlines one of the ways in which software patterns are useful:

> *'Patterns provide several benefits to programmers and system developers. One is as a common language…*
>
> *Another benefit is as a common base to understanding what is important in programming…*
>
> *A third benefit is that with a corpus of patterns a programmer is able to solve problems more rapidly by having available a storehouse of solutions – a cookbook, if you will.'*
>
> *(Gabriel, 1996, p. 51–52)*

We may generalise Gabriel's discussion from software patterns to encompass our consideration of business patterns. Like software patterns, we can expect business patterns to provide a common language, understanding and a cookbook. In evaluating a business pattern, we may ask three things of a pattern:

- Is the pattern useful?
- Does the pattern possess wholeness itself?
- Does the pattern contribute to the generation of wholeness?

The answer to the first of these questions largely depends on the reader's point of view and experience. Answering the second and third is difficult, because we do not have an objective standard for determining if a pattern actually possesses wholeness.

Patterns both describe and exist in a changing environment; thus a pattern possessing and generating wholeness in one environment, say 1960s America, might not be viewed in the same way in another environment, say, twenty-first century Europe. So, while Alexander and Gabriel claim the quality itself is objective, the changing environment makes it hard to validate this claim.

This author believes that, taken together, these arguments render the second and third questions subjective. Who is to be the final arbiter of pattern wholeness? Who is qualified to judge whether a given pattern creates wholeness?

Given these limitations, all we may ask a pattern writer is that they aspire to answer 'yes' to these three questions.

Events or Things

Patterns are not just about physical things we build, they are about events too. Although we often consider patterns to describe something we can build, for example a MARRIAGE BED (Alexander, 1977, p. 187) or a MEMENTO (Gamma et al, 1995, p. 283), it should be recognised that Alexander actually starts by considering patterns of events:

> *'We must begin by understanding that every place is given its character by certain patterns of events that keep on happening there.'*
>
> *(Alexander, 1979, p. 55)*

The building and the events are entwined and co-dependent:

> *'Those of us who are concerned with buildings tend to forget too easily that all the life and soul of a place, all of our experiences there, depend not simply on the physical environment, but on the patterns which we experience there.'*
>
> *(Alexander, 1979, p. 62)*

Indeed, patterns about events are not hard to find, such as DO FOOD (Manns & Rising, 2005, p. 132) and SELF-SELECTING TEAM (Coplien & Harrison, 2004, p. 124) So, a pattern can describe a thing or a set of events, and the two are frequently related.

Sustainability: Living and Dead Patterns

Now we understand the need to aspire to wholeness, we need to understand the limits of pattern writing. Obviously, unique events with unique solutions are not patterns, but what of events that recur and produce recurring solutions, but which do not contribute to wholeness? For example, the smog creating highways that blight cities such as Los Angeles?

Alexander draws a distinction:

> *'These patterns of events are always interlocked... The specific patterns out of which a building or a town is made may be alive or dead. To the extent they are alive, they let our inner forces loose, and set us free; but when they are dead, they keep us locked in inner conflict.'*
>
> *(Alexander, 1979, p. x)*

Simply, some patterns, dead patterns, perpetuate the conflict. This is not to say that all 'alive' patterns resolve all forces: far from it. After the application of a living pattern, some forces are resolved, some mitigated, some unresolved and some new ones created. This creates the environment for the next pattern; this is a living process in which each solution flows from the next.

Conversely, a dead pattern fails to resolve forces, enhances others and creates new ones in ways that restricts change and resolution. Our ability to create wholeness is reduced.

Consider then these examples:

- Architectural patterns describing the creation of slum housing.
- Software patterns describing the creation of a highly coupled monolithic application.
- Business patterns describing Enron-style accounting.

We could write patterns about these subjects, but the resulting patterns would not contribute to wholeness; they would be 'dead patterns' in Alexander's terms.

Things become clearer if we substitute *sustainability* for *wholeness*. Living patterns contribute to the sustainability of architecture, software applications and businesses; conversely, dead patterns reduce sustainability. In fact, Alexander comes close to saying this himself:

> *'In short, saying these patterns are alive is more or less the same as saying they are stable.'*
>
> *(Alexander, 1979, p. 118)*

A business run according to the hypothetical ENRON PATTERN LANGUAGE might well grow, employ thousands of people, increase shareholder value and reward the business leaders, but eventually it would prove to be unstable and unsustainable.

Classifying Patterns: Good, Bad, Dead and Alive

It is useful to explore the subject of *alive* and *dead* patterns a little further. In fact, Alexander initially describes *good patterns* and *bad patterns*:

> *'A pattern which prevents us from resolving our conflicting forces, leaves us almost perpetually in a state of tension.*
>
> *This stress is then no longer functional at all. It becomes a huge drain on the system…*

> *And so 'bad' patterns… stress us, undermine us, affect us continuously.*
>
> *…on the other hand, the corresponding 'good' patterns, when they are correctly made, help us to be alive, because they resolve our conflicts and ourselves.'*
>
> (Alexander, 1979, p. 114–115)

In other words, bad patterns don't really solve our problems; at best they may displace the problem from one place to another. They solve the immediate problem, but create a problem in another place or at a later date.

Some in the patterns community refer to this type of pattern as *dysfunctional*. We may consider a dysfunctional pattern as one that appears to offer a solution to a problem, but does not actually solve the problem in hand, or appears to solve the problem while actually displacing it.

Others have used the term *anti-patterns* (Brown et al, 1998). One problem with some so-called anti-patterns is that they describe a problem that recurs again and again: while interesting, this isn't particularly useful. Some anti-patterns go further and describe the solution to the problem. In effect, now we have an anti-pattern that describes a problem, in a context with a solution: the net effect is that the anti-pattern is little different to an ordinary pattern.

Alexander himself quickly advances the discussion from *good* and *bad* to *living* and *dead*:

> *'Each bad pattern in our environment constantly reduces us, cuts us down, reduces our ability to meet new challenges, reduces our capacity to live, and helps to make us dead…*
>
> *While, on the other hand, the corresponding 'good' patterns, when they are correctly made, help us to be alive, because they allow us to resolve our conflicts ourselves.'*
>
> (Alexander, 1979, p. 115)

And he continues:

> *'Patterns are not merely instruments which help us live: they are themselves alive and dead.'*
>
> (Alexander, 1979, p. 115)

One could argue with the term *dead pattern* on the grounds that something that is dead does not actually exert any force: by definition, a dead thing is inactive and inert. In this way *dead* is not the opposite of *alive*; that which is dead is not destructive, indeed, a *dead thing* is highly stable and changes little. Conversely, something that is living changes and may never reach stability. On the whole it might be simpler to stick with the terms *good* and *bad*.

It is useful to make one further distinction in classifying patterns: that between patterns that are currently in use and patterns that have fallen from use. For example, BATHING ROOM states:

> *'Concentrate the bathing room, toilets, showers and basins of the house in a single tiled area. Locate the bathing room beside the couple's realm – with private access – in a position half-way between the private secluded parts of the house and the common areas; if possible, give it access to the outdoors; perhaps a tiny balcony or walled garden.*
>
> *Put in a large bath – large enough for at least two people to get completely immersed in water; an efficiency shower and basins for the actual business of cleaning; and two or three racks for huge towels, one by the shower, one by the sink.'*
>
> *(Alexander, 1977, p. 685)*

While BATHING ROOM sounds like a wonderful pattern – and this author would certainly like to live in such a house – it is absent from most, if not all, modern constructions. Observation in Europe and North America shows little evidence of large baths being installed. A more current pattern might state:

> *'Provide several small bathrooms, one en-suite for parents, one shared between the children and another en-suite for the guest room. Only the master bathroom need contain a bath.'*

This is not to say BATHING ROOM is necessarily wrong, just that it is seldom used. The context (be it explicit or implicit) that created and sustained BATHING ROOM no longer exists. It may well be that with time the context will return and BATHING ROOM will become common again.

Using the two desiderata of good/bad and used/unused, we may classify and name patterns types as shown in Table 8.

Table 8: Classifying and naming patterns

Current	Pattern (good pattern, living pattern) Builds towards wholeness Sustainable	Dysfunctional pattern Detracts from wholeness Unsustainable
Unused	(Unused) pattern Could build towards wholeness if applicable	– Does not detract from wholeness because it is unused.
	Good (alive)	*Bad (dead)*

Worse is Better: Path Dependency?

If our goal is to address all forces and create wholeness, we must indeed address all forces: technical, social and economic. In some cases it may simply not be possible to address all forces; in other cases a *good enough* solution may suffice to resolve some of the forces, or at least mitigate those that remain.

Gabriel's *Worse is Better* (2006, 1996, 1990) argument suggests that all forces are not equal; the forces of economics and the market can overwhelm technical forces. Similar arguments are made in the pattern BIG BALL OF MUD (Foote & Yoder, 1999a). This describes how shanty towns and monolithic software applications can come to be when the immediate forces of architecture and software design are overwhelmed by the environment we find on the ground.

On the one hand, BIG BALL OF MUD cannot contribute to wholeness, because it describes how we break every rule of good architecture. On the other hand, both the monolithic software application and the shanty town continue to live: the monolithic application continues to be run and the shanty town continues to provide homes for people; both continue to change and evolve as living entities.

The monolithic application stands in contrast to the software application that, no matter how beautifully engineered, has been abandoned and no longer lives. The shanty town contrasts with the rural village that died after the population moved to work in a city and live in the shanty town. Beauty is less important than life: the monolith may be ugly, but it lives; the shanty town may offend our senses, but it lives.

Given the right context, BIG BALL OF MUD makes sense. Sometimes the forces will balance in ways we do not expect; sometimes the virtues of a design may not be apparent until the context changes. For example, shanty towns model many features we now consider virtuous:

> *'These shanties meet many of the ideals of eco-city designers. They are high-density but low-rise; their lanes and alleys are largely pedestrianised; and many of their inhabitants recycle waste materials from the wider city.'*
>
> *(Pearce, 2006)*

We return to the issue of sustainability. The monolithic application and the shanty town are sustainable for a period of time, but maybe not indefinitely. Such applications are fragile and difficult to change, and eventually such applications fail or become unmaintainable: the shanty towns may fail because of natural or social phenomenon such as earthquake, landslides, social breakdown and riots.

Given the disadvantages, how can the BIG BALLS OF MUD survive for so long? Part of the answer may be that they are highly adapted to their environment (the context they live in), but are not adaptable. Another part of the answer may be that, like living organisms. they exist to survive, and the odds of survival increase once they survive childhood.

We may consider life itself to be a force. Once a living thing is brought into being, it is no longer neutral and will exert forces itself. One of the most powerful is the survival force, the force to continue living. The desire to continue living is not unique to biological forms, and de Geus (1997) has suggested that it exists within corporations too.

Consider a situation in which a bad pattern – one that does not contribute to wholeness and has limited sustainability – becomes the dominant solution to a problem. Once in existence, the more established it becomes, the harder it is to dislodge. Such a position is analogous to 'vendor lock-in' and the economic theory of *path dependency.*

According to the path dependency theory, the QWERTY keyboard and VHS video recorders achieved market dominance, not because they were technically superior, but because they were first to market. Because they were first, their position was entrenched by market forces that supported their position. Following this line of argument, once the BIG BALL OF MUD has been brought into being, the cost of replacing it not justified.

A fuller discussion of this theory and the analogy behind it is beyond the scope of this book. For the moment it is sufficient to say that we may draw on the analogy, and that the theory of path dependency is disputed (for example Margolis & Liebowitz, 1998).

Knowledge Management and Patterns

Patterns are written with the objective of communicating some piece of knowledge from the author to the reader. A long list of pattern publications demonstrates some degree of success here. A second objective, less often mentioned, is to allow the authors themselves to understand the pattern better.

The idea that patterns are a form of knowledge management is not new:

> *'A relatively new approach known as patterns has created new possibilities for those who wish to manage knowledge in a more efficient and effective way.'*
>
> *(Manns, 2001)*

> *'The really big opportunity for patterns and pattern languages, an opportunity for exponential growth, comes to light when we perceive patterns as an important part of a larger challenge – that of valuing, exploiting, and managing the knowledge available all around us, in both tacit and explicit forms, ripe for the picking.'*
>
> *(May & Taylor, 2003)*

Patterns both embody knowledge and describe its practical use. Each pattern describes a solution to a problem with supporting evidence of usage and applicability. There is an implied chronology to the pattern that gives it a somewhat story-like nature; for example:

> *'We had a problem, there were these forces… therefore, we did X, and as a result we got here. And now we know of some other folks who did similar things.'*

Software creation is a knowledge-based activity – part of what economists and politicians like to call 'knowledge work' or 'the knowledge economy'. All knowledge work is based on *what you know,* not *what you make.* Individuals and companies with specialist knowledge are able to sell their knowledge. Similarly, individuals and companies derive their competitive advantage from their knowledge and their ability to act on this knowledge.

Before knowledge can be traded for money it must be packaged and delivered. Knowledge may be packaged and delivered by way of a service: for example, a motor mechanic or a management consultant sell their knowledge as a service. Or knowledge may be packaged into products that are sold: for example, Honda packaged knowledge of car engine design into cars, motorbikes, lawn mowers and so on. To best exploit knowledge, a company must know when to sell products, when to sell services, when to switch from one to the other and when, and how, to use one to complement the other.

In writing this book knowledge has been packaged into patterns, the patterns into a book, and the book sold for money. Only when the book is read and the knowledge acted on is the transfer, or sharing, complete. Without the action step these patterns are just information.

There is an emphasis in pattern writing on what you *do* rather than what you *know*; as such, the pattern is a call to action – the 'events' in Alexander's description. The pattern narrative calls for the pattern to be used: the search for wholeness directs us to create and use patterns that live, patterns that are not only knowledge, but action too. The concern with action as well as knowledge gives them a role in closing the so-called *knowing–doing gap* (Pfeffer & Sutton, 2000).

A pattern is a form of structured story. Like poetry the structure may take many forms, and authors are free to devise their own structures. However, there must be a recognisable structure, and it must help express the core elements of a pattern: context, problem, problem forces, solution and consequences.

Patterns are not just structured stories. In describing a set of actions and choices, they outline a design. People must consciously choose to build that which is described in the pattern and modify the pattern to their specific environment. Implementing the pattern is a conscious design-oriented action by one or more individuals. Without the structure, core elements and design imperative, a problem-solution pair may occur again and again and, in common parlance, it may be called *a pattern*, but it is not a pattern in the terms of Alexander, Gabriel and the wider patterns community.

The structured form of the pattern, the emphasis on design and construction, the description of actions, the core elements and tradition of review within the pattern-writing community all serve to help capture in-depth knowledge. In particular it is important to capture the less obvious tacit knowledge within the pattern as well as the better-known explicit knowledge. The structured form of patterns challenges us to capture the tacit knowledge. In particular, it is difficult to write the forces section of a pattern that capture the, often tacit, reasons for applying the pattern. More tacit information is contained in the solution and consequences that detail how to solve the problem and the end result.

Patterns in the Alexandrian tradition do not exist in isolation. True, anyone may pick up a book and read some patterns, but the creation of patterns is seldom done in isolation. A 'community' exists around writers to review the work, guide the author and socialise the pattern knowledge. The community helps the written form and, more importantly, helps authors to capture the nuances and intricacies of the pattern – that is, helps the author capture and document much of the tacit knowledge that hides inside the problem–solution pairing.

The pattern community also serves to keep the writer honest: a writer who ignores *wholeness* will eventually be questioned and his dead patterns exposed.

Storytelling and Patterns

Recently another form of knowledge management has appeared that also seeks to combined action with knowledge: *storytelling* (Denning, 2001; Brown et al, 2005).

> *'Stories are one of the ways knowledge is transmitted, especially social knowledge.'*
>
> *(Prusak in Brown et al, 2005, p. 47)*

> *'Once we understand what knowledge is, where it resides, and how knowledge is communicated, we discover that narrative plays an unexpectedly large role...*
>
> *There are a lot of ways to capture knowledge that kill it stone dead, and it's very hard to spread knowledge when it's dead.'*
>
> *(Brown in Brown et al, 2005, p. 53–54)*

Reading Denning and Brown's works, it is hard not to draw parallels with the pattern community: values and concerns about change, community, abstraction (or *compression* for those subscribing to Gabriel's (1996) definition) and the importance of practice recur. Brown's call to capture *living knowledge* echoes Alexander's call for *living patterns.*

There are also differences between the two techniques. For example, Denning emphasises the role of verbal storytelling, while patterns emphasise the written form; stories are spread by socialisation, while patterns (outside of shepherding and conferences) are spread via books and the web.

Denning (2001, p. 197) provides an appendix describing *Elements for Developing a Springboard Story,* and it is interesting to contrast these elements with accepted pattern norms – see Table 9.

The approach taken by Denning and others to knowledge management through storytelling seems parallel to the approach taken by pattern writers, but the two are not the same. This author hopes that the two communities will be able to learn from one another.

Table 9: Comparison between story elements and patterns

Denning's characteristic	Denning's explanation	Parallel in patterns
The explicit story should be relatively brief and textureless.	The story can be brief and should have only enough texture and detail for the audience to understand it…	Patterns should be short and concise. Patterns should not include needless information.
The story must be intelligible to the specific audience.	The audience needs to understand enough about the protagonist and the initial incident for them to be *hooked*…	Writers should understand who their audience is. Pattern must pose a real, non-trivial, problem; writers should build tension to be resolved later in the pattern.
The story should be inherently interesting.	To capture interest, the *actions* described might be difficult, with a *predicament* that cannot be handled in a routine manner, and some tension between characters in the story; or *unexpected events*…	Patterns should describe a real problem with multiple forces creating tension in the problem statement. The solution should be non-obvious, at least at first, and should describe implementation action.
The story should spring the listener to a new level of understanding.	…it must epitomise or embody the change idea, almost like a premonition of what the future will be like…	The reader should learn something from the pattern. By naming the pattern we move to a new level of abstraction.

Table 9: Comparison between story elements and patterns (continued)

The story must have a 'happy ending'.	The story needs to spring the listener out of the typical negative, questioning, sceptical frame of mind… the listener must [achieve] a positive *aha!*	The solution is an essential element of the pattern, reading it should give the reader an '*aha!*' moment.
The story should embody the change message.	Stories can help persuade people to change… which the audience can discover on its own and make into its own change message.	Patterns do not necessarily embody a change message. The solution may imply some degree of change, but often the solution describes a technical fix.
The change message should be implicit.	…one that lets the listener discover the implicit change message so that it becomes the audience's own idea and meaningful to them.	Patterns contain explicit messages that should be clearly communicated. Readers are encouraged to relate the pattern.
The listener should be encouraged to identify with the protagonist.	Much of the power of the springboard story derives from the fact that the audience identifies with the protagonist…	No direct parallel. Forces and consequences encourage the writer and reader to consider the other protagonists/ stakeholders effected by the problem or solution.
The story should deal with a specific individual or organisation.	People are more likely to project onto single individuals…	Examples are often, but not always, used to build the pattern through a single case. Organisations may be described in worked examples. However most patterns lack a central figure.

Table 9: Comparison between story elements and patterns (continued)

The protagonist should be prototypical of the organisation's main business.	The individual should be a central figure in the business of the organisation...	No direct parallel. Patterns are written for a specific audience.
Other things being equal, true is better than invented.	Our confidence in the veracity of a supposedly true story is usually not on very solid ground.	Patterns should not be works of theory or conjecture. Patterns should be observed in use, in the real world, before documentation. Multiple known uses are valued.
Test, test, test.	...a story can be tested on individuals or small groups before being tried out on a large group in a high-risk setting.	Patterns are not directly tested themselves, but are expected to document known (and therefore tested) solutions. Shepherding, writers workshops and pre-publication review may provide some degree of pattern testing.

Closing Words

Alexander's theories, and the explanations of Gabriel, provide an ethical basis for patterns and pattern languages. These ideas mandate patterns to create benefits, to build *wholeness* and *sustainability*: there should never be an ENRON PATTERN LANGUAGE.

The patterns contained in this book aspire to wholeness and the *quality without a name*. At a minimum they help to create a shared language and understanding for those engaged in the software business. Hopefully readers will find these patterns provide a useful cookbook for company growth.

The patterns exist in an enveloping context, namely, twenty-first century Anglo-Saxon capitalism. Yet this context is itself changing: economic transitions are reliant increasingly on the exchange of knowledge rather than physical goods – the so-called *knowledge economy*. Corporations are asked increasingly to account for themselves and face their social responsibilities.

Even during the writing and development of these patterns and this book, the business context has undergone significant changes. The financial crisis of 2008 has resulted in banks being held to a different standard of accountability than was previously the case.

Patterns are well adapted to the changing context; they are the product of knowledge and have strong ethical roots. This author hopes to hear more of patterns in future.

C

Future Work – Patterns Arising

The patterns in this book are not the only business patterns. Other authors have already captured other patterns; some are referenced, some are not. Other authors are already at work on more business patterns and this author may, or may not, write more business patterns.

In developing these patterns several other potential patterns were identified but have not, as yet, been written. This short appendix lists some of the potential patterns and potential areas of work. The author would be happy to see other writers develop these ideas into full patterns.

While this book contains multiple patterns describing direct and indirect distribution, there are several patterns that could be added to this set:

- Multiple Channels: a pattern describing how companies combine multiple channels while minimising the competition between channels.
- Different Channel, Different Product: a pattern describing how and why companies use different products in different marketing channels.
- Same Product, Different Price: how to market the same product at different price points to maximise revenue. Tactics such as group discounts and time limited special offers deserve more attention.

Several patterns in this book touch on the product manager role, such as Customer Understanding (page 146), Segmented Customers (page 141) and Product Roadmap (page 302). Given the (increasing) importance of product management, it is perhaps surprising that nobody has yet created a pattern language of product management.

Then there are several business models used by companies that deserve their own patterns. Whether all these patterns apply, or could apply, to software business should also be considered:

- FRANCHISE: how and why to create a business in which the services are delivered by franchise holders. Equally there may be one or more patterns about being a franchise holder.
- FAST FOLLOWER: how to organise a business that rapidly copies others' innovations and new ideas.
- PRODUCT INTEGRATOR: a complement to COMPLEMENTOR, NOT COMPETITOR (page 309) describing how a business can be organised to focus on integrating others' products.

If written, these six patterns could easily take their place in the pattern language set out in this book. Beyond this, some of the patterns in this book represent the tip of an iceberg, and some potential pattern languages are possible taking ideas further, possibly into additional books. Examples include:

- A pattern language for product innovation. Such a language would be immensely useful, not just to software companies, but all sorts of technology and non-technology companies alike.
- A pattern language for retail: BRANDED SHOPS (page 172) only scratches the surface in terms of implementation detail. Indeed, there is potential for both a pattern language of high street retail and, more relevant to technology companies, a pattern language of online retail.
- A pattern language for after-sales service. While this book contains several patterns that discuss why companies would offer ongoing service, the variety and innovation in this market warrants a language all of its own.
- Product configuration and customisation. The need for configuration and customisation of software is discussed in several patterns. To the best of this author's knowledge, nobody has yet produced a pattern language on this subject, yet it is surely one that would help many developers and product managers.

There are some potential pattern languages where work is already under way. Hopefully these will come together into one volume before too long:

- Open Source, specifically a pattern language of the organisation and commercial aspects of Open Source development and products. Some work already exists in this field from Michael Weiss and Claudius Link, Christoph

Hannebauer, Vincent Wolff-Marting, and Volker Gruhn. Undoubtedly others have additional work this author is not aware of.

- Product line engineering has been mentioned in several patterns presented here. The technical challenges of product line engineering have been the subject of several recent conference papers from, among others, Christa Schwanninger, Michael Kircher, Dietmar Schütz and Markus Völter. There is a need to marry up the technical side of product line engineering with the business forces and problems that it addresses.

Perhaps overlapping with some of the product line engineering work is the subject of *product ecosystems* – the development of third parties building applications and systems on top of another's platform. Given the recent success of Apple iOS and the AppStore, this is a hot topic at the moment. The 2002 book *Platform Leadership* (Cusumano & Gawer, 2002) already provides a good discussion of this topic, yet there is still potential for a pattern language of product ecosystem creation and exploitation.

Finally, in writing new patterns some of the pattern in this book and elsewhere may need to be reworked, or even discarded entirely. *Pattern refactoring* – to borrow a coding term – will inevitably reveal better ways of communicating concepts in these patterns and show where patterns are better written differently.

References

Alexander, 1977	Alexander, C., Ishikawa, S. & Silverstein, M. 1977. *A Pattern Language*, New York, Oxford University Press.
Alexander, 1979	Alexander, C. 1979. *The Timeless Way of Building*, New York, Oxford University Press.
Alexander, 2002	Alexander, C. 2002. *The Nature of Order: an Essay on the Art of Building and the Nature of the Universe*, Berkeley, Center for Environmental Structure.
Battelle, 2006	Battelle, J. 2006. *The Search: How Google and Its Rivals Rewrote the Rules of Business and Transformed Our Culture*, Nicholas Breadley Publishing.
Beck, 2000	Beck, K. 2000. *Extreme Programming Explained*, Addison-Wesley.
Begg, 2008	Begg, D. 2008. *Economics*, McGraw-Hill Higher Education.
Birkinshaw et al, 2010	Birkinshaw, J., Bouquet, C. & Barsoux, J. -L. 2010. The 5 Myths of Innovation. *MIT Sloan Management Review*, 52.

Bricout et al, 2004	Bricout, V., Heliot, D., Cretoiu, A., Yang, Y., Simien, T. & Hvatum, L. 2004. Patterns for Managing Distributed Product Development Teams. *In:* Marquardt, K. & Schutz, D. (eds.) *EuroPLoP – Proceedings of the 9th European Conference on Pattern Languages of Programs,* 2004.
Bronson, 1998	Bronson, P. 1998. *The First $20 Million is Always the Hardest,* Vintage.
Brooks, 1986	Brooks, F. 1986. No Silver Bullet – Essence and Accident in Software Engineering. *Information Processing.* Proceedings of the IFIP Tenth World Computing Conference: 1069–1076.
Brown et al, 1998	Brown, J. B., Malveau, R. C., McCormick, H. W. & Mowbray, T. J. 1998. *AntiPatterns: Refactoring Software, Architectures, and Projects in Crisis,* New York, NY, John Wiley & Sons.
Brown et al, 2005	Brown, J. S., Denning, S., Groh, K. & Prusak, L. 2005. *Storytelling in Organizations: Why Storytelling Is Transforming 21st Century Organizations and Management,* Elsevier Butterworth-Heinemann.
Burrough & Helyar, 1991	Burrough, B. & Helyar, J. 1991. *Barbarians at the Gate: The Fall of RJR Nabisco,* Harper Business.
Buschmann et al, 1996	Buschmann, B., Meunier, R., Rohnert, H., Sommerlad, P. & Stal, M. 1996. Layers. *Pattern-Oriented Software Architecture: Volume 1, A System of Patterns.* Chichester, John WIley & Sons.
Cagan, 2008	Cagan, M. 2008. *Inspired: How to Create Products Customers Love,* SVPG Press.
Christensen & Bower, 1995	Christensen, C. M. & Bower, J. L. 1995. Disruptive Technologies: Catching the Wave. *Harvard Business Review.*
Christensen & Raynor, 2003	Christensen, C. M. & Raynor, M. E. 2003. *The Innovator's Solution: Creating and Sustaining Successful Growth,* Harvard Business School Press.
Christensen, 1997	Christensen, C. M. 1997. *The Innovator's Dilemma,* Boston, Mass., Harvard Business School Press.
Christensen et al, 2007	Christensen, C. M., Anthony, S. D., Berstell, G. & Nitterhouse, D. 2007. Finding the Right Job For Your Product. *Sloan Management Review,* 48**,** 38–47.

Cockburn, 1998	Cockburn, A. 1998. *Surviving Object-Oriented Projects*, Addison-Wesley.
Conway, 1968	Conway, M. E. 1968. How do committees invent?, *Datamation.*
Cooper & Maskell, 2008	Cooper, R. & Maskell, B. 2008. How to Manage through Worse-Before-Better. *MIT Sloan Management Review,* 49.
Cooper, 2004	Cooper, A. 2004. *The Inmates Are Running the Asylum: Why High Tech Products Drive Us Crazy and How to Restore the Sanity,* Que.
Coplien & Harrison, 2004	Coplien, J. O. & Harrison, N. B. 2004. *Organizational Patterns of Agile Software Development,* Upper Saddle River, NJ, Pearson Prentice Hall.
Coupland, 1996	Coupland, D. 1996. *Microserfs: A Novel (P.S.),* Regan Books/ HarperPerennial.
Coutu, 2002	Coutu, D. L. 2002. Spotting Patterns on the Fly: A Conversation with Birders David Sibley and Julia Yoshida. *Harvard Business Review,* 80**,** 45–50.
Cusumano & Gawer, 2002	Cusumano, M. A. & Gawer, A. 2002. *Platform Leadership: How Intel, Microsoft and Cisco Drive Industry Innovation,* Boston, Harvard Business School Publishing.
Cusumano & Nobeoka, 1998	Cusumano, M. A. & Nobeoka, K. 1998. *Thinking Beyond Lean: How Multi Project Management is Transforming Product Development at Toyota and Other Companies,* Free Press.
De Geus, 1997	De Geus, A. 1997. *The Living Company,* Nicholas Brealey Publishing.
Denning, 2001	Denning, S. 2001. *The Springboard: How Storytelling Ignites Action in Knowledge-Era Organizations,* Butterworth-Heinemann.
Doctorow, 2008	Doctorow, D., Lippert, M. & Srivatsan, V. N. 2008. Rethinking high-tech distribution. *McKinsey Quarterly,* 14.
Doyle, 2002	Doyle, P. 2002. *Marketing Management and Strategy,* Prentice Hall.
Drucker, 1985	Drucker, P. F. 1985. Playing in the Information-Based 'Orchestra'. *Wall Street Journal,* 4 June 1985.

Foote & Yoder, 1999a	Foote, B. & Yoder, J. 1999a. Big Ball of Mud. *In:* Harrison, N., Foote, B. & Rohnert, H. (eds.) *Pattern Languages of Program Design 4.* Boston, MA: Addison-Wesley.
Foote & Yoder, 1999b	Foote, B. & Yoder, J. 1999b. *In:* Harrison, N. B., Foote, B. & Rohnert, H. (eds.) *Pattern Languages of Program Design 4.* Addison-Wesley.
Fowler, 2000	Fowler, M. 2000. *Refactoring: Improving the Design of Existing Code,* Boston, MA, Addison-Wesley Professional.
Gabriel, 1990	Gabriel, R. P. 1990. Worse is Better. *In:* EuroPAL, 1990 Cambridge. Available: `www.dreamsongs.com/WorseIsBetter.html` [Accessed 8 May 2006].
Gabriel, 1996	Gabriel, R. P. 1996. *Patterns of Software: Tales from the Software Community,* Oxford University Press.
Gamma et al, 1995	Gamma, E., Helm, R., Johnson, R. & Vlissides, J. 1995. *Design Patterns: Elements of Reusable Object-Oriented Software,* Reading, MA, Addison-Wesley.
Gartner, 2009	Gartner 2009. Pattern Based Strategy. Genovese, Y. (ed.).
Gentle, 2007	Gentle, M. 2007. *IT Success!: Towards a New Model for Information Technology,* John Wiley & Sons.
Gerstner, 2003	Gerstner, L. V. 2003. *Who says Elephants Can't Dance?,* London, HarperCollins.
Gilb, 2005	Gilb, T. 2005. *Competitive Engineering,* Butterworth-Heinemann.
Hamel & Prahalad, 1991	Hamel, G. & Prahalad, C. K. 1991. Corporate Imagination and Expeditionary Marketing, *Harvard Business Review,* 81–91.
Hamel & Prahalad, 1996	Hamel, G. & Prahalad, C. K. 1996. *Competing for the Future,* Boston, MA, Harvard Business School Press.
Hannebauer et al, 2010	Hannebauer, C., Wolff-Marting, V. & Gruhn, V. 2010. Towards a Pattern Language for FLOSS Development. *PLoP 2010 – 17th Conference on Pattern Languages of Programs.* Reno/Taho Nevada, USA.
Harrison, 2006	Harrison, N. 2006. The Language of Shepherding. *In:* Manolescu, D.-A., Voelter, M. & Nobel, J. (eds.) *Pattern Languages of Program Design 5.* Boston, MA: Addison-Wesley.

Hax & Wilde, 1999	Hax, A. C. & Wilde, D. L. 1999. The Delta Model: Adaptive Management in a Changing World. *Sloan Management Review,* 40**,** 11–28.
Henney, 2004	Henney, K. 2004. Stable Intermediate Forms. *In:* Longshaw, A. & Schütz, D. (eds.) *EuroPLoP – Proceedings of the 9th European Conference on Pattern Languages of Programs.* Irsee, Germany: Universitätsverlag Konstanz GmbH.
Highsmith, 2010	Highsmith, J. 2010. *Agile Project Management: Creating Innovative Products,* Addison-Wesley.
Hoch et al, 1999	Hoch, D. J., Roeding, C. R., Purkert, G., & Linder, S. K. 1999. *The Secrets of Software Success: Management Insights from 100 Software Firms Around the World,* Harvard Business School Press.
Hoffman & Weiss, 2001	Hoffman, D. M. & Weiss, D. M. (eds.) 2001. *Software Fundamentals: Collected Papers by David L. Parnas,* Upper Saddle River, NJ, Addison-Wesley Professional.
Hvatum & Kelly, 2005	Hvatum, L. & Kelly, A. 2005. What do we think of Conway's Law now? *In:* Longshaw, A. & Zdun, U. (eds.) *EuroPLoP – Proceedings of the 10th European Conference on Pattern Languages of Programs,* 2005 Irsee, Germany. Universitätsverlag Konstanz GmbH.
Hvatum, 2009	Hvatum, L. 2009. Applying Distributed Development Patterns Stories and Pattern Sequences. *In:* Kelly, A. & Weiss, M. (eds.) *EuroPLoP – Proceedings of the 14th European Conference on Pattern Languages of Programming,* July 8–12, 2009 Irsee, Germany. `lulu.com`.
Jones, 2008	Jones, C. 2008. *Applied Software Measurement: Global Analysis of Productivity and Quality,* McGraw-Hill.
Kaplan, 1995	Kaplan, J. 1995. *Startup: A Silicon Valley Adventure,* Warner Books.
Kaplan & Norton, 2004	Kaplan, R. S. & Norton, D. P. 2004. *Strategy Maps: Converting Intangible Assets into Tangible Outcomes,* Harvard Business School Press.
Kay, 1998	Kay, J. 1998. Strategic advantage. *Financial Times,* 5 August 1998.
Kelly, 2004a	Kelly, A. 2004a. Business Strategy Design Patterns. *In:* EuroPLoP 2003, July 2004 Irsee, Germany. UVK Universitätsverlag Konstanz GmbH.

Kelly, 2004b	Kelly, A. 2004b. Business Strategy Patterns for the Innovative Company. *In: VikingPLoP – Proceeding of the 3rd Nordic Conference on Pattern Languages of Programming*, 2004, Uppsala, Sweden.
Kelly, 2005	Kelly, A. 2005. A few more business patterns. *In:* Longshaw, A. & Zdun, U. (eds.) *EuroPLoP – Proceedings of the 10th European Conference on Pattern Languages of Programs*, Irsee, Germany. UVK Universitätsverlag Konstanz GmbH.
Kelly, 2006	Kelly, A. 2006. Patterns for Technology Companies. *In:* Hvatum, L. & Zdun, U. (eds.) *EuroPLoP – Proceedings of the 11th European Conference on Pattern Languages of Programs*, 2006 Irsee, Germany. UVK Universitätsverlag Konstanz GmbH.
Kelly, 2008	Kelly, A. 2008. *Changing Software Development: Learning to Become Agile*, John Wiley & Sons.
Kidder, 1981	Kidder, T. 1981. *The Soul of a New Machine,* New York, Avon Books.
Kiechel, 1984	Kiechel, W. 1984. Sniping at Strategic Planning. *Planning Review,* May, 8–11.
Link, 2010	Link, C. 2010. Patterns for the commercial use of Open Source: Legal and licensing aspects. *EuroPLoP 2010.* Irsee, Germany.
Lipsey & Chrystal, 2007	Lipsey, R. & Chrystal, A. 2007. *Economics*, OUP Oxford.
Manns & Rising, 2003	Manns, M. K. & Rising, L. 2003. *Fear Less and Other Patterns for Introducing New Ideas into Organizations* [online]. Addison-Wesley. Available: `www.cs.unca.edu/~manns/intropatterns.html` [Accessed 25 January 2004].
Manns & Rising, 2005	Manns, M. L. & Rising, L. 2005. *Fearless Change: Patterns for Introducing New Ideas,* Boston, MA, Addison-Wesley.
Manns, 2001	Manns, M. L. 2001. Patterns: A Promising Approach to Knowledge Management. *In:* Wibowo, K., ed. ABIT (Association of Business and Information Technology), May, 2001, Monroeville, Pennsylvania.
Manolescu et al, 2006	Manolescu, D.-A., Voelter, M. & Nobel, J. (eds.) *Pattern Languages of Program Design 5,* Boston, MA, Addison-Wesley.

Margolis & Liebowitz, 1998	Margolis, S. E. & Liebowitz, S. J. 1998. *Path Dependence* [online]. Available: `www.utdallas.edu/~liebowit/palgrave/palpd.html` [Accessed 7 May 2006].
Marquardt, 2006	Marquardt, K. 2006. Patterns for Plug-Ins. *In:* Manolescu, D.-A., Voelter, M. & Nobel, J. (eds.) *Pattern Languages of Program Design 5,* Boston, MA, Addison-Wesley.
Maeda, 2006	Maeda, J. 2006. *The Laws of Simplicity,* Cambridge, MA, MIT Press.
May & Taylor, 2003	May, D. & Taylor, P. 2003. Knowledge Management with Patterns. *Communications of the ACM,* 46.
McFarland, 2008	McFarland, K. R. 2008. Should You Build Strategy Like You Build Software? *MIT Sloan Management Review,* 49**,** 7.
McKenzie, 2001	McKenzie, R. 2001. *The Relationship-Based Enterprise: Powering Business Success Through Customer Relationship Management,* McGraw-Hill Ryerson.
Mintzberg, 1978	Mintzberg, H. 1978. Patterns in Strategy Formation. *Management Science,* 24.
Mintzberg, 1994	Mintzberg, H. 1994. *The Rise and Fall of Strategic Planning,* FT Prentice Hall.
Mintzberg, 2009	Mintzberg, H. 2009. *Managing,* San Francisco, Berrett-Koehler Publishers Inc.
Moore, 1999	Moore, G. A., 1999. *Crossing the Chasm,* Capstone Publishing.
Naughton, 1996	Naughton, P. 1996. *The Java Handbook,* McGraw-Hill.
Nonaka & Takeuchi, 1995	Nonaka, I. & Takeuchi, H. 1995. *The Knowledge Creating Company: How Japanese Companies Create the Dynamics of Innovation,* New York, Oxford University Press.
Norman, 1988	Norman, D. A. 1988. *The Design of Everyday Things,* Basic Books.
Parnas & Clements, 1986	Parnas, D. L. & Clements, P. C. 1986. A Rational Design Process: How and Why to Fake It. *IEEE Transactions on Software Engineering,* 12**,** 251–257.
Pearce, 2006	Pearce, F. 2006. Ecopolis now. *New Scientist.*

Pfeffer & Sutton, 2000	Pfeffer, J. & Sutton, R. L. 2000. *The Knowing-Doing Gap: How Smart Companies Turn Knowledge into Action*, Harvard Business School Press.
Pine, 1993	Pine, B. J. 1993. *Mass Customization: The New Frontier in Business Competition,* Boston, Mass., Harvard Business School Press.
Porter, 1980	Porter, M. E. 1980. *Competitive Strategy: Techniques for Analyzing Industries and Competitors,* New York, Free Press.
Porter, 1996	Porter, M. 1996. What is Strategy?. *Harvard Business Review.*
Ries, 2011	Ries, E. 2011. *The Lean Startup: How Today's Entrepreneurs Use Continuous Innovation to Create Radically Successful Businesses,* Crown Business.
Rising, 2000	Rising, L. 2000. Customer Interaction Patterns. *In:* Harrison, N. B., Foote, B. & Rohnert, H. (eds.) *Pattern Languages of Program Design 4.* Addison-Wesley.
Rising, 2002	Rising, L. 2002. *Customer Interaction Patterns* [online]. Available: `members.cox.net/risingl1/Articles/customer.doc` [Accessed October 25 2011].
Schmidt et al, 2000	Schmidt, D., Stal, M., Rohnert, H. & Buschmann, F. 2000. *Pattern-Oriented Software Architecture Volume 2: Patterns for Concurrent and Networked Objects,* Chichester, John WIley & Sons.
Schwaber & Beedle, 2002	Schwaber, K. & Beedle, M. 2002. *Agile Software Development with Scrum,* Prentice Hall.
Schwaber, 2003	Schwaber, K. 2003. *Agile Project Management with Scrum,* Microsoft Press.
Schwartz, 1991	Schwartz, P. 1991. *The Art of the Long View: Planning for the Future in an Uncertain World,* New York, Bantam Doubleday Dell.
Slywotzky et al, 1999	Slywotzky, A., J., Morrison, D. J., Moser, T., Mundt, K. A. & Quella, J. A. 1999. *Profit Patterns: 30 Ways to Anticipate and Profit from Strategic Forces Reshaping your Business,* Chichester, John WIley & Sons.
Stull et al, 2008	Stull, C., Myers, P. & Scott, D. M. 2008. *Tuned In: Uncover the Extraordinary Opportunities that Lead to Business Breakthroughs,* Hoboken, NJ, John WIley & Sons.

Sull, 2007	Sull, D. N. 2007. Closing the Gap Between Strategy and Execution. *MIT Sloan Management Review,* 48, 8.
Tax et al, 2006	Tax, S. S., Colgate, M. & Bowen, D. E. 2006. How to Prevent Your Customers from Failing. *MIT Sloan Management Review,* 47.
Thomas, 2007	Thomas, K. 2007. Skills and learning: Can HR handle IT recruitment? *Financial Times,* March 14 2007.
Ward, 2006	Ward, J. 2006. Delivering Value from Information System and Technology Investments: Learning from success. Cranfield, Bedford: Cranfield School of Management.
Waters, 2006	Waters, R. 2006. IBM repackages its brain power. *Financial Times,* 10 July 2006.
Watson et al, 2005	Watson, R. T., Wynn, D. & Boudreau, M-C. 2005. JBoss: The Evolution of Professional Open Source Software. *MIS Quarterly,* 4.
Weick, 1997	Weick, K. E. 1997. Improvisation as a Mindset for Organizational Analysis. *Organization Science,* 9.
Weick, 1999	Weick, K. E. 1999. The aesthetic of imperfection in orchestras and organizations. *Comportamento Organizacional e Gestão,* 5, 5–22.
Weir, 1997	Weir, C. 1997. Patterns for designing in teams. *In:* Martin, R. C., Riehle, D. & Buschmann, F. (eds.) *Pattern Languages of Program Design 3,* Addison-Wesley.
Weiss, 2007	Weiss, M. 2007. In Bed with the Enemy. *In:* Hvatum, L. & Schümmer, T. (eds.) *EuroPLoP – Proceedings of the 12th European Conference on Patterns Languages of Programs,* 2007 Irsee, Germany. UVK Universitätsverlag Konstanz GmbH.
Weiss, 2009	Weiss, M. 2009. Performance of Open Source Projects. *In:* Kelly, A. & Weiss, M. (eds.) *EuroPLoP – Proceedings of the 14th European Conference on Patterns Languages of Programs,* 2009 Irsee, Germany. `lulu.com`.
Weiss, 2010	Weiss, M. 2010. Profiting from Open Source. *EuroPLoP – Proceedings of the 15th European Conference on Patterns Languages of Programs,* 2010 Irsee, Germany.
Welch, 2001	Welch, J. 2001. *Jack: What I've Learned Leading a Great Company and Great People,* London, Headline Book Publishing.

Welch & Welch, 2006	Welch, J. & Welch, S. 2006. *Winning*, HarperCollins.
Womack & Jones, 2005	Womack, J. P. & Jones, D. T. 2005. *Lean Solutions*, London, Simon & Schuster.

Index